M000078445

THE MESSAGE OF
A COURSE IN MIRACLES

VOLUME TWO

FEW CHOOSE TO LISTEN

THE MESSAGE OF
A COURSE IN MIRACLES

Volume Two

FEW CHOOSE TO LISTEN

Kenneth Wapnick, Ph.D.

Foundation for *A Course in Miracles*®

Foundation for *A Course in Miracles*®
Teaching Organization of the Foundation for Inner Peace
1275 Tennanah Lake Road
Roscoe, NY 12776-5905

Copyright 1997 by the
Foundation for *A Course in Miracles*®

All rights reserved under International and Pan-American Copyright Conventions. No part of this book may be reproduced or transmitted in any form or by any means, electronic or mechanical, including photocopying, recording, or by any information storage and retrieval system, without permission in writing from the publisher. For information, contact the Director of Publications at the Foundation for *A Course in Miracles*® • 1275 Tennanah Lake Road • Roscoe, NY 12776-5905.

Printed in the United States of America

Portions of *A Course in Miracles*® copyright 1975, 1992,
Supplements to A Course in Miracles:
Psychotherapy: Purpose, Process and Practice
The Song of Prayer, copyright 1976, 1978, 1992, 1996,
The Gifts of God, copyright 1982,
reprinted by permission of the Foundation for Inner Peace.

A Course in Miracles is a registered service mark and trademark
of the Foundation for Inner Peace. Used by permission.

Library of Congress Cataloging in Publication Data

Wapnick, Kenneth
    The message of A course in miracles / Kenneth Wapnick.
        p. cm.
    Includes bibliographical references and indexes.
    Contents: v. 1. All are called -- v. 2. Few choose to listen.
    ISBN 0-933291-25-6 (set : pbk.)
    1. Course in miracles. 2. Spiritual life. I. Title.
BP605.C68W3595   1997
299'.93--dc21   97-16732

CONTENTS

Introduction

HUMILITY VERSUS ARROGANCE

This book—Volume Two of *The Message of A Course in Miracles*—is the companion to *All Are Called* and, as explained in the Introduction to that book, could indeed carry the subtitle, juxtaposed with the suggested subtitle of the first book: "What *A Course in Miracles* does *not* say." Its focus therefore is not really on what the Course teaches, since this is the burden of the first volume, but rather on the ways in which students have understood *A Course in Miracles* to say something it simply does not say or mean; in other words, their choosing *not* to listen to its message. In this sense, *Few Choose to Listen* is a guide for errors to be avoided. Thus my purpose in this book is to guide students in how to avoid certain potential mistakes or confusions as they read, study, and implement into their daily lives the teachings of *A Course in Miracles*. Such sidestepping of errors will, it is hoped, be of help in clearing the way for the student to be more accessible to the Holy Spirit's "particular care and guidance" (M-29.2:6).

The misunderstandings of its students have led to conclusions, both theoretical and practical, directly opposite to what *A Course in Miracles* actually teaches. On one level we should not expect otherwise. Following upon our discussion in *All Are Called*, we can recognize the tremendous investment egos have in holding to the beliefs that reinforce and support its thought system and very existence. These beliefs include, in one way or another and however subtly they may be practiced, our making real the error of separation. To remove our investment in perpetuating this error is to undo the very foundation of the ego's thought system.

Thus, in general, we can see that these errors in understanding are defenses against the truth that we find in the Course. As Jesus points out in *A Course in Miracles*, and as I have emphasized, when the ego is confronted by the loving truth of the Holy Spirit it becomes afraid, for the truth of our reality as God's Son is the greatest threat to the integrity of its thought system. The Course explains:

> The ego is... particularly likely to attack you when you react lovingly, because it has evaluated you as unloving and you are going against its judgment.... This is when it will shift abruptly from suspiciousness to viciousness, since its uncertainty is increased.... It remains suspicious as long as you despair of yourself. It shifts to viciousness when you decide not to tolerate self-abasement and seek relief. Then it offers you the illusion of attack as a "solution."... When the ego experiences threat, its only decision is whether to attack now or to withdraw to attack later.... Even the faintest hint of your reality literally drives the ego from your mind, because you will give up all investment in it.... The ego will make every effort to recover and mobilize its energies against your release (T-9.VII.4:5,7; T-9.VIII.2:8-10; 3:4; 4:2,5).

Therefore, if the ego cannot attack directly—because the Son would find that totally unacceptable—then it "withdraws" to attack later through distortion, its form of passive resistance. Thus the ego follows the axiom: "If you can't lick 'em, join 'em." Unable to convince us *not* to pursue *A Course in Miracles*, the ego nonetheless is able to distort the Course's teachings sufficiently to allow its truth to be clouded over, protecting the ego's belief system from ever being looked at openly and honestly. Jesus asks each of us in the Course to "Be very honest with yourself... for we must hide nothing from each other" (T-4.III.8:2). Thus we must openly look at these errors and bring them to his love, *after* which they can be released. Without such honest examination, the truth will continue to be obstructed, and its light "forbidden" entry into the hidden portals of the ego's darkened mind, where it would surely heal our mistaken thoughts. In his Introduction to the fourth review in the workbook, Jesus urges his students to look at and understand their defenses as part of the preparation for the application of the truth to their daily lives (W-pI.rIV.in.1:1):

> Let us begin our preparation with some understanding of the many forms in which the lack of true forgiveness may be carefully concealed. Because they are illusions, they are not perceived to be but what they are; defenses that protect your unforgiving thoughts from being seen and recognized. Their purpose is to show you something else, and hold correction off through self-deceptions made to take its place (W-pI.rIV.in.3).

This fear of the truth leading to the defense of distortion has striking parallels to the early history of Christianity, where the followers of Jesus quite clearly changed his teachings to suit their own fear and guilt. As Jesus comments in the text, specifically referring to the aforementioned "upside-down" interpretations given to his crucifixion:

> If you interpret the crucifixion in any other way [i.e., than a loving and *un*sacrificial act], you are using it as a weapon for assault rather than as the call for peace for which it was intended. The Apostles often misunderstood it, and for the same reason that anyone misunderstands it. Their own imperfect love made them vulnerable to projection, and out of their own fear they spoke of the "wrath of God" as His retaliatory weapon. Nor could they speak of the crucifixion entirely without anger, because their sense of guilt had made them angry.... I do not want you to allow any fear to enter into the thought system toward which I am guiding you (T-6.I.14; 16:2).

Finally, we may recall again the Course's statement:

> To learn this course requires willingness to question every value that you hold. Not one can be kept hidden and obscure but it will jeopardize your learning (T-24.in.2:1-2).

This important teaching refers to our willingness to generalize the Course's principles totally, without exception. To hold out

3

any situation or belief from its uncompromising non-dualism is to make some aspect of the illusory world real. A serious student of *A Course in Miracles* recognizes the absoluteness of its thought system. To quote again one of Jesus' statements about his Course:

> This course will be believed entirely or not at all. For it is wholly true or wholly false, and cannot be but partially believed (T-22.II.7:4-5).

Almost all mistakes students make regarding the Course result from what I sometimes refer to as level confusion; namely, not understanding the important distinction *and* interface between the metaphysical (Level I) and practical (Level II) levels on which *A Course in Miracles* is written. It is from the metaphysical absoluteness of the Course's thought system that its practical teachings of forgiveness derive their power and meaning.

We must therefore be careful not to bring the truth to the illusion, but rather to bring our illusory beliefs to the truth *A Course in Miracles* holds out to us. This requires an openness within ourselves to examine our investments in perpetuating the ego's thought system. The errors we shall be discussing ultimately result from the unconscious unwillingness to bring our fears to the Holy Spirit's Love and truth.

This book is therefore written in the same spirit as *A Course in Miracles* itself. As Jesus explains to his students, the Course does not aim at having us learn what is positive or true, but rather at *un*learning the confusing thought system the ego has taught us in order to conceal and obscure the truth. Thus, for example, we are instructed right at the Course's beginning, and indeed all the way through:

> The course does not aim at teaching the meaning of love, for that is beyond what can be taught. It does aim, however, at removing the blocks to the awareness of love's presence, which is your natural inheritance (T-in.1:6-7).

4

> Your task is not to seek for love, but merely to seek and
> find all of the barriers within yourself that you have built
> against it. It is not necessary to seek for what is true, but it
> *is* necessary to seek for what is false (T-16.IV.6:1-2).

> It is the function of God's teachers to bring true learning to
> the world. Properly speaking it is *un*learning that they
> bring, for that is "true learning" in the world (M-4.X.3:6-7;
> italics mine).

Therefore, a major theme of this book is to emphasize
again to students of *A Course in Miracles* that they are *not*
asked to bring the truth of God's Love to the illusions of the
ego's guilt and fear, but rather to bring the darkness of their
ego's specialness to the light of Jesus' forgiveness. In other
words, students are encouraged by Jesus to bring the belief in
the reality of their problems *to him*, rather than asking or even
demanding that he solve their problems *for them*, or meet their
specific needs.

The reader may recall our discussion in *All Are Called*
(pp. 133-34) about people sitting in a movie theater, when
suddenly the picture on the screen begins to flutter up and
down. No one in the theater would expect the management to
rush to the screen and try to remedy the problem there. One
would go instead to the usually *unseen* or *unnoticed* projection
booth in back of the theater, where the fault lies either in the
motion picture projector, or the film itself passing through the
projector. Only then could the problem of the poor image on
the screen be truly solved. In this analogy, the screen represents our external lives and behavior, the projection booth represents our minds, and the projector itself represents the
mind's capacity to project (or extend) the film, which in turn
represents either the thought system of the ego or the Holy
Spirit, depending on our choice. Therefore, the problem never
rests on the form or behavior of what we perceive or experience (the image on the screen), but always on the content in
our minds, the thoughts with which we choose to identify (the
film running through the projector).

In *Psychotherapy: Purpose, Process and Practice*, Jesus makes the same point in the context of the body's sickness (the screen) and the mind's unforgiveness (projection booth, projector, and film):

> These testimonies which the senses bring have but one purpose; to justify attack and thus keep unforgiveness unrecognized for what it is. Seen undisguised it is intolerable. Without protection it could not endure. Here [in the mind] is all sickness cherished, but without the recognition that this is so. For when an unforgiveness is not recognized, the form it takes seems to be something else. And now it is the "something else" [the physical symptom] that seems to terrify. *But it is not the "something else" that can be healed. It is not sick, and needs no remedy. To concentrate your healing efforts here is but futility. Who can cure what cannot be sick and make it well?* (P-2.VI.4; italics mine)

If we do not like how we feel about something going on in our lives, or in the lives of those with which we are identifying, *A Course in Miracles* is teaching us to go to the source of our distress: the decision our minds have made to choose the ego's attack instead of the Holy Spirit's forgiveness. If the ego is our choice, the resultant guilt will be what is projected from the mind onto a world we perceive to be outside the mind and filled inevitably with fear, hopelessness, and despair. If the Holy Spirit is chosen, on the other hand, the resultant peace will be what the mind has extended, and it is this peace and joy that will remain with us regardless of what appears to be external to us. This world, which is experienced without fear and sparkling with hope, is the world the guiltless Son perceives. This is so even if he finds himself in Auschwitz, for the peace comes not from outside the mind in the external world, but from what is certain and stable in the guiltless world within, termed the *real world* in the Course. It is this reality that envelops the entire Sonship with its love.

Therefore, Jesus is not offering to help us solve our external problems, nor to remove the fears we experience in our everyday lives, but rather he is teaching us how to join with him in undoing the *causes* of our fear, which lie in the mind's decision to be separate from him and therefore from God. He states in a passage partially quoted in *All Are Called*, in what originally was meant specifically for Helen Schucman, scribe of *A Course in Miracles*:

> The correction of fear *is* your responsibility. When you ask for release from fear, you are implying that it is not. You should ask, instead, for help in the conditions that have brought the fear about. These conditions always entail a willingness to be separate.... If I intervened between your thoughts and their results, I would be tampering with a basic law of cause and effect; the most fundamental law there is. I would hardly help you if I depreciated the power of your own thinking. This would be in direct opposition to the purpose of this course (T-2.VI.4:1-4; T-2.VII.1:4-6).

To return to our movie screen analogy and restate this essential point: The fluttering image on the screen is the *effect* of the malfunction that is located in the projection booth, which is the true *cause* of the problem. And so Jesus is exhorting his students to pay careful attention to their mind's decision to be unhappy, and to correct that *cause*, rather than continually seeking his help in remedying the *effect*, which ultimately makes no sense at all. Thus he is not so much teaching his students what is good about themselves (although certainly many, many beautiful passages in the Course describe this truth), as he is helping them to recognize their own wrong ego choices, so that they can make the correct ones now with him. His repeated plea throughout *A Course in Miracles* that we choose again reflects the need to choose him as our teacher instead of the ego. And so he urges all his students: "Resign now as your own teacher....for you were badly taught" (T-12.V.8:3; T-28.I.7:1).

The premise underlying this book is that by helping students of *A Course in Miracles* avoid certain mistakes— having chosen the ego as their teacher instead of Jesus,

7

perhaps without even knowing they had done so—their minds would be left clear and open. And so to come back to the central theme in this Introduction, they would then allow the Holy Spirit to teach them in the way that would be most appropriate and helpful. However, if people are certain that they *do* understand (when they truly do *not*), then they will never be open to learn or ask for help from the Course, already believing that there is nothing more to learn. This important point is underscored in the following passage in the workbook, related to looking at objects freshly, having withdrawn preconceived ideas from them:

> You will not question what you have already defined. And the purpose of these exercises is to ask questions and receive the answers (W-pI.28.4:1-2).

And if we do not ask the right question, how can we possibly hear the answer? The answer is always there in our right minds, but without the appropriate question posed by our decision maker, the Holy Spirit's answer of forgiveness is meaningless and totally irrelevant to us.

Thus, the reader who I hope is reading this book is one who comes with an open mind, choosing to *listen* to Jesus rather than wishing to speak to him; it is the open-minded student who has chosen the humility of wanting to learn, rather than having chosen the arrogance of believing the learning is already completed and perfect. I shall return to this important theme of humility in a later chapter, but for now would like to relate it to the famous story of the six blind men and the elephant.

Each blind man in the story feels a different part of the elephant—trunk, tusk, side, leg, tail, or ear—and then mistakenly and arrogantly proclaims that the elephant is, respectively, like a snake, spear, wall, tree, rope, or fan. He knows nothing else but his very limited perception, and foolishly trusts that this perceptual experience is valid. We know from *A Course in Miracles* that perception is a lie, as it was made to conceal and protect the original lie of the ego's thought system of separation and duality. This thought system in turn was made to conceal the truth of the Atonement: the separation never truly happened. Therefore, Jesus repeatedly urges his students *not* to trust their bodies and perceptions. On one level, at best, our sensory organs provide limited reflections of the external "truth"; on another level, at worst, they provide total distortions of the real truth that is our spiritual, non-material reality. In one place in the text, speaking of the "transient stranger" that is the ego thought system they have welcomed into their minds instead of the truth, Jesus issues a word of caution to his students. The reader may recall our discussion of this important passage in Chapter Three of *All Are Called*:

> Ask not this transient stranger, "What am I?" He is the only thing in all the universe that does not know. Yet it is he you ask, and it is to his answer that you would adjust. This one wild thought, fierce in its arrogance, and yet so tiny and so meaningless it slips unnoticed through the universe of truth, becomes your guide. To it you turn to ask the meaning of the universe. And of the one blind thing in all the seeing universe of truth you ask, "How shall I look upon the Son of God?" (T-20.III.7:5-10).

Therefore, it is the mistaken and arrogant students of *A Course in Miracles* who proclaim the "truth" about the Course from very limited data that have come through what their past history and present perceptions have taught them is true. And it is these students who no longer are open to being taught the fullness of that truth, and even resent being told that the elephant is not what they think, *because their experience has seemed to be so real and therefore valid.* Borrowing the imagery of the opening pages of *The Song of Prayer*, we may say that these students are willing to settle for a mere part or aspect of the song, when they could have the complete song instead (S-1.I.3). I discussed this in *All Are Called* (pp. 233-34), and the reader may recall Jesus' words to his students in the workbook: "You do not ask too much of life, but far too little"

(W-pI.133.2:1), a caution echoed in the text: "Here [the world] does the Son of God ask not too much, but far too little" (T-26.VII.11:7). We shall discuss in the next chapter that one of the primary motivations behind the dictating of *The Song of Prayer* was Jesus' desire to help students of his Course not settle for less than the everything he has promised them.

As with any great spiritual text, *A Course in Miracles* can be understood on many different levels. It has been said of the Hindu spiritual gem the *Bhagavad Gita* that while its message is for all, peoples' understanding will be equal to their varying stages of spiritual development. One could say the same about *A Course in Miracles*, and so regardless of where students are on their spiritual journey, they will find something of value in its pages. And as they grow spiritually, so will the treasures of the Course increasingly open up for them.

Therefore, students may work with *A Course in Miracles* in any way they choose, and at any level on which they feel comfortable, as they feel guided by the Holy Spirit. And their understanding and the benefit they derive from their study is that study's own justification. However, it would be a mistake for them then to conclude, again like the blind men with the elephant, that their level of understanding constituted the reality or truth of the Course. Once that occurs, we have seen the crossing of the line from humility to arrogance. As their capacity to understand would expand, these students would then be able to take in more and more of the Course's richness. But if they think that the water held in their little cup is the ocean, then they will never learn of the ocean's vastness and real nature. Similarly, with *A Course in Miracles*, if students believe their limited understanding *is* the Course, then their learning will be stunted and their learning potential limited. It is to help free students of that littleness at the expense of their true magnitude that is, in the final analysis, this book's goal.

Few Choose to Listen is divided into chapters that reflect the different kinds of errors students are prone to make. We begin with a discussion of the three books of *A Course in*

Miracles themselves, and how each is an important part of the integrated curriculum. This includes a consideration as well of the two supplements that were scribed after the Course— *Psychotherapy: Purpose, Process and Practice* and *The Song of Prayer*—and their relationship with *A Course in Miracles*. This chapter is followed in turn by discussions of the Course's use of language, the roles of Jesus and the Holy Spirit, including the important distinction between form and content, the relevance or irrelevance of groups on *A Course in Miracles*, with specific reference to students joining together in networks, communities, churches, etc., and finally a discussion of making the error real and the dangers of minimizing the ego. One final note: It has probably already been apparent from this Introduction that there is some overlap between *All Are Called* and *Few Choose to Listen*. This is inevitable, as discussion of students' misunderstandings of *A Course in Miracles* often necessitates some treatment of what it does say. Thus, some important common themes end up being discussed in both books, and some passages from the Course presented in both places as well.

Chapter 1

A COURSE IN MIRACLES
AN INTEGRATED CURRICULUM

Introduction

From the beginning, *A Course in Miracles* was conceived
as an integrated curriculum, and Jesus always made it clear to
his scribe Helen Schucman that the Course's three books were
never to be separated (not to mention never to be abridged or
excerpted), and that the successful completion of its curriculum depended on the student's study and practice of the text,
workbook for students, and manual for teachers. The actual
sequence of study, however, was left to the individual student
and the Holy Spirit:

> The curriculum is highly individualized, and all aspects are
> under the Holy Spirit's particular care and guidance
> (M-29.2:6).

Clearly, again, Jesus conceived of his Course as an integrated
work in which each book had its own particular place, making
a unique contribution to the student's learning and growth, as
well as being integrated with the other two books. Thus, for
example, the workbook begins with this statement:

> A theoretical foundation such as the text provides is nec-
> essary as a framework to make the exercises in this
> workbook meaningful. Yet it is doing the exercises that
> will make the goal of the course possible. An untrained
> mind can accomplish nothing. It is the purpose of this
> workbook to train your mind to think along the lines the
> text sets forth (W-in.1).

In the context of becoming a teacher of God, Jesus' term for
his students, the manual states:

> He [a teacher of God] cannot claim that title until he has
> gone through the workbook, since we are learning within
> the framework of our course (M-16.3:7).

Moreover, throughout *A Course in Miracles* Jesus sets forth
his teachings within the framework of a definite curriculum.
The books refer back to each other with the unverbalized,
though clearly implied premise that the student has been or is
currently working with them, or at the very least is familiar
with all three books and the importance each plays in the total
curriculum.

In this chapter we shall examine each of the Course's three
books separately, and will consider their relationship to each
other as well. We begin, however, with a very brief overview
of the basic teaching of *A Course in Miracles* so that we can
see how the three books contribute to the understanding and
integration of its teaching message. For the reader interested
in a more in-depth discussion of the Course's teachings, any
one of the Foundation for *A Course in Miracles*' publications
would do, including, of course, the companion volume to this
book, *All Are Called.*

We have already quoted the statement from the very beginning of the text that in effect summarizes the entire purpose of
A Course in Miracles:

> The course *does not aim* at teaching the meaning of love,
> for that is beyond what can be taught. It *does aim*, however,
> at removing the blocks to the awareness of love's presence,
> which is your natural inheritance (T-in.1:6-7; italics mine).

Jesus teaches us in the Course that the truth about who we are
is our Identity as Christ, and that this, in fact, has never
changed. What *has* changed, however, is our belief in, and
identification with this Self. This change occurred when, as
one Son, we seemed to fall asleep and believed that our dream
of separation were reality. More pointedly, the core of this insane dream is that we have indeed covered this light of Christ

with layers upon layers of defenses—our special relationships—which "protect" us from this truth.

The principal defenses the ego employs to accomplish its purpose of preserving its individualized and separated identity are denial (or repression) and projection. *Denial* causes us to become mindless, wherein we forget, first, our having chosen to fall asleep and then, second, our continuing decision to remain in that alien state. *Projection* continues the ego's defensive strategy by placing the contents of our minds—the ego's illusory thought system of separation and specialness—outside of us in the equally illusory world and body. Thus we now see in others—or in our personal and physical selves—the mind's decision to be separate from God that we do not wish to see within our own minds. Doing so, of course, would force us to accept responsibility for this decision that the ego labels sin, leading us to change the decision from the ego to the Holy Spirit.

It should be emphasized here that while these dynamics of denial and projection appear to operate sequentially, in truth they occur simultaneously, so that one without the other is impossible. In other words, once guilt is made real it must be denied, and automatically and inevitably projected outside the mind, either onto another's body (attack) or onto one's own body (pain and sickness).

Our task, therefore, is to allow the Holy Spirit or Jesus—through the miracle—to teach us to remember who we are by returning to our awareness the power of our minds to choose between the two mutually exclusive thought systems of the ego and the Holy Spirit. Forgiveness is the means by which this mind retraining is accomplished as we undergo the process—step by step—of learning to choose to remove the ego's illusory layers of specialness which block our "awareness of love's presence" *in* our Self and *as* our Self.

Simply stated then, the text—in great depth and detail—explains this paradoxical situation to us of being "at home in God, [yet] dreaming of exile" (T-10.I.2:1): how this insane belief in separation seemed to arise in our *minds*, how it is maintained in our *minds*, and how it finally is undone in our *minds*. *A Course in Miracles* is thus, as the text says, a "mind-training" (T-1.VII.4:1) curriculum designed to help us change our thought system from the ego's to the Holy Spirit's.

The workbook for students provides the one-year training program that seeks to teach us, through the daily exercises, that we do indeed have a mind that believes it can think these thoughts. Furthermore, we are taught that we can change these thoughts, allowing the Holy Spirit's thought system of forgiveness to replace the ego's thought system of attack and judgment.

The manual for teachers, among other things, reminds us what it truly means to be a teacher of God, the Course's term, again, for those who pursue *A Course in Miracles* as their spiritual path. Included are specific teachings that relate to how a teacher reacts and behaves in the world. Here the clear emphasis is placed *not* on behavior, but on the teacher-student's change of mind that allows actions to be guided by Jesus or the Holy Spirit, and not the ego.

We turn now to a brief examination of each book, elaborating on its place in the total curriculum.

Text

Many years ago while on an international speaking tour, Gloria and I continually heard from people how they had been studying *A Course in Miracles* for a number of years. We were somewhat taken aback by this, as many of these students seemed to have very little real understanding of what the Course was actually saying. The mystery was solved for us, however, when we eventually realized that by "studying the Course" the people meant that they had "done" the workbook. Most had hardly studied the text, or even read it at all, and so

it was understandable that they did not recognize what
A Course in Miracles taught.

The text, which was scribed first, provides the basic
theoretical foundation for *A Course in Miracles*, as the Introduction to the workbook, quoted above, makes clear. The
Course, and especially the text, is unique in the non-linear presentation of its ideas. I quote now from the Introduction to my
Glossary-Index for A Course in Miracles, which discusses this
non-linear aspect of the Course's presentation, again most
clearly seen in its text:

> Unlike most thought systems, *A Course in Miracles* does
> not proceed in a truly linear fashion with its theoretical
> structure built upon increasingly complex ideas. Rather,
> the Course's development is more circular with its themes
> treated symphonically: introduced, set aside, reintroduced,
> and developed. This results in an interlocking matrix in
> which every part is integral and essential to the whole,
> while implicitly containing that whole within itself.
>
> This structure establishes a process of learning instead of
> merely setting forth a theoretical system. The process re-
> sembles the ascent up a spiral staircase. The reader is led in
> a circular pattern, each revolution leading higher until the
> top of the spiral is reached, which opens unto God. Thus,
> the same material consistently recurs, both within the
> Course as a thought system as well as in learning opportu-
> nities in our personal lives. Each revolution, as it were,
> leads us closer to our spiritual goal. The last two paragraphs
> of the first chapter in the text particularly emphasize this
> cumulative impact of the Course's learning process (p. 1).

Therefore, the text should be read straight through, since its
development is symphonic, and its pedagogical impact is developed through the process of working through the material
as it was given. One would not, for example, be able fully to
appreciate a great Beethoven symphony with its inherent
thematic development—inner and outer—by listening to its
four or five movements in a random fashion. This is certainly

not to say that students cannot read the text anyway they choose, "dowsing" here, "dowsing" there, just as music lovers frequently listen to and enjoy symphonic excerpts. However, consistently following such a practice with *A Course in Miracles* will inevitably cause students to miss the *process* of learning that is inherent in the text's structure. One does not successfully complete a journey without taking steps in their proper sequence, *one step after another.*

Thus, the very first principle of miracles that begins the text proper (and actually was the very first thing Helen took down after Jesus' introductory line, "This is a course in miracles. Please take notes.") contains the whole thought system of the Course. In that sense the rest of the text is a commentary on this first principle—"There is no order of difficulty in miracles" (T-1.I.1:1)—which is the cornerstone of the teaching. Indeed, one could even liken the fifty miracle principles themselves to a great Wagnerian prelude that presents the principal themes to be introduced and developed later in the music-drama.

Just to cite a few more examples, guilt, the central dynamic in the ego's thought system and its preserver, is introduced in the Course slowly, as the student is ready to learn of it. And special relationships, the ego's brilliant and most vicious strategy to exclude God and the Holy Spirit, is not brought in until Chapter 15, discussed at great length for the next nine chapters, when it is then scarcely mentioned again by name, although its dynamics of hate and deception are clearly described throughout the text's final chapters.

Victimization, another central concept in the ego's thought system, is discussed all the way through the text, especially in the sections on cause and effect. The theme crescendos inexorably toward the final chapter where the ultimate ego goal is summarized in a succinct fortissimo passage that, in effect, is the climax of all Jesus is teaching his students about this insane thought system of murder and death:

If you can be hurt by anything, you see a picture of your secret wishes. Nothing more than this. And in your suffering of any kind you see your own concealed desire to kill (T-31.V.15:8-10).

To make the point again, if the text is to be properly understood and experienced as Jesus meant it to be in the curriculum, it should in general be read and studied straight through, as it was given. Jesus made this clear to Helen and Bill in the passage that now closes Chapter 1. It is of such importance that I shall end this section by quoting it as it was originally dictated to Helen, in which form the passage is provided with a more personal and direct emphasis. Thus, the two paragraphs as they now appear in the text were part of a larger message to Helen and Bill, and actually came somewhat later in the scribing, at a time when Jesus obviously felt that his first two students were not being diligent enough in studying his "notes," his term for the dictation. Jesus' plea to them, however, is also clearly meant for everyone, and should be mandatory reading for all Course students as a reminder of how Jesus saw this material, and the importance of it being studied in the order in which he gave it. Therefore, I ask that readers imagine themselves as one of Jesus' students, who is *not* studying his material as he envisioned it, thus necessitating this gentle though firm rebuke and reminder:

All learning involves attention and study at some level. This course is a *mind-training* course. Good students assign study period for themselves. However, since this obvious step has not occurred to *you*, and since we are co-operating in this, I will make the obvious assignment now [of studying the notes]....

The next part of this course rests too heavily on the earlier part not to *require* its study. Without this, you will become much too fearful when the unexpected *does* occur to make constructive use of it. However, as you study the notes, you will see some of the obvious implications....

The reason why a solid foundation is necessary at this

point is because of the highly likely confusion of "fearful" and "awesome," which most people do make.

A brief discussion followed on awe related to God, which is found in the opening chapter of the text in the published Course, and the message concluded with:

> The next step, however, *does* involve the direct approach to God Himself. It would be most unwise to start on this step at all without very careful preparation, or awe will surely be confused with fear, and the experience will be more traumatic than beatific.
>
> Healing is of God in the end. The means are carefully explained in the notes. Revelation has occasionally *shown* you the end, but to reach it the means are needed (*Absence from Felicity*, pp. 258-59).

Workbook for Students

The workbook, on the other hand, aims only at training the mind "along the lines the text sets forth" (W-in.1:4). Although certainly it does contain some important passages bearing on a number of themes in the text, it does not aim at presenting or explaining the thought system of *A Course in Miracles*. For example, as was just stated, special relationships constitute the core of the ego's defensive system against God and the Holy Spirit, not to mention against the unity of the Sonship. Large portions of the text, again, deal extensively with this crucial topic, and yet it is not mentioned at all in the workbook (nor in the manual for teachers), though it is alluded to. Significant passages related to the Course's metaphysical formulations about the illusory nature of the physical world of time and space can be found within the workbook, but it is only in the text that these concepts are discussed in depth. In short, students wishing to know what *A Course in Miracles* teaches, would hardly find such information in the workbook.

One could better understand the purpose of the workbook as being to provide a one-year training program in helping students recognize experientially that there are *two* thought systems in their minds—the ego and the Holy Spirit—and that they can choose between their inherent meaninglessness and meaningfulness, respectively. This purpose can be clearly seen in Lessons 1-50, a brilliant series of exercises that are directly taken from the text's metaphysical formulations, and yet are presented in such simple language that most students of *A Course in Miracles* are not even aware of the path to total egolessness they are being gently led along.

The first thirty-two lessons present in exercise form, with a relatively minimal amount of explanation, the ego thought system that we perceive because it is what we have chosen in our minds, and the first twenty-five specifically aim at the beginning of the process of correcting or undoing our faulty perceptions. Emphasis is also placed in these early lessons upon the cause-effect relationship that exists between our thoughts and our perceptions, reflecting the text's principle: "projection makes perception" (T-13.V.3:5; T-21.in.1:1). Lessons 33-50 shift to emphasizing the alternative in our minds, and that we can just as easily "see peace instead of this" (W-pI.34). These lessons in general reflect the *other* way of seeing ourselves, and teach that the light of God is our true Identity that we can choose over the ego's darkness, emphasizing "the happy things to which [we] are entitled" (W-pI.40.1:1).

The later Lesson 93 expresses very clearly the workbook's purpose. Its title—"Light and joy and peace abide in me"—reflects our right-minded self, while the lesson's opening paragraphs set forth the wrong-minded ego, beginning with the line: "You think you are the home of evil, darkness and sin" (W-pI.93.1:1). Throughout the lesson, the ego self of sin and guilt is clearly contrasted with the sinless Self that God created:

> Salvation requires the acceptance of but one thought;—
> you are as God created you, not what you made of yourself.
> ... One Self is true; the other is not there (W-pI.93.7:1; 9:2).

And so students are asked to recognize *both* alternatives within their minds, and then to make the correct choice of undoing the ego thought system which will inevitably lead to the true happiness of being free from guilt and fear.

Recall the statement that the ego's goal is to render us mindless, wherein we believe that our bodies are at the mercy of forces and events beyond our control. There is no hope within such a system, which *is* the thought system of the world, but there is hope when we can remember that the world and our experiences within it are aspects of the dream that *we* are dreaming in our minds. The workbook, therefore, helps us to redirect our attention to this mind where the decisions are made, for it is here that our only hope can be found.

This procedure of undoing the ego's thought system is expressly set forth in the introduction to the workbook, where Jesus explains its two main sections: "the first dealing with the undoing of the way you see now, and the second with the acquisition of true perception" (W-in.3:1). And then: "The purpose of the workbook is to train your mind in a systematic way to a different perception of everyone and everything in the world" (W-in.4:1).

It should also be mentioned that in *A Course in Miracles* Jesus never says that the workbook need be done more than once. That does not mean that it cannot be, if the student feels so guided. But, as always, it does mean that students should be vigilant of their egos, and aware of possible, if not probable ego involvement in their work with the Course. In this case, ego involvement could take the form of urging repeated run-throughs of the workbook exercises in the magical hope that "this time I'll get it right." Working through one's dependency on *A Course in Miracles* itself—an expression of the special relationship—is as integral a part of a student's curriculum as is forgiving the special relationships in one's personal life.

Finally, one of the more important aspects of the workbook is its capacity to serve as a projective device, similar to the role that the Rorschach inkblots (and other projective tests) play in a clinical psychologist's attempt to diagnose psychopathology. No one comes to *A Course in Miracles* without unresolved authority issues—the problem that the text refers to as the "root of all evil" (T-3.VI.7:3)—as no one comes into this world without an authority problem. A central theme in *All Are Called* was that our individual lives within the world's dream consist of *nothing more nor less* than the shadowy fragments of the ontological thought of the original split mind. It should come as no surprise therefore to observe how everyone in this world struggles with authority figures, the projected images of our belief that God is seeking to dominate and control us, and to suffocate our very existence by His Will. "Who is the author of my existence?" is the fundamental question everyone's life attempts to answer, and as a result all believe that others are competitors for the position as well:

> The issue of authority is really a question of authorship. When you have an authority problem, it is always because you believe you are the author of yourself and project your delusion onto others. You then perceive the situation as one in which others are literally fighting you for your authorship. This is the fundamental error of all those who believe they have usurped the power of God (T-3.VI.8:1-4).

It should be mentioned that although the need to assert one's authority in defiance of God and all substitute authority figures is shared by everyone, it certainly does not mean that behaviorally people should meekly allow tyrants—political, religious, or supervisory: physically or psychologically—to subject them to abuse. However, it does mean that one should be aware of the *unconscious need* to feel victimized by abusive authorities—real or imagined—so as to feel justified in perceiving themselves unfairly treated. Consequently, it would be most naive to think that these conflicts, whose ultimate focus is our relationship with God, would not be manifest in practicing instructions given by Jesus, the Western world's ultimate symbol of the Authority of God.

Simply stated, this conflict can manifest itself in two basic ways. On the one hand, students can either openly rebel by *not* doing the exercises as they are given. This occurs, for example, whenever they try to change or adapt the workbook to a way they believe works for them, out of the belief that they know what is best for them. Some forms this acting out has taken include "forgetting" the lesson throughout the day, sometimes even "forgetting" to do the lesson at all, or becoming outright angry and judgmental of what is being taught in them. Some students of the Course actually believe they are "receiving guidance" that there are short-cuts to doing the workbook (combining lessons, omitting "non-essential" lessons, etc.), or to the forgiveness process itself. These short-cuts also can entail the attempt to make the workbook easier to understand and practice, because it is conceived to be too difficult as it stands now. Moreover, the "revealed message" may continue, while these short-cuts may not be for everyone, for the more "advanced" student (including, of course, the recipient of the message) they are approved at the "highest level," meaning Jesus himself. And so these special ones are urged to share their inspired short-cuts to the workbook (or to *A Course in Miracles* itself) with others who may also be "ready" for such "advanced" procedures.

On the other hand, students may go to the other extreme and become totally submissive and docile, doing *exactly* what Jesus says, in the magical and usually unconscious hope that they will please the Authority who will then in turn grant them special favor. These are the students who strive to do the workbook perfectly. I remember once in the very early years of *A Course in Miracles*' public life an earnest young man who boasted to his Course group that he had been doing the workbook for twenty-one days, and he was still on Lesson 1! He was going to do it *perfectly* before moving on. I reminded him that if Beethoven had had that attitude with his first symphony, he never would have written the other eight.

Sometimes this tactic of pleasing Jesus by trying to be perfect in his eyes goes to the extreme of students purchasing an alarm wristwatch that reminds them throughout the day to remember the lesson's assignment. These well-meaning students thus aim to fulfill the *letter* of the lessons, but totally violate the *spirit* of the workbook's purpose of disciplining one's mind to *want* to think about God. The "wristwatch approach" thus inadvertently undermines the workbook's aim of *training* its students to become aware of the mind's split nature, and its resistance to choosing the Holy Spirit. Only with such awareness can they meaningfully change their minds and correct their former choice. Instead, however, the wristwatch enables students to train themselves, like Pavlov's dogs, to "salivate" the workbook lesson whenever the alarm goes off. Again, the form of the lesson may have been satisfied, but the content of mind-training has been totally sabotaged and undermined.

It has always struck me as interesting that students who come to *A Course in Miracles* after having "suffered" through a rigid religious background, in which pleasing the authority —a rabbi, minister, priest, nun, guru, Jesus, or God—was sacrosanct, and which adherence to rules and rituals had become tantamount to obeying God Himself, simply transfer onto the Course and Jesus the same authority issues. You can almost feel in many students their unconscious thoughts about a harsh and judgmental Jesus hovering over them with a scorecard, keeping track of how often they "slip up" in doing the workbook, not being able to think of the lesson hourly (let alone six times an hour!).

It should be obvious to students of *A Course in Miracles* that Jesus does not expect them to learn his curriculum overnight. If he did, he would have stopped dictating after the first principle of miracles and would not have given 365 lessons, nor concluded the workbook by stating that "This course is a beginning, not an end" (W-ep.1:1). A much healthier and gentler way of doing the workbook—and one much more in keeping with the whole tone and nature of Jesus' instruction—is to see the purpose of the workbook lessons as being to forgive oneself when one inevitably fails to do the lesson perfectly. To be sure, Jesus is the authority, but his is a *gentle* authority. It is the ego's projections of guilt that turn him into a cruel and condemnatory judge, and the student into a sin-laden failure unworthy to be pursuing such a "holy course of study."

The student of *A Course in Miracles* should never forget that this is not a curriculum in form, achievement, receiving a passing grade, or in success in the usual sense of the word. Rather, this is a curriculum in learning forgiveness, both theoretically as a thought system *and* as a personal experience. This is but another way of saying that the workbook's purpose —reflecting *A Course in Miracles*' general purpose—is to *undo* our faulty images about ourselves. Since, again, the Course's process is to bring the darkness of the ego's illusions to the light of Jesus' truth, the workbook's aim can be seen to expose the student's ego thought system which can then be brought to Jesus to be forgiven and let go. Therefore, seeking to avoid making mistakes (by doing the lessons perfectly) very craftily undercuts Jesus' goal for his students.

Lesson 95 provides us with a clear statement of Jesus' purposes, and the reader may recall discussion of this lesson in Chapter Seven of *All Are Called.* We shall not repeat that discussion here, except to emphasize again Jesus' instructions there about *not* feeling guilty for failing to do the lessons perfectly. Failure to recall the structured practice periods asked of us is not a sin, but as was stated above, is an opportunity to forgive ourselves for our mistakes of forgetting about God, choosing the ego's world of specialness instead of His Love.

Another error many students are prone to make, which I cited briefly above, comes from forgetting the workbook's place in the curriculum and becoming victims of the form of level confusion that leads them to think that salvation has been achieved because they satisfactorily completed the workbook. They do not realize the *process* involved, which entails the "little steps" students are asked to take each day as they practice learning to think with the Holy Spirit instead of their ego. Thus Lesson 193 ends with these important lines, referring to the end of the journey:

> God will take this final step Himself. Do not deny the little steps He asks you take to Him (W-pI.193.13:6-7).

This theme of the *process* of learning is nowhere more clearly summarized than in Lesson 284, where, in the context of the teaching that all suffering "is nothing but a dream," Jesus states:

> This is the truth, *at first* to be but said and *then* repeated many times; and *next* to be accepted as but partly true, with many reservations. *Then* to be considered seriously more and more, and *finally* accepted as the truth (W-pII.284.1:5-6; italics mine).

Finally, mention should be made of the basic resistance all students would have in doing the workbook, whether they are aware of it or not. As the workbook aims at the ultimate reversal of the ego thought system, held in place by our commitment to anger and judgment, it stands to reason that our identification with this anger would interfere with our learning, thus promoting the resistance we have been discussing. Again, it would be naive and foolhardy for students to believe they can so easily let this investment go. Rather, once again, students of *A Course in Miracles*, and the workbook specifically, would be far better off to see that the lessons provide a classroom in which the student's ego can "act up," so that its thought system can at last be recognized and chosen against. It is this process of looking without guilt at our repressed anger and judgments—our investment in specialness—that is the prerequisite to making "progress" with the Course. The workbook for students plays an essential part in helping us achieve our goal of moving beyond the ego to the truth.

The Relationship between the Text and Workbook

To restate this important point: The workbook is the mind-training arm of *A Course in Miracles*, whose text sets forth in great detail the two thought systems of the ego and the Holy Spirit. The relationship of the text and workbook can therefore be understood as being somewhat similar to that between a class in biology or chemistry and the laboratory section that students must take as part of the science curriculum. In the lab, students have the opportunity of putting into practice what they have learned in the more formal classroom situation. The principles and theory are taught in the more formal class, and then applied to the laboratory experience.

Clearly, the text is the most difficult of the three books, and it can be tempting for students who find the text rough going, and do not consider themselves intellectually inclined, to skip over it and focus almost exclusively on the workbook. On the other hand, students of *A Course in Miracles* who find the text's intellectual formulations interesting and challenging might dismiss the workbook as simple-minded or irrelevant to their spiritual progress. Both errors should be avoided if a student hopes to benefit from the Course's integrated curriculum. While the text and workbook need not be done concurrently, and the development of one book is *not* synchronized with the other—that is, as an example, particular sections in the text are not necessarily intended to be studied with certain workbook lessons—the two books do most certainly complement each other.

One of the more common mistakes students fall into when they focus almost exclusively on the workbook and virtually ignore the text is to misunderstand the role of the Holy Spirit, a central theme to which we shall devote two later chapters.

The workbook places much greater emphasis on hearing the Holy Spirit's Voice, encouraging students to ask the Holy Spirit for very specific help in all situations. In fact, Lesson 71 even instructs the student to ask God the Father for help, suggesting we pose the following very specific questions to our Creator:

> What would You have me do?
> Where would You have me go?
> What would You have me say, and to whom?
>
> Give Him full charge... and let Him tell you what needs to be done by you in His plan for your salvation (W-pI.71. 9:3-6; italics omitted).

This is all the more astounding given the fact that later in the workbook and the manual, not to mention the supplement *The Song of Prayer* as will be discussed in the next chapter, Jesus states clearly that God does not even understand words, let alone answer specific requests.

In the text, this idea of asking the Holy Spirit for specific help with one's external life is barely touched upon. Instead, students are urged to go to the Holy Spirit (or Jesus) with their guilt and judgment, so that together they can look at the ego and let it go. That process—the core of forgiveness—is the Holy Spirit's real function according to the Course, and again a later chapter will discuss this at length. On the other hand, as part of its training program the workbook's emphasis is to help us learn that the Holy Spirit is our friend and not the enemy the ego would have us believe. Therefore, students of *A Course in Miracles* are encouraged to trust the Voice that speaks for God, and learn that they are indeed worthy of His Love. The issue here is the use of symbols, including the repeated references to the Holy Spirit, and in the next chapter we shall discuss the Course's inconsistent use of language, and the dangers inherent in *not* understanding how flexibly Jesus uses words—"symbols of symbols" (M-21.1:9)—in the Course.

However, mistakes enter as well when students work exclusively with the text. They then run the risk of intellectualizing its principles, unconsciously working against the Course's attempts to have us integrate its abstract teachings in our everyday experiences in the world. Repeatedly, Jesus emphasizes his goal of the practical application of the Course's theoretical ideas, also discussed in *All Are Called* (pp. 317-19), as the following repeated excerpts from the text and manual make clear:

> You have surely begun to realize that this is a very practical course, and one that means exactly what it says.... This is not a course in the play of ideas, but in their practical application.... This course is always practical....and it is the practical with which this course is most concerned (T-8.IX.8:1; T-11.VIII.5:3; M-16.4:1; M-29.5:7).

The Introduction to the workbook highlights the important place that *using* the Course's ideas has in the curriculum:

> Some of the ideas the workbook presents you will find hard to believe, and others may seem to be quite startling. This does not matter. You are merely asked to *apply* the ideas as you are directed to do. You are not asked to judge them at all. You are asked only to *use* them. It is their *use* that will give them meaning to you, and will show you that they are true....and whatever your reactions to the ideas may be, *use* them (W-in.8; 9:4; italics mine).

It is instructive to recognize, however, that nowhere in the text does Jesus let his students off the hook in this way. Clearly, the text is to be *studied, understood*, and *believed*; the workbook, on the other hand, is meant to be *practiced*. This is not to say, by the way, that students should not also read and study the workbook carefully after completing the one-year training period, nor that they should not use any of the lovely workbook prayers or meditations for daily inspiration, encouragement, or as reminders. It really need not be said that anything that is helpful should be utilized. However, these individualized practices should not—if the Course's curriculum is to be satisfied—be taken as substitutes for the systematic study and application of the text and workbook.

To restate this very important point: It should be noted, as *Absence from Felicity* documents, that early in the dictation Jesus repeatedly urged Helen and Bill not only to *study* the "notes," as I discussed above, but also to *apply* the principles to their everyday experience. He spent considerable time in going through daily situations in Helen's and Bill's lives, showing them how what he was teaching them on a more abstract level in the dictated "notes," should be applied directly to their everyday situations. At that point, of course, there was no workbook, and the dictation of the text had just barely begun. Yet we can see in these messages, even at the very beginning of the Course's scribing, the important dual emphasis Jesus was placing on *both* study and practice.

Manual for Teachers

The manual for teachers, scribed last, provides a summary of *some* of the themes and principles of the text. It is organized in question and answer form, and is a most useful adjunct to the other two books. It is the smallest of the three and the most simply written, and thus is perhaps the most accessible of the Course books for students to read and study. For that reason, many students prefer to begin their study of *A Course in Miracles* with the teacher's manual.

The manual is the only book in which the teacher of God is discussed by name, and it is extremely important to understand what *A Course in Miracles* means by that phrase, and even more so, what it does *not* mean. As we shall see later, all too frequently students remove from the Course's context passages that reinforce their ego's specialness desires, distorting the true meaning of these passages in the Course's overall thought system.

Thus for example, the manual makes it very clear in meaning—although certain excerpted words may seem to suggest the opposite—that teachers of God need merely accept the Atonement for themselves, and that salvation of the world depends on their simply doing just that *and only that*. This is not an insignificant point. However, without first understanding the underlying metaphysical principles that there is literally no world outside oneself, it is impossible to understand what *A Course in Miracles*, and specifically here the manual really means. Otherwise, the ego's need to make the world and itself special will distort the words to mean that the Course student, now a seemingly advanced teacher of God, is asked by Jesus *behaviorally* to teach other students, heal the sick, or preach to the world.

Let us briefly reconsider a passage from the manual, discussed in *All Are Called* (pp. 299-300), that emphasizes the importance of God's teachers changing their minds, their behavior being essentially irrelevant—the behavior, of course, being the *effect* of the mind, and not its *cause*. In his discussion of "The Function of the Teacher of God," Jesus states:

> The simple presence of a teacher of God is a reminder. His thoughts ask for the right to question what the patient has accepted as true. As God's messengers, His teachers are the symbols of salvation. They ask the patient for forgiveness for God's Son in his own Name. *They stand for the Alternative. With God's Word in their minds they come in benediction, not to heal the sick but to remind them of the remedy God has already given them. It is not their hands that heal. It is not their voice that speaks the Word of God.* They merely give what has been given them. Very gently they call to their brothers to turn away from death: "Behold, you Son of God, what life can offer you. Would you choose sickness in place of this?" (M-5.III.2:2-12; italics mine)

A later section (M-12) answers the question "How Many Teachers of God are Needed to Save the World?" The answer is "one," since there is only *one* Son, despite the illusion of many. And in that one Son's healed mind is the thought that heals the world, because it remains outside the world's dream of suffering, sickness, and death. Nothing need be done to heal, since in that one mind all healing is already accomplished:

> It [the redemption or healing of God's Son] is not really a change; *it is a change of mind. Nothing external alters, but everything internal now reflects only the Love of God....* God's teachers appear to be many, for that is what is the world's need. Yet being joined in one purpose, and one they share with God, how could they be separate from each other? What does it matter if they then appear in many forms? Their minds are one; their joining is complete. And God works through them now as one, for that is what they are (M-12.2:2-3,5-9; italics mine).

Therefore, all that need be done is for the teacher of God to accept the truth that is already present within his mind, what is repeatedly referred to in *A Course in Miracles* as accepting the Atonement for oneself. One does not heal *others,* minister to *others,* or teach *others*; one simply accepts the truth within oneself by realizing the illusory nature of the ego. And in that holy instant of healing is the Sonship healed as well: "When I am healed I am not healed alone" (W-pI.137). Of course, as was pointed out in *All Are Called* (e.g., p. 346), this does not mean that people may not be guided on the behavioral level to heal, help, or teach others. However, one's investment, again, should always be *only* on accepting the Atonement, leaving the Holy Spirit's Love the freedom to flow as it does.

Even more to the point, one cannot heal others because ultimately, if the world is an illusion, who is there to help? The Sonship cannot be understood quantifiably—as in how *many* teachers are needed to save the world—because the student needs to understand that the appearance of many conceals the underlying oneness of the Sonship. There is, in the end, only *one* Son. And that, of course, is the meaning of the moving poem that ends the manual, which speaks of the "help" for which God turns to us in order to "save the world" (M-29.8:2).

Our "helping" God has nothing to do with going out into the world as the Christian missionaries did, for example, but rather with the simple acceptance of our own holiness as Christ. Needless to say, the whole concept of *helping* presupposes a dualistic universe, of which God knows nothing. And so, as we shall discuss in the next chapter, passages like this poem are meant to be taken as *symbols* of God's Love, and not as literal truth.

This acceptance of the holiness of God's one Son ushers in the real world, "unseen, unheard, yet truly there" (M-29.8:5). The real world, as we have seen, is a state of mind of *unified* perception, not an external reality of differences that can be perceived through the body's sensory organs. Again, a student's understanding of the Course's metaphysics would ensure against misinterpretation of passages such as this. We shall return to this idea in Chapter Three when we discuss the Course's teachings of forgiveness in light of our discussion of symbol and reality, duality and non-duality.

The appendix to the manual, which clarifies some of *A Course in Miracles'* terminology, was scribed three years after the completion of the Course. It was a kind of "afterthought" that came in response to a need, expressed by some early students, to clarify the Course's language. However, this appendix is really not comprehensible without first having some understanding of the terms themselves from a prior study of the text. On the other hand, the poetic "definitions" of the "Clarification of Terms" are wonderful reminders of what *A Course in Miracles* itself has taught, and can therefore be a helpful aid to the student in summarizing certain of its concepts.

Some Reflections on *A Course in Miracles*

Certainly Jesus presumes an intellectual level of his students that is average at the very minimum, and thus on the one hand we may state that, *in general, A Course in Miracles* would not be the path for those seekers lacking in intellectual ability. However, here too one must guard against the temptation to legislate who is to study the Course and who should not study it. *A Course in Miracles* is written on several different levels, as we discussed in the Introduction. Among these are differing layers of teaching, and so students can benefit regardless of where they are on the essentially non-existent spiritual continuum, not to mention the intellectual one. Thus, for example, "non-intellects" may find the Course's metaphysics too difficult to comprehend, or even irrelevant to their experience. Nonetheless, they are able to learn from the Course that God is Love and not vengeance, forgiveness is preferable to attack, and that Jesus is a far better and wiser teacher than the ego. While *A Course in Miracles* is certainly not the only spirituality that teaches these ideas—and the three we have mentioned, moreover, do not do justice to the *totality* of the Course's thought system—who would wish to deprive spiritual seekers of a tool that brought them closer to God and His Love, regardless of what else they may not understand or even miss?

But nonetheless, a student should understand that to omit any aspect of *A Course in Miracles* is to change it. We recall again Jesus' words about his Course:

> This course will be believed entirely or not at all. For it is wholly true or wholly false, and cannot be but partially believed (T-22.II.7:4-5).

And so when students omit something from the Course, or even change one of its principles, they have in effect changed the whole thing. Thus, for all intents and purposes, these students are then pursuing a *different* spiritual path from *A Course in Miracles*. Again, this is not to say there is anything *wrong* with doing this—it is always the content that is important and not the form in which this content appears—but it *is* to say that to whatever extent they are able, people should be aware of what is happening and what they are choosing.

Otherwise, they may believe that they are "doing" the Course, when they are really in fact practicing something else.

It is also important to note here that *A Course in Miracles* itself makes no claim to universality, nor to its being the only spiritual path, let alone the only form of truth. Thus we read at the beginning of the manual for teachers:

> This is a manual for a special curriculum, intended for teachers of a special form of the universal course [which teaches that "God's Son is guiltless, and in his innocence is his salvation" (M-1.3:5)]....There are many thousands of other forms, all with the same outcome (M-1.4:1-2).

This being said, however, it is also important to state that *A Course in Miracles* presents an entirely new and different theology that cannot be blended in with any other. This does not mean that the Course is necessarily better (or worse) than any other spirituality, but it does reflect the fact that it *is* unique and different, and radically so. Therefore we find this exhortation in the text, originally meant specifically for Helen, to respect the Course's uniqueness, but also not to judge other paths:

> This [joining with another in forgiveness] is the special means this course is using to save you time. You are not making use of the course if you insist on using means which have served others well, neglecting what was made for *you* (T-18.VII.6:4-5).

And in a verbal communication to Helen a number of years after the Course's scribing was completed, Jesus echoed his earlier statement and said: "Do not take another's path as your own, but neither should you judge it."*

Thus we return to the point that one of the clear characteristics of the Course's presentation is that it is written on a relatively high intellectual level. When Helen, herself a very intellectual woman, finished taking down the manuscript, she

---

* *Absence from Felicity: The Story of Helen Schucman and Her Scribing of A COURSE IN MIRACLES*, p. 450.

exclaimed to Jesus: "Thank God there is at last something [on the spiritual life] for the intellectual." Therefore, attempting to change *A Course in Miracles* from what it is in terms of over- or under-playing the text or workbook—instead of simply finding a more compatible spiritual path—does a disservice both to the Course itself as well as to its students, regardless of how sincere and devoted they may be.

In addition, students of *A Course in Miracles* are occasionally heard complaining about the sometimes idiosyncratic and free nature of its syntax and grammar, not to mention the seemingly excessive use of pronouns.* The Course's writing style is therefore said to be confusing, especially to those who have been accustomed to more precise verbal expression. However, to simplify the writing style, or even to "improve" upon it, would be to violate Jesus' very specific pedagogical intention. It is the purpose of this style to demand that the student pay very careful attention to what has been written, oftentimes calling for multiple readings of the same sentence or paragraph to get its proper meaning and specific pronoun reference. This is not material that can be speed-read, to say the very least. The very process of working out what particular passages mean reflects the underlying process of letting go of one's ego defenses—layer by layer—that are the true impediments to understanding what Jesus refers to repeatedly as his simple, clear, and direct Course.† Still further, students have the experience, once they "get" the meaning of a sentence or passage, of being astounded that they were not able to see it so clearly before; that is, of course, until their fear causes them to forget again!

Finally, a student of *A Course in Miracles* must also be wary of other self-proclaimed channels offering short-cuts to

---

* The capitalization of *A Course in Miracles*, also the subject of considerable comment and criticism by students, falls into another category, and is addressed in the Appendix.
† See the Appendix for Gloria's and my article, "A Simple, Clear, and Direct Course."

understanding the Course's teachings, as well as to learning and practicing forgiveness, as we mentioned above. *The Course, as it is, is the short-cut!* It is precisely because it is this short-cut that the egos of its students become so threatened. If they could only realize how preposterous, let alone arrogant it is to think that they could devise or conceive of a short-cut to *A Course in Miracles*, students would simply step back and laugh, just as the Holy Spirit asked them to do in the original instant when the Son of God believed he had a better way than God, and could improve upon Heaven. It is one of the principal purposes of this book to alert students to the subtle temptation of their egos to set themselves up as "alternatives" to the Course (which really means in opposition to it), without even understanding what it is saying.

The other writings of "Jesus" that purport to come from the same person who wrote *A Course in Miracles* are all equally impressive in demonstrating the phenomenon of "Jesus" *not* understanding his own Course. Thus we can see that otherwise well-meaning people are not in touch with their unconscious specialness needs and the ego's demands that their individuality and world, in which their special and unique self appears to live, be real. As a result, their egos have "Jesus" (or some other highly evolved being) dictate material to suit their special requests, totally disregarding what *A Course in Miracles* really teaches about the process of honestly looking at their specialness and thereby giving it up. This is not to pass judgment on the quality of the writings, but simply to comment on the unmistakable and objective differences between their teachings and those of *A Course in Miracles*.

In an essay "On the Playing of Beethoven,"* the distinguished British music scholar Eric Blom wrote about the

---

* The essay is unfortunately out of print, but it can be found in the notes to the recording of Artur Schnabel playing the thirty-two Beethoven piano sonatas published as part of the Angel "Great Recordings of the Century" series, GRM 4005.

Beethoven piano sonatas. He told the story of the Swiss music publisher Nägeli's attempts to "improve" upon the Master's 16th sonata in G major by inserting four measures into the coda of the first movement in the hope of "balancing the phrases." However, all he succeeded in doing was providing a rather conventional, redundant, and hackneyed musical phrase to an otherwise wonderfully understated conclusion to the movement. Blom was pointing out how people—publishers and pianists alike—tried to improve on Beethoven, when in fact they did not understand this great genius at all. Thus he states:

> But to add anything, even as little as a note to a chord or an extra pause, merely because it appears rhyme or reason to the player, is inadmissible. It cannot possibly mean that the player knows better than Beethoven; it can only show that he has no notion of what Beethoven was about.

One could certainly make the same statement about many students' attempts to improve upon *A Course in Miracles*— form *and* content—without really understanding Jesus' pedagogical "rhymes and reasons" for his Course being the way it is. Humility accepts *A Course in Miracles* as it is; arrogance seeks to improve upon it.

The Two Supplements
Psychotherapy: Purpose, Process and Practice
The Song of Prayer

These two supplements were scribed by Helen after *A Course in Miracles* was completed. *Psychotherapy: Purpose, Process and Practice* begun in early 1973 and completed in early 1975, while *The Song of Prayer* waited another two years, and was scribed in the latter part of 1977. For the full story of the interesting circumstances behind their scribing, see *Absence from Felicity* (pp. 389-91,461-77). It is enough to say at present that *Psychotherapy* was dictated for Course students who were

39

also practicing therapists as the framework for the "special training" (P-3.II.2:2) that would be required of them if they were to become true healers in their profession. *The Song of Prayer*, on the other hand, came to correct students' already growing misunderstandings and misapplications of prayer and what it meant to ask the Holy Spirit for help.

Both supplements in their own way provide beautiful summaries of the teachings of the Course. *Psychotherapy* specifically applies the principle of healing—two people joining in Christ's Name—to the profession of psychotherapy. *The Song of Prayer* brings together forgiveness and healing within the context of prayer, and introduces a term not found in *A Course in Miracles* itself—"forgiveness-to-destroy"—though the concept is discussed in both text and workbook.

However, as a summary, neither work is really capable of being understood, let alone appreciated, independent of *A Course in Miracles* itself. Pregnant ideas are introduced, with little or no preparation or subsequent development; ideas that in no way could be comprehended without the more in-depth treatment that *A Course in Miracles* itself provides. For example, there are the following profound comments—on sickness, the mind-body relationship, the unreality of time, forgiveness, and healing—that are almost dropped into the supplements, as it were, *in media res* (i.e., in the middle of things):

> Once God's Son is seen as guilty, illness becomes inevitable....Illness can be but guilt's shadow, grotesque and ugly since it mimics deformity (P-2.IV.2:1,6).

> The ear translates; it does not hear. The eye reproduces; it does not see....They answer the decisions of the mind, reproducing its desires and translating them into acceptable and pleasant forms (P-2.VI.3:1-2,4).

> In time there can be a great lag between the offering and the acceptance of healing. This is the veil across the face of Christ. Yet it can be but an illusion, because time does not

exist and the Will of God has always been exactly as it is (P-3.II.10:9-11).

> The secret of true prayer is to forget the things you think you need. To ask for the specific is much the same as to look on sin and then forgive it (S-1.I.4:1-2).

The body's healing will occur because its cause has gone. And now without a cause, it cannot come again in different form (S-3.III.6:3-4).

Thus, we can see that these two supplements were not given to supplant the Course, nor to be a shortened version or summary of its content. Quite to the contrary; they are meant to augment or extend for students what has already been taught and learned in *A Course in Miracles*. That is why each supplement contains the subtitle: "An Extension of the Principles of *A Course in Miracles*." Standing on their own, the two supplements would be prone to misunderstanding or justified accusations of obfuscation. Alongside *A Course in Miracles*, on the other hand, they become useful, and in many places inspiring adjuncts to the basic teachings.

An example of the "misuse" of the supplements can be seen in the unfortunate actions of many students of *A Course in Miracles* who are in psychotherapy with a non-Course therapist. They become tempted by their unconscious resistance to treatment to "hit their therapists over the head" with the Course by giving them *Psychotherapy: Purpose, Process and Practice* and saying—implicitly or explicitly—your approach is not spiritual enough; *this* is how you should be doing therapy with me. Therapists in this situation, of course, usually have no understanding of what has been handed to them since, again, the supplement was not meant to be understood independently of the context of *A Course in Miracles* itself.

We shall return to *The Song of Prayer* in a later chapter when we discuss the particular role of correction that Jesus gave the supplement in the curriculum, both in the understanding and application of his teachings in the Course.

Chapter 2

THE COURSE'S USE OF LANGUAGE – I
The Symbolism of Duality

Introduction

Perhaps the greatest source of confusion to students of *A Course in Miracles* is its inconsistent and metaphoric use of language, especially since most students are probably not even aware of such usage. This confusion unfortunately can well serve the ego as a tempting justification for those who would already be prone to misinterpreting the Course's teachings in light of the strong investment in maintaining and defending their own belief system. Thus, the Course's poetic style can be one of the greatest obstacles for those students whose bent is towards more literal if not fundamentalist interpretations of what they read. This approach may work well with more scientific writings, where precision of statement is essential, but such rigidity regarding *form* wreaks havoc with the Course's *content*. While some discussion of this theme occurred in *All Are Called* (e.g., pp. 32-35), the current chapter addresses this very important issue in greater depth.

The Course's Metaphoric Language

We begin therefore by stating simply that *A Course in Miracles* is not written as a scientific tract, nor as a professional research paper, as was Helen's usual style of writing. Rather, the Course's use of language is frequently poetic, and its style symphonic and not linear, as we saw in the preceding chapter. While this is certainly an advantage to readers familiar and comfortable with such a style, such writing, again, can become extremely frustrating to those who prefer more technically precise prose. I shall always remember the man who stood up at a workshop Gloria and I were giving many years ago, after our discussion of some of the translations of *A Course in Miracles* that were then either already in progress, or being considered. He spoke quite forcefully of his background as a Ph.D. in Engineering, as well as his being a rather literate and intelligent man, but yet one who was not able to understand the Course at all. "When," he concluded his remarks by saying, "are you going to translate this Course into English?"

We quoted earlier Jesus' comment from the text: "You have surely begun to realize that this is a very practical course, and one that means exactly what it says" (T-8.IX.8:1). The problem is, however, that the Course's words often do not mean what they say *literally*, and further, are not meant to be taken that way. But the words certainly do mean what they say when they are understood *metaphorically* or *symbolically*, and this meaning can be discerned when the content behind their form is recognized.* Consider a few examples:

Jesus makes some statements about the incorruptibility of the body, suggesting that it cannot die (T-19.IV-C.5:2; M-12.5:5), which when taken out of context certainly do seem to suggest that the body's life can be immortal. And those students of the Course who subscribe to other spiritualities that do emphasize the immortality of the body leap for joy as they seize upon the Course's literal words to support the claims of their own spiritual path. Their conclusion then is that *A Course in Miracles* is "just like" this other path because they both advocate the immortality of the body, and hold that up therefore as an important if not essential goal for the spiritual seeker and student of the Course.

However, what these passages in the Course really mean is that the body does not die because *the body does not live*. As the text says:

---

* Again, this issue is explored in depth in Gloria's and my article "A Simple, Clear, and Direct Course," which is reprinted in the Appendix.

> The body no more dies that it can feel. It does nothing. Of
> itself it is neither corruptible nor incorruptible. It *is* nothing
> (T-19.IV-C.5:2-5).

Therefore, in that sense *only* can we say that the body does not
die, for what does not possess life cannot lose it. It would
make no sense if Jesus in *A Course in Miracles* advocated the
immortality of a body that throughout the three books he
teaches is not real and *has no life*. Yet this is an example of
where well-meaning students can become confused by not
recognizing, again, where specific statements are not to be
wrenched from their context and taken as literal truth.

A group of examples dealing with God make the point very
well of paying attention to the content behind the form. Incidentally, the italics in the following quotations are mine, and
in the last quote I have omitted those found in the Course since
they related to stylistic considerations and not to the passage's
meaning:

> God is *lonely* without His Sons, and they are *lonely* without
> Him.... God Himself is *lonely* when His Sons do not know
> Him (T-2.III.5:11; T-7.VII.10:7; italics mine).

> God *weeps* at the "sacrifice" of His children who believe
> they are lost to Him (T-5.VII.4:5; italics mine).

> "God Himself is *incomplete* without me." ...For by it [sin]
> God Himself is changed, and rendered *incomplete* (T-9.
> VII.8:2; T-19.II.2:7; italics mine).

Indeed, throughout *A Course in Miracles* God is referred to as
having Arms, Hands, and a Voice, and with this "body" of His
reacts to His Son's mistakes by taking steps, reaching down,
speaking words, creating plans, etc.

It would be obvious to even a casual reader of *A Course in
Miracles* that God is not and cannot be corporeal. He does not
have a body, nor does He live in a *place* called Heaven. In fact,
we are taught that the physical world was made as an attack on
Him (W-pII.3.2:1), and that the body is a limit on love (T-18.
VIII.1:2). And yet in the passages above we are specifically

told that God is lonely, weeps, and is incomplete without us. Not only do these words clearly imply that God exists in a body—as other passages do as well by referring to Him as Father, denoting His masculine humanity by use of the human pronouns "He" and "Him," and referring to the body parts noted above—but also these passages clearly suggest that the separation from Him actually happened; otherwise, He could not be reacting to it as He is clearly described in places as doing. However, it is the principle of the Atonement, upon which rests the whole thought system of the Course, that the sin of separation never happened at all. Thus our resultant guilt and fear make no sense. And just as nonsensical is the thought that God—our perfect Creator and undifferentiated and unified Source—could weep, suffer loneliness, or even believe that He were incomplete.

In the sections to come, I shall explain what Jesus truly means in these symbolic references, but I continue now with a brief presentation of some passages that involve the creation of the Holy Spirit. *A Course in Miracles* says that He was created by God as His Answer to the ego's thought of separation. For example:

> [The Holy Spirit] came into being with the separation as a protection, inspiring the Atonement principle at the same time....The Holy Spirit is God's Answer to the separation. ...The principle of the Atonement and the separation began at the same time. When the ego was made, God placed in the mind the call to joy (T-5.I.5:2; T-5.II.2:5–3:2).

Later the text states, in another reference to the creation of the Holy Spirit, that when God's extension outward was blocked by the separation, "He thought, 'My children sleep and must be awakened'" (T-6.V.1:8).

In these quotations, only a few among many, many others, it is clear that the words themselves directly imply a human God, who thinks, feels, and acts as would a loving parent when confronted by a wayward child. The God of the gospel parables naturally is portrayed in exactly the same way. The

Creator-God of the Old Testament is also clearly depicted as a very human father, though not always in a positive fashion, to say the very least. Given our strong bodily identification, such an image of God is understandable:

> Can you who see yourself within a body know yourself as an idea? Everything you recognize you identify with externals, something outside itself. You cannot even think of God without a body, or in some form you think you recognize (T-18.VIII.1:5-7).

In addition, the Judaeo-Christian tradition with which almost all students of *A Course in Miracles* identify—whether they are conscious of it or not—would make it practically impossible *not* to conceptualize the Creator in human terms, both physically and psychologically. How then should we understand these continual references in the Course to a very human- (if not at times ego-) sounding deity? The next sections address this question.

Non-Duality versus Duality

At this point it would be helpful to introduce two terms that, although they are not specifically used in *A Course in Miracles*, nonetheless characterize the two dimensions of experience that are reflected in the Course's teachings, and therefore the two levels of language we have been discussing. These terms are *non-duality* and *duality*, respectively reflecting the pre-separation state of Heaven, the only true reality, and the separated world of the ego thought system, the world of illusion. These two levels are also frequently characterized in the Course by the terms *knowledge* and *perception*.

As has already been said, so much of the misunderstandings and confusion about what *A Course in Miracles* teaches, inevitably leading to distortions in students' teachings of others, can be traced back to not recognizing these two very different levels, and why Jesus' material has come in this form. The basic process in the Course's undoing of guilt is summarized in its emphasis, to restate this very important principle, on bringing the illusions of the ego's darkness to the light of the Holy Spirit's truth. As Jesus says of himself early in the text:

> I was a man who remembered spirit and its knowledge. As
> a man I did not attempt to counteract error with knowledge,
> but to correct error from the bottom up (T-3.IV.7:3-4).

This statement reflects the fact that the correction of the ego thought system that he brought to the world's awareness occurred at the dualistic level of the error, not at the non-dualistic level of truth. Thus he did not bring the truth of Heaven down to the world magically to shine away the darkness of sin, as is implied in the theology of Christianity. Furthermore we see in the Bible that Jesus is God's only Son who incarnated into the world of real sin. In John's gospel, the last of the four gospels to be written, Jesus is portrayed as the cosmic Christ, barely on earth and thus one who does not act or speak in human terms. Yet he is nonetheless one who has interceded in human affairs to take away the sins of those who believe in him.

On the other hand, the Jesus in *A Course in Miracles* is clearly different from the biblical character who bears his name for, among other things, he makes it very clear that he *will not*, because he *cannot*, remove our sins from us. One such example is seen in this passage:

> God and His creations remain in surety, and therefore
> know that no miscreation exists. Truth cannot deal with
> errors that you want....By uniting my will with that of my
> Creator, I naturally remembered spirit and its real purpose.
> I cannot unite your will with God's for you, but I can erase
> all misperceptions from your mind *if you will bring it under
> my guidance. Only your misperceptions stand in your way.*
> Without them your choice is certain. Sane perception
> induces sane choosing. *I cannot choose for you, but I can*

help you make your own right choice (T-3.IV.7:1-2,6-11;
italics mine).

In addition, the Jesus of *A Course in Miracles* speaks of living
and teaching in the world, *in the world's terms*, a world that he
never denigrates nor dismisses, though he clearly insists to us
is illusory. For example, he says of the body that

it is almost impossible to deny its existence in this world.
Those who do so are engaging in a particularly unworthy
form of denial (T-2.IV.3:10-11).

And clearly this is a denial he is not advocating.

This speaking to us in the world's terms is what Jesus does
as well in the form of *A Course in Miracles*. He states repeatedly in the Course how what he is *really* saying cannot be
understood. In one telling passage he even dismisses all the
arrogant pretensions of the intellectual by saying:

You are still convinced that your understanding is a
powerful contribution to the truth, and makes it what it is.
Yet we have emphasized that you need understand nothing
(T-18.IV.7:5-6).

And so in *A Course in Miracles* Jesus teaches his students in
the symbolic and metaphoric language of the myth, reaching
them on the worldly level they can accept and understand.
And yet, as we shall see presently, he occasionally points to
the non-dualistic, abstract, and non-specific truth that is the
content beyond the dualistic and specific symbols he employs.

Finally, we need to clarify what is meant by non-dualistic
and dualistic systems, since this distinction reflects the crucial
difference between *A Course in Miracles* and almost all other
spiritual thought systems. By *non-duality* we are referring to
the part of *A Course in Miracles* that reflects the two mutually
exclusive dimensions—knowledge and perception, spirit and
matter, Heaven and the world—*only one of which is real.*
Therefore, the clear conclusion of this non-dualistic metaphysics is that God cannot be present in the illusory world,

49

since this would compromise the absolute nature of God's Oneness by implying that there could actually exist a state that is *outside* of perfect unity, an evident and logical impossibility. Duality, on the other hand, reflects the belief that both dimensions—the spiritual *and* the material—are real and co-exist. Consequently, it *is* possible within such spiritual systems that God be present if not active in the phenomenal universe, since the world originated with Him, is really out there, and obviously in need of His help and intervention. Moreover, the very fabric of materiality somehow carries within itself some aspect, traces, or reflection of the divine.

We now consider the nature of non-duality and the problem it presents for a dualistic world.

Non-Duality
The Problem for Students of A COURSE IN MIRACLES

A fuller treatment of the nature of God and Heaven can be found in *All Are Called,* Chapter One, but for our purposes here, a brief overview of the dimensions of this non-dualistic reality is sufficient. We begin with what alone is true: God and His creation. *A Course in Miracles* is quite emphatic that Heaven is the only reality and as Christ, our "only real relationship" is with God (T-15.VIII.6:6). This relationship is of total oneness, with no differentiation between Creator and Created, Cause and Effect, God and Christ. As Jesus teaches about Heaven in the Course:

> Heaven is not a place nor a condition. It is merely an awareness of perfect Oneness, and the knowledge that there is nothing else; nothing outside this Oneness, and nothing else within (T-18.VI.1:5-6).

This is the state of non-duality, where there is no dualistic presence in Heaven, but only One: "nowhere does the Father end, the Son begin as something separate from Him"

(W-pI.132.12:4). In an earlier book, Gloria and I described Heaven this way:

> ...in the Beginning, before there was even a concept of beginning, there is God, our Source and the Source of all creation: a perfection and resplendence whose magnificence is beyond comprehension; love and gentleness of such an infinite nature that consciousness could not even begin its apprehension; a pristine stillness of uninterrupted joy; a motionless flow without friction to impede it; a vast, limitless, and all-encompassing Totality, beyond space, beyond time, in which there is no beginning, no ending, for there was never a time or place when God was not....
>
> Creation, like spirit, is abstract, formless, and unchanging. Its nature is unity, knowledge of which is that there is nowhere the Creator ends and the created begins. There is no boundary, no differentiation, no separation. Yet, included in this knowledge is the fact that we are not the Source of creation, though we remain One within It.
>
> Can the Mind of God begin? Can the Mind of God end? Can a Thought that is part of that Mind be something other than that Mind? Surely not, since there is no subject or object in the state of Heaven; no observer or observed. There is no perception, simply the total knowledge of who we are: a glory of such unified resplendence that concepts of within-without have no meaning (*Awaken from the Dream*, pp. 3-4).

A Course in Miracles itself provides many lovely passages that depict this non-dualistic state of Oneness, and many of these statements emphasize Heaven's inherent ineffability:

> It should especially be noted that God has only *one* Son. If all His creations are His Sons, every one must be an integral part of the whole Sonship. The Sonship in its oneness transcends the sum of its parts (T-2.VII.6:1-3).

> Love cannot judge. As it is one itself, it looks on all as one. *Its meaning lies in oneness. And it must elude the mind that thinks of it as partial or in part.* There is no love but God's, and all of love is His. There is no other principle that

rules where love is not. Love is a law without an opposite. *Its wholeness is the power holding everything as one, the link between the Father and the Son which holds Them Both forever as the same* (W-pI.127.3; italics mine).

Communication, unambiguous and plain as day, remains unlimited for all eternity. And God Himself speaks to His Son, as His Son speaks to Him. *Their language has no words, for what They say cannot be symbolized.* Their knowledge is direct and wholly shared and wholly one (W-pI.129.4:1-4; italics mine).

As nothingness cannot be pictured, so there is no symbol for totality. Reality is ultimately known without a form, unpictured and unseen (T-27.III.5:1-2).

Oneness is simply the idea God is. And in His Being, He encompasses all things. No mind holds anything but Him. We say "God is," and then we cease to speak, for in that knowledge words are meaningless. There are no lips to speak them, and no part of mind sufficiently distinct to feel that it is now aware of something not itself. It has united with its Source. And like its Source Itself, it merely is.
We cannot speak nor write nor even think of this at all (W-pI.169.5:1–6:1).

We can see clearly that there is no way the state of a non-dualistic Heaven can be understood by a brain that has been programmed by the guilty and dualistic mind *not* to understand non-duality, the state that constitutes the gravest threat to individual and specific existence. And so we come to the crux of the issue: how to speak of the non-dualistic truth to dualistic minds—and therefore brains—that can literally not understand this truth. That is the challenge met by Jesus in *A Course in Miracles*, which teachings come from truth to a world of illusion that does not believe in, nor even recognize this truth.

Inconsistent Form and Consistent Content
The Solution for Students of A COURSE IN MIRACLES

It is the language of metaphor and symbol that supplies the solution to this problem, and the following key passage from the text provides the clearest explanation in *A Course in Miracles* of the principle underlying how Jesus has gone about teaching the truth of the non-duality of perfect oneness to his younger siblings who believe they live in the duality of separation, and experientially know of no other dimension:

> *Since you believe that you are separate, Heaven presents itself to you as separate, too. Not that it is in truth, but that the link that has been given you to join the truth may reach to you through what you understand* [i.e., the language of duality]. *Father and Son and Holy Spirit are as One, as all your brothers join as one in truth. Christ and His Father never have been separate, and Christ abides within your understanding, in the part of you that shares His Father's Will. The Holy Spirit links the other part—the tiny, mad desire to be separate, different and special—to the Christ, to make the oneness clear to what is really one. In this world this [non-dualistic truth] is not understood, but can be taught [through the symbol and metaphor of dualistic language].*
>
> The Holy Spirit serves Christ's purpose in your mind, so that the aim of specialness can be corrected where the error lies. Because His purpose still is one with Both the Father and the Son, He knows the Will of God and what you really will. But this is understood by mind perceived as one, aware that it is one, and so experienced. It is the Holy Spirit's function to teach you how this oneness is experienced, what you must do that it can be experienced, and where you should go to do it.
>
> All this takes note of time and place [the world of duality] as if they were discrete, *for while you think that part of you is separate, the concept of a Oneness joined as One is meaningless.* It is apparent that a mind so split could never be the Teacher of a Oneness which unites all things

within Itself. And so What is within this mind, and does unite all things together, must be its Teacher. *Yet must It use the* [dualistic] *language that this mind can understand, in the* [separated and dualistic] *condition in which it thinks it is.* And It must use all learning to transfer illusions to the truth, taking all false [dualistic] ideas of what you are, and leading you beyond them to the [non-dualistic] truth that *is* beyond them (T-25.I.5:1–7:5; italics mine, except for "is" in the last sentence).

The preceding discussion is not the only place in *A Course in Miracles*, however, where Jesus elucidates this idea of having to couch his non-dualistic truth in a dualistic form. We see it also clearly reflected in the section in the manual, referred to in the previous chapter, that deals with the one teacher of God who saves the world. Importantly, in this passage as in the characteristics of God's teachers presented in an earlier section in the manual, Jesus is here clearly referring to *advanced* teachers, in contrast to the "non-advanced" level of Course students who have yet to learn the Course and are still "at the beginning stages of their functioning" (M-4.1-2). The first part of his passage was cited in the previous chapter.

God's teachers appear to be many, for that is what is the world's need. Yet being joined in one purpose, and one they share with God, how could they be separate from each other? What does it matter if they then appear in many forms? Their minds are one; their joining is complete. And God works through them now as one, for that is what they are.

Why is the illusion of many necessary? Only because reality is not understandable to the deluded. Only very few can hear God's Voice at all, and even they cannot communicate His messages directly through the Spirit which gave them. They need a medium through which communication becomes possible to those who do not realize that they are spirit. A body they can see. A voice they understand and listen to, without the fear that truth would encounter in them. Do not forget that truth can come only where it is welcomed without fear. *So do God's teachers need a body, for their unity could not be recognized directly....* The teachers of God appear to share the illusion of separation, but because of what they use the body for, they do not believe in the illusion despite appearances (M-12.2:5–3:8; 4:6; italics mine).

Thus, we see again that a non-dualistic truth—i.e., *one* teacher —is presented in a dualistic context—i.e., *many* teachers—so that it could be understood within the dream of duality. And so never let it be said that Jesus does not clearly state his purpose in speaking dualistically, nor that he compromises the non-dualistic truth that his Course came to teach.

These two references above make it clear that Jesus did not mean that the *form* of his message be taken for the message's *content* itself. The reader will perhaps recall the strong emphasis he places in *A Course in Miracles* on recognizing the importance in the ego thought system of the *forms* of its special relationships, and how they are always substituted for the *content* of love. One such passage will suffice:

Whenever any form of special relationship tempts you to seek for love in ritual, *remember love is content, and not form of any kind.* The special relationship is a ritual of form, aimed at raising the form to take the place of God at the expense of content. *There is no meaning in the form, and there will never be* (T-16.V.12:1-3; italics mine).

These words can be taken as a caveat for all students of *A Course in Miracles* who would seek to understand its principles by almost slavishly holding to the literal meaning of the words, rather than using them as symbols to go beyond to their true meaning. This is why Jesus offers the following statement in the "Clarification of Terms," explaining that his words by their very nature will be inconsistent and *not* the literal truth, and that therefore his students should look *beyond* the inconsistent words to the consistent content of truth:

> This course remains within the ego framework [i.e.,
> duality, the utilization of words and concepts], where it is
> needed. It is not concerned with what is beyond all error
> [i.e., non-duality] because it is planned only to set the
> direction towards it. Therefore it uses words, which are
> symbolic, and cannot express what lies beyond symbols....
> *The course is simple.* It has one function and one goal [i.e.,
> content]. Only in that does it remain wholly consistent
> because only that can *be* consistent (C-in.3:1-3,8-10).

Again, we can see how clearly Jesus is making the distinction
between his inconsistent words and consistent content.

There are still other examples in *A Course in Miracles* of
Jesus "explaining" his use of dualistic language. These evidence how central to the presentation of the Course curriculum is this procedure of utilizing symbols to reflect the non-
dualistic truth of Oneness beyond all symbols, a reality that
cannot be understood within the dualistic world of separation.
We cite some of these passages here:

> In this world, because the mind is split, the Sons of God
> appear to be separate. Nor do their minds seem to be joined.
> In this illusory state, the concept of an "individual mind"
> seems to be meaningful. It is therefore described in the
> course *as if* it has two parts; spirit and ego (C-1.2).

> The idea for today...applies to your inner and outer
> worlds, which are actually the same. *However, since you
> see them as different*, the practice periods for today will
> again include two phases, one involving the world you see
> outside you, and the other the world you see in your mind.
> In today's exercises, try to introduce the thought that both
> are in your own imagination (W-pI.32.2; italics mine).

> God is a Means as well as End. In Heaven, means and end
> are one, and one with Him. This is the state of true creation,
> found not within time, but in eternity. *To no one here is this
> describable.* Nor is there any way to learn what this condi-
> tion means. Not till you go past learning to the Given; not
> till you make again a holy home for your creations is it
> understood.

A co-creator with the Father must have a Son. Yet must this Son have been created like Himself. A perfect being, all-encompassing and all-encompassed, nothing to add and nothing taken from; not born of size nor place nor time, nor held to limits or uncertainties of any kind. Here do the means and end unite as one, nor does this one have any end at all. *All this is true, and yet it has no meaning to anyone who still retains one unlearned lesson in his memory, one thought with purpose still uncertain, or one wish with a divided aim.*

This course makes no attempt to teach what cannot easily be learned. Its scope does not exceed your own, except to say that what is yours will come to you when you are ready. Here are the means and the purpose separate because they were so made and so perceived. *And therefore do we deal with them as if they were* (T-24.VII.6:5–8:4; italics mine).

Learning is change. Salvation does not seek to use a means as yet too alien to your thinking to be helpful, nor to make the kinds of change you could not recognize. Concepts are needed while perception lasts, and changing concepts is salvation's task. *For it must deal in contrasts, not in truth, which has no opposite and cannot change* (T-31.VII.1:1-4; italics mine).

This last passage about the non-dualistic (i.e., "simple") nature of truth is echoed in the following brief statement from the supplement *Psychotherapy: Purpose, Process and Practice*. It deals with the need to couch such simplicity in terms understandable to a complicated world of duality:

While truth is simple, it must still be taught to those who have already lost their way in endless mazes of complexity. This is the great illusion (P-2.V.1:1-2).

Finally, this passage from the text, to be examined again later, also makes the point that God's non-dualistic truth must be reflected in the dualistic world of illusion if the Son is to be awakened from his dream. As the bridge or link between these two dimensions, the Holy Spirit (the "Maker" and "Corrector") is the means for such awakening:

> God's laws do not obtain directly to a world perception
> rules, for such a world could not have been created by the
> Mind to which perception has no meaning. Yet are His laws
> reflected everywhere. Not that the world where this reflec-
> tion is, is real at all. Only because His Son believes it is, and
> from His Son's belief He could not let Himself be separate
> entirely. He could not enter His Son's insanity with him,
> but He could be sure His sanity went there with him, so he
> could not be lost forever in the madness of his wish....
>
> There is another Maker of the world, the simultaneous
> Corrector of the mad belief that anything could be estab-
> lished and maintained without some link that kept it still
> within the laws of God; not as the law itself upholds the
> universe as God created it, *but in some form adapted to the*
> *need the Son of God believes he has* (T-25.III.2; 4:1; italics
> mine).

Therefore, we can clearly see from these few examples
how Jesus is "admitting" to inconsistency in the *form* of his
teaching, although his *content* is absolutely consistent. This is
an extremely important point for students of *A Course in*
Miracles to understand, which is why I keep underscoring it.
Without such understanding, they will inevitably lapse into
misinterpretations that will seriously impede their progress on
the journey Home, which is *A Course in Miracles*' ultimate
goal for them.

A parallel example of how a spiritual teacher uses words
that might suggest one thing while his message is quite
another is found in the teachings of Ramana Maharshi, the
20th-century Indian holy man. He is questioned by a disciple
about an earlier statement that the Heart is "the seat of consciousness and ... identical with the Self." The student is confused because his Master seems to be treating the heart—this
spiritual symbol—as a distinctive physical organ, carefully
situated within the body. Maharshi's answer is reminiscent of
Jesus' teachings in the Course of the need to present a non-
dualistic truth in a dualistic (i.e., physical) context:

...the person who puts the question about the position of the Heart, considers himself as existing with or in the body. While putting the question now, would you say that your body alone is here but that you are speaking from somewhere else? No, you accept your bodily existence. It is from this point of view that any reference to a physical body comes to be made.

Truly speaking, pure Consciousness [i.e., spirit] is indivisible, it is without parts. It has no form and shape, no "within" and "without." There is no "right" or "left" for it. Pure Consciousness, which is the Heart, includes all; and nothing is outside or apart from it. That is the ultimate Truth.

From this absolute stand-point, the Heart, Self or Consciousness can have no particular place assigned to it in the physical body. What is the reason? The body is itself a mere projection of the mind, and the mind is but a poor reflection of the radiant Heart. How can That, in which everything is contained, be itself confined as a tiny part within the physical body...?

But people do not understand this. They cannot help thinking in terms of the physical body and the world.... It is by coming down to the level of ordinary understanding that a place is assigned to the Heart in the physical body (*Maharshi's Gospel*: Books I and II; T.N. Venkataraman; Tiruvannamalai, 1939; pp. 73-74; italics mine).

One more important point need be made regarding the Course's dualistic language, and it is one which Jesus did not need to explain, because it was self-evident to Helen as she was taken down his dictation. This relates to the fact that Jesus' original teaching was to *two* people: Helen Schucman and William Thetford. And so his teachings on forgiveness, which ultimately can occur only *within* the mind of the individual student, were couched in the dualistic language which reflected the mutual classroom that constituted Helen and Bill's relationship. And a classroom, it should be added, they both believed consisted of two people: each other. It was through that classroom that Jesus hoped to lead them both to the non-dualistic content of his love, which existed in their joined *minds* beyond the dualistic form.

While on the subject of Helen and Bill being the original recipients of the message, let me briefly digress to mention that another potential source of confusion for students is in not knowing that certain statements in the Course had direct specific reference to Helen and Bill, and *not* the general audience. A major reason for the writing of *Absence from Felicity: The Story of Helen Schucman and Her Scribing of A COURSE IN MIRACLES* was to help students of the Course better understand the context in which *A Course in Miracles* came, which would help them better understand how certain statements should be taken. Let me give one example which makes the point.

Many students of *A Course in Miracles* have taken the opening lines of the Introduction—"This is a course in miracles. It is a required course."—to mean something to the effect that this is a required course for the world, although the specific form may be different. However, the meaning of these lines was nothing of the sort. The statement was originally part of Jesus' humorous response to Helen's complaint about the "notes" she was taking down and supposed to study. She wondered to Jesus one day whether this course was an elective, which she wrongly (and her ego hopefully) assumed it was. Jesus' emphatic response, which then later became incorporated into the text's Introduction, was:

> *No, it* [this course] *isn't* [an elective]. It's a definite *requirement.* Only the time you take it is voluntary. (*Absence from Felicity*, p. 219).

In like manner, the famous passage from the gospels where the biblical Jesus says that it would be easier for a camel to go through the eye of the needle than for a rich man to enter the Kingdom of God (Matthew 19:24) has been a temptation throughout the centuries for some biblical students to conjecture about the metaphysical meaning of the camel and the needle. The truth, however, is that the reference was to the "needle" or narrow stone arch that kept camels from coming into the sacred temple area that was decidedly off-limits to them. Similarly, students of the Course would do well to remember that the form and context of *A Course in Miracles* was very much influenced by Helen's individual personality and the unforgiving circumstances of her relationship with Bill.

Let us now consider six other examples of this inconsistency in the Course's language, where Jesus appears to be saying something that would clearly contradict the basic tenets of the Course:

1) There are several instances in the workbook where Jesus uses the word *God* when it is really *the Holy Spirit* Who is meant. Lesson 193 is entitled "All things are lessons God would have me learn," and yet throughout the Course it is the Holy Spirit Who is clearly designated as our Teacher, and certainly not the real God Who does not even know we are here. And in fact, the lesson begins with the statement:

> God does not know of learning. Yet His Will extends to what He does not understand....
>
> God sees no contradictions [i.e., duality]. Yet His Son believes he sees them. Thus he has need for One [the Holy Spirit] Who can correct his erring sight, and give him vision that will lead him back to where perception ceases. God does not perceive at all (W-pI.193.1:1-2; 2:1-4).

Clearly then, the word "God"—a one syllable word that fulfills the metric demands of the title's iambic pentameter (a not uncommon reason for Jesus' choice of certain words)—is a symbol for the Holy Spirit, itself a symbol, as we shall see later.

2) Earlier in the workbook come the two lessons, 29 and 30, that are probably more misunderstood than any other: "God is in everything I see." and "God is in everything I see because God is in my mind." Taken literally, the lessons seem

to reflect pantheism, the religious belief that has God present in all material form. Yet the meaning of the workbook lessons, as is indeed explained in them, is that it is the *purpose* of God that is "seen" in everything because that purpose is in our minds (e.g., see W-pI.29.1-3; W-pI.30.2). And that purpose is the forgiveness taught to us by the Holy Spirit. Lesson 193 carries this idea through in a more sophisticated fashion. But clearly Jesus does not mean for his students to believe that God Himself is present in a world of form He does not and can not even know about, *because* it is not real. Again, the word "God" should not always be taken literally by Course students to mean the non-dualistic Creator.

3) Another frequently misunderstood passage comes in Lesson 184:

> Think not you made the world. Illusions, yes! But what is true in earth and Heaven is beyond your naming (W pI.184.8:1-3).

Students who believe that God did indeed make the physical world of individual existence use this passage as "proof" of their position; namely, that we made up the illusory world of pain, suffering, and death, but that God created the physical world of beauty, joy, and happiness. However, what has not been understood is that the passage is referring to the *real world*, which is "made" by the Holy Spirit and not by the Son's ego. This can be seen in these statements from "Perception and Choice" in the text, which we presented earlier in this chapter in another context:

> God's laws do not obtain directly to a world perception rules, for such a world could not have been created by the Mind to which perception has no meaning. Yet are His laws reflected everywhere. Not that the world where this reflection is, is real at all....
> *There is another Maker of the world....*
> There is another purpose [forgiveness] in the world that error made, because *it has another Maker* Who can reconcile its goal with His Creator's purpose [creation]....

> *The Maker of the world of gentleness* [the real world]...
> (T-25.III.2:1-3; 4:1; 5:1; 8:1; italics mine).

Further still, the statement quoted above from the workbook, "what is true in earth and Heaven," finds its meaning in this concept of truth being reflected in the world.

Earlier statements in the text also establish clearly that the Son of God does not make the real world, as we see in the following passages, cited earlier in Chapter One. Quoting from the famous verse from the gospel of John (3:16), Jesus makes a correction in the Course:

> The statement "God so loved the world that He gave His only begotten Son, that whosoever believeth in Him should not perish but have everlasting life" needs only one slight correction to be meaningful in this context; "He gave it *to* His only begotten Son" (T-2.VII.5:14).

And then he clarifies this point later on:

> I said before that God so loved the world that He gave it to His only-begotten Son. God does love the real world, and those who perceive its reality cannot see the world of death. For death is not of the real world, in which everything reflects the eternal. *God gave you the real world* [through the Holy Spirit] *in exchange for the one you made out of your split mind,* and which is the symbol of death (T 12.III.8:1-4; italics mine).

4) In the workbook for students, Jesus very clearly states that God does not understand words and does not hear prayers:

> Think not He hears the little prayers of those who call on Him with names of idols [of specialness] cherished by the world. They cannot reach Him thus. *He cannot hear requests that He be not Himself,* or that His Son receive another name than His....
> Turn to the Name of God for your release, and it is given you. *No prayer but this is necessary, for it holds them all within it. Words are insignificant,* and all requests unneeded when God's Son calls on his Father's Name. His

Father's Thoughts become his own. He makes his claim to all his Father gave, is giving still, and will forever give. He calls on Him to let all things he thought he made be nameless now, and in their place the holy Name of God becomes his judgment of their worthlessness (W-pI.183.7:3-5; 10; italics mine).

That workbook passage is similar to the discussion at the beginning of *The Song of Prayer* where Jesus addresses the issue of asking (or praying to) God for specifics. Our Creator and Source does not hear our prayers for what does not exist (in the world of duality), but calling upon Him recalls to us the non-dualistic truth in which is found the answer to all our supposed needs. That is why, incidentally, there is no order of difficulty in miracles. All problems—regardless of their seeming magnitude—are solved in the same way: by recognizing, through the miracle of choosing the Holy Spirit's truth instead of the ego's illusion, that all problems are equally unreal. And so Jesus says to his students, in an important passage the reader will recall from our discussion in *All Are Called* (pp. 316-17), as well as having been cited earlier in this book:

To ask for the specific is much the same as to look on sin and then forgive it. Also in the same way, in prayer you overlook your specific needs as you see them, and let them go into God's Hands.... What could His answer be but your remembrance of Him? Can this be traded for a bit of trifling advice about a problem of an instant's duration? God answers only for eternity. But still all little answers are contained in this (S-1.I.4:2-3,5-8).

And this is underscored, as we have seen, by this statement in the manual: "God does not understand words, for they were made by separated minds to keep them in the illusion of separation" (M-21.1:7).

Yet given all this, the thoughtful student of the Course is astounded to find that virtually the entire second part of the workbook, Lessons 221-360, consists of one beautiful prayer after another addressed to God the Father, not to mention the above-cited workbook Lesson 71 where we are told to ask our Creator and Source for very specific help. And so students may feel justified in complaining to Jesus that he has presented them with contradictory messages. In fact, Jesus anticipates this complaint and specifically addresses it in *The Song of Prayer*, in a passage we discussed at great length in the section on prayer in Chapter Seven of *All Are Called*:

> You have been told to ask the Holy Spirit for the answer to any specific problem, and that you will receive a specific answer if such is your need [See, for example, T-11.VIII. 5:5-6; T-20.IV.8:4-8; there were also early personal messages to Helen in that regard, see for example *Absence from Felicity*, p. 293]. You have also been told that there is only problem and one answer [See W-pI.79-80]. In prayer this is not contradictory (S-1.I.2:1-3).

These seemingly mutually exclusive statements are not contradictory because they represent different levels of teaching, meant to be commensurate with students' differing levels of readiness. At the beginning of what later in the supplement is called "the ladder of prayer" (S-1.II)—the process of forgiveness—the belief in specifics dictates that God's Love be expressed in those terms. As students make their way up the ladder—i.e., lessen their identification with the ego's specialness—they can experience this Love more and more abstractly, and draw closer and closer to its true nature.

Therefore, teaching to those on the higher reaches of the ladder, Jesus states that God is not involved in the illusory dualistic world of specifics at all. However, when he teaches to those on the first levels, as he so frequently does in *A Course in Miracles*, he refers to a God whose Love for His children extends into the dream, where specific needs *seem* to be met and requests for specialness *seemingly* granted. And so we can understand Jesus' "higher" teachings on prayer as reflecting our choosing again so that we now can identify with the right mind (the Holy Spirit; i.e., the memory of God) instead of the wrong mind. From this perspective, then, prayer is *not* literally asking God for things, even though that may be our experience, but rather it refers to our turning to a right-minded image of God that for us *metaphorically* represents the abstract non-dualistic God that is beyond our dualistic experience and understanding.

5) A wonderfully clear example of how loosely Jesus uses his words—letting them mean one thing in one place, and another thing elsewhere—is with the phrase "miracle of healing." Early in the text he is quite emphatic in saying:

> Our emphasis is now on healing. The miracle is the means, the Atonement is the principle, and healing is the result. *To speak of "a miracle of healing" is to combine two orders of reality inappropriately. Healing is not a miracle.* The Atonement, or the final miracle, is a remedy and any type of healing is a result (T-2.IV.1:1-5; italics mine).

One could not ask for a more precise statement. And yet there are five places elsewhere in the Course where Jesus speaks of a "miracle of healing" (T-19.I.14:5; T-27.II.5:2; T-27.V.1:3; T-28.IV.10:9; and M-22.4:4), clearly violating his own earlier injunction to his students. Again, a student would seem justified in asking Jesus why he presents conflicting messages in a Course that claims to be so clear and direct. Here is what his answer would be:

> In the original statement, which is made early in the text, I am teaching my students that the miracle is the means and healing is the result, establishing a cause and effect relationship between them, the understanding of which is crucial to the learning process in those early parts of the text. That point having been made and the distinction established, however, I am now able to use the poetic phrase "miracle of healing" more freely later in the Course. I repeatedly emphasize in my teaching that purpose is everything, for it alone provides meaning to behavior and circumstances. And so here the inconsistency on the level

of form is reconciled by the differing purpose for the passages in question.

6) A constant and consistent inconsistency in the Course is Jesus' juxtaposing statements that speak of salvation coming happily and joyously in an instant (e.g., T-26.VIII; W-pI.182) with statements that urge patience in what is a long and painful process of forgiveness (e.g., M-4.I-A.3-8; VIII). Here, too, there is no contradiction, as long as one remembers that Jesus is speaking on different levels. From the point of view of timelessness or the holy instant—the dimension that transcends the ego's time-bound view of sin (past), guilt ("present"), and fear (future)—all that is required is the change of mind from the ego to the Holy Spirit. Since time is an illusion, this can only occur in an instant, as stated in Lesson 182: "I will be still an instant and go home."

On the other hand, however, within the illusion of time— where students of the Course believe they are while at the beginning of the ladder—the undoing of guilt takes a very long time, as is reflected in the six stages of the development of trust in the manual for teachers. The transition from the fifth to the sixth stage, which is the real world, is spoken of like this: "And now he must attain a state that may remain impossible to reach for a long, long time" (M-4.I-A.7:7).

As can be seen from the above discussion, if a person's ego wishes to invalidate the authority of *A Course in Miracles*, it can easily find "cause" by pointing to these seeming incongruities in the language. Similarly, people seeking to change the Course's teachings around to suit their own needs can also find innumerable passages to "support" their position. As a safeguard against making these mistakes, a student should always evaluate any particular statement in the Course in the light of the Course's overall metaphysical teaching. In summary, therefore, we can observe once again that Jesus is reflecting different aspects of the process of forgiveness, as seen from different rungs of the ladder. When one holds the true teaching of *A Course in Miracles* in mind, then the differing statements in form are understood as teaching metaphors or symbols that gently reflect the different stages of our journey home.

Symbols

There are several places in *A Course in Miracles* where Jesus discusses the nature and role of symbols, and it would be instructive to look at some of these now, as further evidence of *his* awareness of the difference in his Course between symbol and reality. We begin with the question in the manual for teachers that specifically addresses the role of words (or symbols). This provides us with the clearest statement in the Course, already considered in part, about the difference between words and meaning, form and content:

> Strictly speaking, words play no part at all in healing. The motivating factor is prayer, or asking. What you ask for you receive. But this refers to the prayer of the heart, not to the words you use in praying. Sometimes the words and the prayer are contradictory; sometimes they agree. It does not matter. God does not understand words, for they were made by separated minds to keep them in the illusion of separation. Words can be helpful, particularly for the beginner, in helping concentration and facilitating the exclusion, or at least the control, of extraneous thoughts. *Let us not forget, however, that words are but symbols of symbols. They are thus twice removed from reality.*
>
> As symbols, words have quite specific references. Even when they seem most abstract, the picture that comes to mind is apt to be very concrete. Unless a specific referent does occur to the mind in conjunction with the word, the word has little or no practical meaning, and thus cannot help the healing process....

Pausing for a moment, we can better understand Jesus' relatively abstract words here with a specific example. As we have seen, *A Course in Miracles* speaks of God weeping over His separated Sons (T-5.VII.4:5). This clearly implies, if taken literally, that God has a body containing tear ducts, not to mention His having thoughts that have made the separation real and powerful. But given this teaching about words being symbols of symbols, we can understand the passage about God's tears this way: "Tears" is the *word* (the first symbol) that contains the *image* or *picture* (the second symbol) of God's weeping, and this represents the *reality* that God loves us. Since the Love of God is abstract and non-dualistic, beyond the split mind's ability to understand, Jesus resorts to the symbol that reflects this Love. Rather than our believing in the God of the ego's fairy tale Who is angry and vengeful, Jesus would have us believe instead, in these early stages of our journey of awakening, in the God of his corrected fairy tale Who truly loves us, independent of what we believe we have done to Him. And all this presented in a way we can relate to and understand. But if these words are taken literally, we would find ourselves back in our childhood world of fairy godmothers, Santa Claus, and a Sugar Daddy for a God.

To continue now with our passage from the manual:

> The sleeping Son of God has but this power left to him [the power to decide]. It is enough. His words do not matter. Only the Word of God [the Atonement] has any meaning, because it symbolizes that which has no human symbols at all. The Holy Spirit alone understands what this Word stands for. And this, too, is enough.
>
> Is the teacher of God, then, to avoid the use of words in his teaching? No, indeed! *There are many who must be reached through words, being as yet unable to hear in silence* [Jesus obviously would have his own Course students in mind here]. The teacher of God must, however, learn to use words in a new way [as Jesus is exemplifying for these teachers in *A Course in Miracles*]. Gradually, he learns how to let his words be chosen for him by ceasing to

69

> decide for himself what he will say. This process is merely
> a special case of the lesson in the workbook that says, "I
> will step back and let Him lead the way." [W-pI.155] The
> teacher of God accepts the words which are offered him,
> and gives as he receives. He does not control the direction
> of his speaking. He listens and hears and speaks....God's
> teachers have God's Word behind their symbols. And He
> Himself gives to the words they use the power of His Spirit,
> raising them from meaningless symbols to the Call of
> Heaven itself (M-21.1:1–2:3; 3:7–4:9; 5:8-9 italics mine).

Truth, therefore, cannot be really be expressed in words,
but only pointed to. It is the truth that is essential, not the
symbol itself. In an important passage from Lesson 189, we
see another clear statement of the need to move beyond
symbols to what alone is real—God:

> Simply do this: Be still, and lay aside all thoughts of what
> you are and what God is; all concepts you have learned
> about the world; all images you hold about yourself. Empty
> your mind of everything it thinks is either true or false, or
> good or bad, of every thought it judges worthy, and all the
> ideas of which it is ashamed. Hold onto nothing. Do not
> bring with you one thought the past has taught, nor one be-
> lief you ever learned before from anything. Forget this
> world, forget this course, and come with wholly empty
> hands unto your God (W-pI.189.7).

Another specific example where Jesus clarifies the seeming inconsistency of his words, discussed before in *All Are
Called* (pp. 317-21), comes in workbook Lesson 194, "I place
the future in the Hands of God." At first blush this title seems
incongruous with the timeless reality of God Who can
obviously have no notion of a future, not to mention the incon-
gruity of the lesson's obvious symbolism of our formless
Creator having Hands. But one must go beyond the words and
symbols to the lesson's real meaning, which is clearly stated
in the fourth paragraph of the lesson:

God holds your future as He holds your past and present.
They are one to Him, and so they should be one to you. *Yet
in this world, the temporal progression still seems real.
And so you are not asked to understand the lack of
sequence really found in time.* You are but asked to let the
future go, and place it in God's Hands. And you will see by
your experience that you have laid the past and present in
His Hands as well, because the past will punish you no
more, and future dread will now be meaningless
(W-pI.194.4; italics mine).

One of Freud's great contributions to the study of dreams
was his delineation of the *manifest* dream content versus its
latent content. The manifest content referred to the parts of the
dream—the figures, objects, and events that constitute its
form, the story of the dream—while the latent content pointed
to the meaning that lay beyond the dream's manifest symbolism. Thus, two analysts of differing persuasions could obviously agree on the dream's manifest content, but could ascribe
totally different meanings to what the dream is saying. To use
a simple example, a Freudian would tend to interpret a church
steeple in a person's dream as a phallic symbol, possibly reflecting sexual conflict, while a Jungian might see instead a
symbol of the dreamer's spiritual strivings.

Returning to the workbook lesson, what Jesus is teaching
is not the manifest content that we should literally place our
future in God's Hands, but rather the latent content that we
should abandon the ego's insane yet vicious notion that our
guilt demands punishment at the *hands* of a vengeful deity.
And therefore we can trust His Love and safely place our
future in His *Hands*. In other words, Jesus is *not* teaching us
that we should blithely give up our personal, social, and work
responsibilities, destroy our insurance policies, etc., because
the world is an illusion and God will provide if only we place
our future in His Hands. But he *is* teaching us that the ego's
insane thought system of sin, guilt, and fear is unreal. Thus,
God is not the vengeful Father of our ego's fairy tale, but the

loving Creator of Jesus' corrected fairy tale that is the symbolic substitute for the ego's distorted set of images.

To digress briefly, students make the same mistake with the section in Chapter 18 in the text, "I Need Do Nothing" (T-18.VII), or the statement in Lesson 135: "A healed mind does not plan" (W-pI.135.11:1). These statements are often interpreted to mean that one need do nothing in the world (like hold a job, meet family responsibilities, plan for the future, etc.) because God or the Holy Spirit will take care of us. But what these passages *really* mean is that one should not do anything or plan *on one's own* (with the ego), but rather should always go to the Holy Spirit or Jesus for help. Thus, these are not calls to turn one's back on the world, but rather calls to bring one's ego perceptions of the world to the Holy Spirit's truth within. In that way, one's responses will be filled with His forgiveness and love, rather than with the ego's hate-filled specialness which is sometimes veiled by denial, appearing to be holiness, advanced spirituality, or love. We shall leave an in-depth discussion of the Holy Spirit's function for a later chapter.

And so this lesson of the ego's inherent untrustworthiness is taught to Jesus' students in the language and form they can understand. You do not tell little children, for example, upset that they have done something wrong and therefore have run away from home, that they do not have to be afraid since Daddy does not even know that they exist, and besides, they only *think* that they have misbehaved and have run away. Rather, you comfort them by letting them know that Daddy is not upset with them, will not punish them, and moreover, that he weeps over his loss and yearns for the children's return. Therefore, once again Jesus concludes for his younger siblings who are studying his Course: You *can* entrust your future to your Father's Hands, since He only loves you and will not cause you any harm.

In summary, therefore, these various passages must be understood on the level of the *content* of God's Love for His children (itself, of course, an anthropocentric metaphor), expressed through the *form* of an earthly father's love for his child. Since we are still very much children in the spiritual life —"You are very new in the ways of salvation" (T-17.V.9:1) Jesus tells us—the Course's gentle and loving use of language at this level is certainly more than appropriate.

It cannot be emphasized enough that a student of A *Course in Miracles* must always be able to distinguish between the symbol (manifest content) and its meaning (latent content). The reader should recall this telling passage from the third obstacle to peace, which has Jesus issuing just such a warning about this potential confusion:

> Remember, then, that neither sign nor symbol should be confused with source, for they must stand for something other than themselves. *Their meaning cannot lie in them, but must be sought in what they represent* (T-19.IV-C.11:2-3; italics mine).

The Course's dualistic words are the symbols or signs that point to their non-dualistic source of truth, and students of A *Course in Miracles* should always heed Jesus' clear admonition not to confuse them; otherwise, the meaning of his teachings will inevitably become distorted and lost.

A student of A *Course in Miracles* must therefore understand metaphoric language ("sign and symbol"), just as a student of poetry must understand *how* and *why* words are used, without taking them literally. For example, Macbeth laments at the end of his life:

> Out, out, brief candle!
> Life's but a walking shadow; a poor player,
> That struts and frets his hour upon the stage,
> And then is heard no more: it is a tale
> Told by an idiot, full of sound and fury,
> Signifying nothing (V.5).

Clearly, Shakespeare is not having his fallen hero speak here about candles or actors in a play, but rather is using poetic symbols as a way of offering a tragic commentary about the meaninglessness of life. Needless to say, analyzing these words would literally destroy their meaning and significance in the play, not to mention ruining the genius of Shakespeare's poetry.

The following passages well illustrate Jesus' clear awareness of the use of symbols in *A Course in Miracles* as *reflections* of the truth, since the non-dualistic nature of truth cannot be expressed directly from one to another:

> ...God is not symbolic; He is Fact (T-3.I.8:2).

> True vision is the natural perception of spiritual sight, but *it is still a correction rather than a fact.* Spiritual sight is symbolic, and therefore not a device for knowing. It is, however, a means of right perception, which brings it into the proper domain of the miracle. A "vision of God" would be a miracle rather than a revelation. The fact that perception is involved at all removes the experience from the realm of knowledge. That is why visions, however, holy, do not last (T-3.III.4; italics mine).

> The reflections you accept into the mirror of your mind in time but bring eternity nearer or farther. But eternity itself is beyond all time. Reach out of time and touch it, with the help of its reflection in you.... Reflect the peace of Heaven here, and bring this world to Heaven. *For the reflection of truth draws everyone to truth, and as they enter into it they leave all reflections behind.*

> In Heaven reality is shared and not reflected. By sharing its reflection here, its truth becomes the only perception the Son of God accepts.... *You on earth have no conception of limitlessness, for the world you seem to live in is a world of limits* (T-14.X.1:2-4,6-7; 2:1-2,4; italics mine).

Very specifically in this next passage, we see Jesus' clearly implied "admission" that he has at other times in the Course used words symbolically (or allegorically), although in this instance he is making it clear that he has not:

It is only the awareness of the body that makes love seem limited. For the body *is* a limit on love. The belief in limited love was its origin, and it was made to limit the unlimited. Think not that this is merely allegorical, for it was made to limit *you* (T-18.VIII.1:1-4).

In one of Helen's letters to me, dealing with circumstances that are tangential to our subject here, she discussed symbols and a mutual friend's inability to understand how to use them. She wrote:

This is a letter I feel just has to be written, and written as soon as possible. It has to do with fact and allegory and the somewhat uncertain borderline between them.... Freddie does not understand symbolism; the dear boy can't even understand how a thing can stand for something else. Bill [Thetford] went over this with him, and all he could grasp was if you see something it's there. It's not that he's stupid, Heaven knows, but *he just can't seem to get beyond facts, so he can be mistaken just because of that* (*Absence from Felicity*, pp. 346-47; italics mine).

Thus, if students of *A Course in Miracles* are not able to get "beyond facts (or symbols)," they can be easily mistaken in their understanding of what is truly being said. And so the deeper meaning of the Course will always remain hidden to them, not by Jesus' design, but by their own fear. It was in anticipation of this difficulty leading to inevitable distortion, that Helen would frequently comment that *A Course in Miracles* was only for five or six people. She recognized how difficult this Course was, and how terrifying it would be for people's egos. And so, in light of all the distortions students have made and continue to make with the Course, based upon their fear of what it says, one can very easily be tempted to make the statement that *A Course in Miracles* was *not* written for students of *A Course in Miracles*; that is, the Course is not for those who so readily jump on their own bandwagon and seek to make *A Course in Miracles* into something it is not.

Rather, it is for those relative few who would be willing to "step back and let him lead the way" (W-pI.155), allowing Jesus' wisdom in the Course to lead them through the ego's dark tunnel to the light that awaits at the end of the journey.

Chapter 3

THE COURSE'S USE OF LANGUAGE – II
THE SYMBOLISM OF FORGIVENESS

Introduction

The issue of Jesus correcting our mistakes at the level we can accept and understand has already been discussed, but we return to it now more specifically in this chapter to see how forgiveness serves as the great *symbol* of *A Course in Miracles*.

As the correction for the ego's story of sin, guilt, and fear of punishment, forgiveness cannot be real (since it corrects what never happened) but is rather a symbol for what alone is real: the Love of God. However, as the Course teaches us, this correction does not oppose reality for it *reflects* the non-dualistic and non-oppositional truth. Forgiveness thus gently undoes the ego's voice, which allows the Son to hear the only Voice in this dualistic and symbolic world that can lead him beyond it to the truth of God's Love. Incidentally, it is this gentle process of correcting our errors through intermediate steps that makes *A Course in Miracles* unique in the history of non-dualistic spiritualities. It retains the integrity of a non-dualistic metaphysical system, yet allows its truth to be reflected into the dualistic world where the Son believes he lives. One wonderful example of this gentleness is seen in the following passage which discusses awakening from the ego's dream of terror. It is a nice entrée to our discussion:

> So fearful is the dream, so seeming real, he [the Son of God] could not waken to reality without the sweat of terror and a scream of mortal fear, unless a gentler dream preceded his awaking, and allowed his calmer mind to welcome, not to fear, the Voice that calls with love to waken him; a gentler dream, in which his suffering was healed and where his brother was his friend. God willed he

waken gently and with joy, and gave him means to waken without fear (T-27.VII.13:4-5).

Forgiveness As a Dualistic Symbol

Forgiveness, of course, is the means of awakening from the ego's dream of terror. And it is a means which, Jesus emphasizes, *is* illusory, as shown in the following passages:

Illusion makes illusion. Except one. Forgiveness is illusion that is answer to the rest.

Forgiveness sweeps all other dreams away, and though it is itself a dream, it breeds no others. All illusions save this one must multiply a thousandfold. But this is where illusions end. Forgiveness is the end of dreams, because it is a dream of waking. *It is not itself the truth. Yet does it point to where the truth must be*, and gives direction with the certainty of God Himself. It is a dream in which the Son of God awakens to his Self and to his Father, knowing They are one (W-pI.198.2:8–3:7; italics mine).

Forgiveness might be called a kind of happy fiction; a way in which the unknowing can bridge the gap between their perception and the truth. *They cannot go directly from perception to knowledge because they do not think it is their will to do so.* This makes God appear to be an enemy instead of what He really is. And it is just this insane perception that makes them unwilling merely to rise up and to return to Him in peace.

And so they need an illusion of help because they are helpless; a Thought of peace because they are in conflict (C-3.2:1–3:1; italics mine).

Forgiveness is thus the process of correcting the ego's symbols (belonging to the dualistic world), thereby undoing the ego thought system and making room for the non-dualistic truth to be recognized and accepted.

We turn to two passages from the workbook where Jesus makes it clear, again, that forgiveness itself is unreal and illusory, being simply a *reflection* of the non-dualistic Love of Heaven:

> God not does forgive because He has never condemned.... Yet forgiveness is the means by which I [the student] will recognize my innocence. *It is the reflection of God's Love on earth.* It will bring me near enough to Heaven that the Love of God can reach down to me and raise me up to Him (W-pI.60.1:2,4-6; italics mine).

> For Love must give, and what is given in His Name takes on the form most useful in a world of form.
> These are the forms which never can deceive, because they come from Formlessness Itself. *Forgiveness is an earthly form of love, which as it is in Heaven has no form. Yet what is needed here is given here as it is needed.* In this form you can fulfill your function even here, although what love will mean to you when formlessness has been restored to you is greater still (W-pI.186.13:5–14:4; italics mine).

We examine now a brief passage that describes forgiveness' role in undoing the ego's illusions—substituting a happy illusion for the ego's illusions of fear—and clearing the way for the return of truth:

> Yet although God does not forgive, His Love is nevertheless the basis of forgiveness. Fear condemns and love forgives. Forgiveness thus undoes what fear has produced, returning the mind to the awareness of God. For this reason, forgiveness can truly be called salvation. It is the means by which illusions disappear (W-pI.46.2).

Our final passage in this section on forgiveness provides yet another clear description of the dualistic nature of forgiveness, which is based upon the contrast of opposites, but which should not be confused with the non-dualistic reality that has no opposite. The reader may recall, incidentally, the earlier quoted passage from the obstacles to peace (T-19.IV-C.11:2-3) where Jesus emphasizes the importance of distinguishing between symbol and source, form and content.

Unweakened power, with no opposite, is what creation is. For this there are no symbols. Nothing points beyond the truth, for what can stand for more than everything? Yet true undoing must be kind. And so the first replacement for your picture is another picture of another kind.

As nothingness cannot be pictured, so *there is no symbol for totality. Reality is ultimately known without a form, unpictured and unseen.* Forgiveness is not yet a power known as wholly free of limits. Yet it sets no limits you have chosen to impose. *Forgiveness is the means by which the truth is represented temporarily.* It lets the Holy Spirit make exchange of pictures possible, until the time when aids are meaningless and learning done. No learning aid has use that can extend beyond the goal of learning. When its aim has been accomplished it is functionless. Yet in the learning interval it has a use that now you fear, but yet will love....

Forgiveness vanishes and symbols fade, and nothing that the eyes have ever seen or ears have heard remains to be perceived. A Power wholly limitless has come, not to destroy, but to receive its own. There is no choice of function anywhere. The choice you fear to lose you never had. Yet only this appears to interfere with power unlimited and single thoughts, complete and happy, without opposite. You do not know the peace of power that opposes nothing. Yet no other kind can be at all. Give welcome to the power beyond forgiveness, and beyond the world of symbols and of limitations. He [God] would merely be, and so He merely is (T-27.III.4:4–5:9; 7; italics mine).

And so forgiveness is a temporary correction—a means to an end—for the belief in the reality of the ego's insane thought system. It is a "kind (though illusory) undoing" of the ego's illusory "doing" of attack. To state this important point once again, understanding the important distinction between the truth of non-duality and the illusion of duality, emphasized again in this passage, is essential if one is truly to understand *A Course in Miracles.* Since, once again, forgiveness corrects what never *was*, it too must not truly *be.* Thus it is we speak of forgiveness as a symbol, and all the passages in the Course where Jesus speaks of forgiving your brother can be understood to be metaphors for the process of undoing the illusion that occurs only within the mind. We turn now to a discussion of this essential point.

Forgiveness As Correction within the Dream of Duality

It is because students of *A Course in Miracles* do not understand the dualistic framework of the Course's *form* as opposed to the non-dualistic framework of its *content*, that they misunderstand the meaning of forgiveness, believing that it is a process that actually occurs between two people; i.e. in a dualistic reality. To be sure, Jesus' language in the Course suggests this, for the reasons we have already explored, and thus *A Course in Miracles* seems in many places to be similar to other spiritual or religious paths that emphasize forgiveness of others. But as we have seen, the teachings of *A Course in Miracles* would be seriously distorted, not to mention misapplied in practice, if it is not recognized by its students that forgiveness can only truly occur within the *mind* of the student, although it is experienced *within* the belief system and perceptual dream that says that there is someone outside us to forgive.

The same is true of course with a holy relationship, which can only exist in the *mind* of the perceiver of the relationship. Relationships are not holy in *form*, but only in *purpose*. And purpose exists, once again, in the individual's mind, its source coming either from the ego or the Holy Spirit. But one often finds expression of the ego's unconscious arrogance when students claim that a specific relationship is a holy one. They know not what they say for the chances are that their egos have succeeded once again in repressing its true purpose of hiding guilt behind a shield of seeming holiness, expressed here in the form of spiritual specialness. One must never underestimate this need to defend against the repressed un-holiness we believe is our true reality. It is so great that we need not only to deny its presence, but to assert its opposite. And so we seek to convince ourselves (and others) how holy our relationships are. We shall return to a discussion of this spiritual specialness in Chapters Four and Six.

The error has its root in the confusion of the nature of the Sonship. In the text, quoted in the previous chapter, Jesus explains that contrary to the famous axiom in Euclidean geometry, "The Sonship [the whole] in its Oneness transcends the sum of its parts" (T-2.VII.6:3). In other words, one cannot appreciate the pure wholeness and oneness of Christ by simply adding up the billions and billions of fragments that the world thinks is the Son of God, as if the Sonship were like a huge pie, a quantifiable entity consisting of a certain amount of separated fragments. Christ in His very nature is a perfect and undivided One, *as Mind*, and He loses that essential character-istic which defines His Being if fragmentation in any of its forms is acknowledged as real. Similarly, returning to our ear-lier example of the elephant and the six blind men (p. 8), if each man described his piece of the elephant to the others, and an outside observer recorded their observations, the sum total of their perceptions would not constitute the essence of the pachyderm. Thus, believing that a fragment of the Sonship—for example, a human being—is Christ, the true Son of God, would be as gross a mistake as one of the blind men examining the elephant's leg and proclaiming that the elephant is a tree! Again, even though the *language* of *A Course in Miracles* sug-gests that the Son is a member of *homo sapiens*, a proper understanding of Jesus' *meaning* beyond his words would keep students from reaching such an erroneous conclusion. Recalling the statement in workbook Lesson 93, "The self you made is not the Son of God" (W-pI.93.5:1).

Therefore, to summarize this essential thought, we may say that forgiveness is mediated by the *process* that is the holy relationship, and occurs within a dualistic framework of relationships with others. It must be so, for otherwise how could one correct the misperceptions that have been projected from within the guilt-ridden *non-human* mind onto someone else? Since the experience is the unforgiveness we have projected onto others, the correction—forgiveness—will likewise appear to be between oneself and this other. One cannot skip over the "little steps" and recall our true Self as Christ, as the fear of losing our special identity and individual uniqueness is too overpowering. As we have just seen, we first must experience the gentle dreams of forgiveness before we can awaken from the ego's nightmare dreams of terror. Thus, the Holy Spirit's dualistic correction of forgiveness undoes the ego's dualistic thoughts of attack. Only then can the world of duality fade away, its place to be taken by the truth of God that has always been present in our minds.

In this next very important passage, Jesus expresses in more depth the role of the dualistic correction—i.e., forgiveness—in helping to restore the Son of God to his non-dualistic Identity. There is no choice possible in a non-dualistic state, by definition, but there is the illusion of choice within the dualistic world of the dreams of fear which we believe to be our reality. And so, through the Holy Spirit, forgiveness is that choice available to us within the dualistic dream that undoes all the other choices, and restores to our awareness the non-dualistic reality of Heaven. What follows are excerpts from Lesson 138: "Heaven is the decision I must make," which expresses the inherently illusory nature of choice:

> In this world Heaven is a choice, because here we believe there are alternatives to choose between. We think that all things have an opposite, and what we want we choose. If Heaven exists there must be hell as well, for contradiction is the way we make what we perceive, and what we think is real.
>
> Creation knows no opposite. But here is opposition part of being "real." It is this strange perception of the truth that makes the choice of Heaven seem to be the same as the

relinquishment of hell. *It is not really thus. Yet what is true in God's creation cannot enter here until it is reflected in some form the world can understand.* Truth cannot come where it could only be perceived with fear. For this would be the error truth can be brought to illusions. Opposition makes the truth unwelcome, and it cannot come....

You need to be reminded that you think a thousand choices are confronting you, when there is really only one to make. And even this but seems to be a choice. Do not confuse yourself with all the doubts that myriad decisions would induce. You make but one. And when that one is made, *you will perceive it was no choice at all.* For truth is true, and nothing else is true. There is no opposite to choose instead. There is no contradiction to the truth.

Choosing depends on learning. And the truth cannot be learned, but only recognized. In recognition its acceptance lies, and as it is accepted it is known. But knowledge is beyond the goals we seek to teach within the framework of this course. Ours are teaching goals, to be attained through learning how to reach them, what they are, and what they offer you. Decisions are the outcome of your learning, for they rest on what you have accepted as the truth of what you are, and what your needs must be....

Heaven is chosen consciously. The choice cannot be made until alternatives are accurately seen and understood. All that is veiled in shadows must be raised to understanding, to be judged again, this time with Heaven's help....

The conscious choice of Heaven is as sure as is the ending of the fear of hell, when it is raised from its protective shield of unawareness, and is brought to light. Who can decide between the clearly seen and the unrecognized? Yet who can fail to make a choice between alternatives when only one is seen as valuable; the other as a wholly worthless thing, a but imagined source of guilt and pain? Who hesitates to make a choice like this? And shall we hesitate to choose today? (W-pI.138.1-2; 4-5; 9:1-3; 10; italics mine)

This choice between truth and illusion (Heaven and hell), is reflected in the rhetorical question that closes Chapter 23.

Indeed, the entire Course is Jesus' attempt to join with us so that we could make, finally, this one choice that would save us and all the world:

> Who with the Love of God upholding him could find the choice of miracles or murder hard to make? (T-23.IV.9:8)

This next passage, from the text, provides still another very clear example of how Jesus contrasts the non-dualistic reality of God and His creation with the Holy Spirit's world of reflected reality, "the real world." It is an important passage, for it helps to summarize our discussion of the need for students of *A Course in Miracles* to recognize the uncompromising nature of its non-dualistic metaphysics, yet a metaphysics which is integrated with a gentle approach to our experiences within the dream of duality. It begins with a two-paragraph restatement of this non-dualistic foundation: Only God is real and sane; *everything else* is illusory and insane. These lines, incidentally, should be read carefully and thoughtfully, again and again, by every student of the Course:

> Let us go back to what we said before, and think of it more carefully. It must be so that either God is mad, or is this world a place of madness. Not one Thought of His makes any sense at all within this world. And nothing that the world believes as true has any meaning in His Mind at all. What makes no sense and has no meaning is insanity. And what is madness cannot be the truth. If one belief so deeply valued here were true, then every Thought God ever had is an illusion. And if but one Thought of His is true, then all beliefs the world gives any meaning to are false, and make no sense at all. This is the choice you make. *Do not attempt to see it differently, nor twist it into something it is not.* For only this decision can you make. The rest is up to God, and not to you.
>
> To justify one value that the world upholds is to deny your Father's sanity and yours. For God and His beloved Son do not think differently. And it is the agreement of their thought that makes the Son a co-creator with the Mind

Whose Thought created him. So if he chooses to believe one thought opposed to truth, he has decided he is not his Father's Son because the Son is mad, and sanity must lie apart from both the Father and the Son. This you believe. Think not that this belief depends upon the form it takes. Who thinks the world is sane in any way, is justified in anything it thinks, or is maintained by any form of reason, believes this to be true. Sin is not real *because* the Father and the Son are not insane. This world is meaningless *because* it rests on sin. Who could create the changeless if it does not rest on truth? (T-25.VII.3-4; italics mine in paragraph 3)

Despite its uncompromising treatment of the difference between reality and illusion, as we have repeatedly noted, *A Course in Miracles* is practical and gentle in its advocacy of specific application of these principles within the dream. And so the words of Jesus meet his students in the unreal world of duality, where they believe they are. These next paragraphs, from the same section we have just quoted, therefore deal solely with our perception of the dualistic world, but now corrected by the Holy Spirit to *reflect* only truth. More specifically, our "special function" of forgiveness that is discussed below becomes the reflection of Heaven's Love, expressed in the specific forms (the classrooms of our relationships) that meet the specific needs established by our specialness:

The Holy Spirit has the power to change the whole foundation of the world you see to something else; a basis not insane, on which a sane perception can be based, another world perceived. And one in which nothing is contradicted that would lead the Son of God to sanity and joy. Nothing attests to death and cruelty; to separation and to differences. For here is everything perceived as one, and no one loses that each one may gain....

Your special function is the special form in which the fact that God is not insane appears most sensible and meaningful to you. The content is the same. *The form is suited to your special needs, and to the special time and place in*

*which you think you find yourself, and where you can be
free of place and time, and all that you believe must limit
you. The Son of God cannot be bound by time nor place nor
anything God did not will. Yet if His Will is seen as madness, then the form of sanity which makes it most
acceptable to those who are insane requires special choice.*
Nor can this choice be made by the insane, whose problem
is their choices are not free, and made with reason in the
light of sense.

It *would* be madness to entrust salvation to the insane.
Because He is not mad has God appointed One as sane as
He to raise a saner world to meet the sight of everyone who
chose insanity as his salvation. To this One is given the
choice of form most suitable to him; one which will not
attack the world he sees, but enter into it in quietness and
show him he is mad. This One but points to an alternative,
another way of looking at what he has seen before, and recognizes as the world in which he lives, and thought he
understood before.

Now must he question this, because the form of the alternative is one which he cannot deny, nor overlook, nor fail
completely to perceive at all. To each his special function
is designed to be perceived as possible, and more and more
desired, as it proves to him that it is an alternative he really
wants. From this position does his sinfulness, and all the sin
he sees within the world, offer him less and less. Until he
comes to understand it cost him his sanity, and stands
between him and whatever hope he has of being sane
(T-25.VII.5; 7:1–9:4; italics mine in paragraph 7).

The foregoing paragraphs introduce the important role in
salvation the Holy Spirit has as "the Alternative," that presence within the Son's split mind that represents the other
choice. We shall discuss this role in more depth in a later chapter, but for now we shall continue our discussion of symbols
by examining the Holy Spirit's role in the context of translating the ego's symbols of hate and separation into forgiveness
and joining. The following two passages from the text, for example, express quite specifically the Holy Spirit's function of

reinterpreting the ego's symbols, thus *reflecting* the laws of God.

> The Holy Spirit is the mediator between the interpretations of the ego and the knowledge of the spirit. His ability to deal with symbols enables Him to work with the ego's beliefs in its own language. His ability to look beyond symbols into eternity enables Him to understand the laws of God, for which He speaks. He can therefore perform the function of reinterpreting what the ego makes, not by destruction but by understanding. Understanding is light, and light leads to knowledge. The Holy Spirit is in light because He is in you who are light, but you yourself do not know this. It is therefore the task of the Holy Spirit to reinterpret you on behalf of God (T-5.III.7).

> I have said that the last step in the reawakening of knowledge is taken by God. This is true, but it is hard to explain in words because words are symbols, and nothing that is true need be explained. However, the Holy Spirit has the task of translating the useless into the useful, the meaningless into the meaningful, and the temporary into the timeless. He can therefore tell you something about this last step [which of course is inherently illusory since God does not take steps] (T-7.I.6:3-6).

Just as forgiveness remains an illusion because it corrects the sin that never was, so too must the Holy Spirit be an illusion as well, because He corrects (or translates) what is useless and meaningless. And they are useless and meaningless because they are not real. Again, we shall return to the nature of the Holy Spirit in a later chapter.

Lesson 184, "The Name of God is my inheritance," provides perhaps the clearest description in *A Course in Miracles* of the need for symbols in the dualistic, separated, and unreal world which we made and in which we find ourselves. And yet we recognize the total unreality of such symbols when compared to the pure truth of our non-dualistic reality as Christ. The excerpts from this lesson, which the reader may recall from *All Are Called* (pp. 362-63), focus first on the ego's dualistic world of separation, the little names made to substitute for God's Name.

> You live by symbols. You have made up names for everything you see. Each one becomes a separate entity, identified by its own name. By this you carve it out of unity. By this you designate its special attributes, and set it off from other things by emphasizing space surrounding it. This space you lay between all things to which you give a different name; all happenings in terms of place and time; all bodies which are greeted by a name....
>
> What are these names by which the world becomes a series of discrete events, of things ununified, of bodies kept apart and holding bits of mind as separate awarenesses? You gave these names to them, establishing perception as you wished to have perception be. The nameless things were given names, and thus reality was given them as well. For what is named is given meaning and will then be seen as meaningful; a cause of true effect, with consequence inherent in itself....
>
> This is the sum of the inheritance the world bestows. And everyone who learns to think that it is so accepts the signs and symbols that assert the world is real. It is for this they stand. They leave no doubt that what is named is there. It can be seen, as is anticipated. What denies that it is true is but illusion, for it is the ultimate reality. To question it is madness; to accept its presence is the proof of sanity (W-p.I.184.1,3,6).

These paragraphs, then, clearly describe the ego's world of separation and differentiation. The sleeping Son of God dreams that he has shattered the unity of Christ into billions and billions of fragments, each of which is seen as different and then named; thus each fragment is set off one from the other. The mind then programs the sensory organs of the body to perceive this fragmentation, and the brain to interpret and classify these data into a world that appears to be understandable and certainly very real. The workbook lesson continues by describing the Holy Spirit's different interpretation of such data or symbols, how His use of the world's symbols or names, by their very nature dualistic and illusory, can yet lead us back to the unity of the one Name we share with God:

> It would indeed be strange if you were asked to go beyond all symbols of the world, forgetting them forever; yet were asked to take a teaching function. You have need to use the symbols of the world a while. But be you not deceived by them as well. *They do not stand for anything at all, and in your practicing it is this thought that will release you from them. They become but means by which you can communicate in ways the world can understand, but which you recognize is not the unity where true communication can be found.*
>
> Thus what you need are intervals each day in which the learning of the world becomes a transitory phase; a prison house from which you go into the sunlight and forget the darkness. Here you understand the Word, the Name which God has given you; the one Identity which all things share; the one acknowledgment of what is true. And then step back to darkness, not because you think it real, but only *to proclaim its unreality in terms which still have meaning in the world that darkness rules.*
>
> Use all the little names and symbols which delineate the world of darkness. *Yet accept them not as your reality.* The Holy Spirit uses all of them, but He does not forget creation has one Name, one meaning, and a single Source which unifies all things within Itself. Use all the names the world bestows on them but for convenience, yet do not forget they share the Name of God along with you (W-pI.184.9-11; italics mine).

And so we recognize, on the one hand, the basic unreality of the world, and yet still are taught by Jesus in *A Course in Miracles* how to operate within such a world as to be able to teach its unreality in the world's terms, understandable to ourselves and to others. Thus is the non-dualistic metaphysics of the Course united with its loving and gentle application in the dualistic world of separation and form.

Our final example in this section of the Course's use of symbols is from the end of the text. This incisive passage from "Self-Concept versus Self" discusses the role that concepts (symbols) play in the dualistic ego thought system, and the importance of ultimately moving beyond all thoughts *about* ourselves—which are inherently dualistic—to the non-dualistic truth: our Identity as Christ, our real Self.

> Concepts are learned. They are not natural. Apart from learning they do not exist. They are not given, so they must be made. Not one of them is true....
>
> A concept of the self is meaningless, for no one here can see what it is for, and therefore cannot picture what it is. Yet is all learning that the world directs begun and ended with the single aim of teaching you this concept of yourself, that you will choose to follow this world's laws, and never seek to go beyond its roads nor realize the way you see yourself. Now must the Holy Spirit find a way to help you see this concept of the self must be undone, if any peace of mind is to be given you. *Nor can it be unlearned except by lessons aimed to teach that you are something else. For otherwise, you would be asked to make exchange of what you now believe for total loss of self, and greater terror would arise in you....*

Thus, we need first exchange the Holy Spirit's concepts of forgiveness and healing for the ego's guilt and hate, the gentle precursors to moving beyond concepts entirely. The section continues:

> Salvation can be seen as nothing more than the escape from concepts. It does not concern itself with content of the mind [i.e., the different forms duality takes], but with the simple statement that it thinks [i.e., that the mind has chosen duality over non-duality, illusion over truth]....
>
> Seek not your Self in symbols. There can be no concept that can stand for what you are.... The world can teach no

images of you unless you want to learn them. There will come a time when images have all gone by, and you will see you know not what you are. It is to this unsealed and open mind that truth returns, unhindered and unbound. Where concepts of the self have been laid by is truth revealed exactly as it is. When every concept has been raised to doubt and question, and been recognized as made on no assumptions that would stand the light, then is the truth left free to enter in its sanctuary, clean and free of guilt. There is no statement that the world is more afraid to hear than this:

I do not know the thing I am, and therefore do not know what I am doing, where I am, or how to look upon the world or on myself.

Yet in this learning is salvation born. And What you are [the Self] will tell you of Itself (T-31.V.7:1-5; 8; 14:3-4; 15:1-2; 17; italics mine in paragraph 8).

Elsewhere in the Course Jesus emphasizes that this experience of the Self cannot be taught (e.g., W-pI.157.9), for It is beyond all the symbols and concepts of the world. Thus this Self can only be shown to be the end product of using the symbol of forgiveness to undo the ego's symbols of separation.

We can understand from our discussion in this chapter, therefore, that Jesus' actual words in *A Course in Miracles* cannot be taken literally. They are not themselves "the truth," yet they "point to where the truth must be, and give(s) direction with the certainty of God Himself" (W-pI.198.3:5-6). Jesus' actual words in the final analysis then are but "an illusion of help," because without them his little brothers and sisters would be help-*less.* This is no different from a psychotherapist needing to go beyond the patient's dream symbolism to the underlying meaning, which would otherwise be inaccessible to both of them. Moreover, the meaning of the dream can only be truly understood within the context of the patient's life, also, as it were, a set of symbols. Similarly, one cannot understand any particular passage in the Course without a proper appreciation of the whole. This is the same point as we saw earlier in the twice-quoted statement where, speaking of the Oneness of Christ, Jesus teaches us that "the Sonship in its Oneness transcends the sum of its parts" (T-2.VII.6:3). Later in the text he adds that the Atonement message he is bringing to us, in its totality transcends the sum of its parts (T-4.III.1:6).

Thus, to recapitulate, a student of *A Course in Miracles* will never really be able to understand any one passage in it without first understanding the whole, just as a therapist would be irresponsible to attempt to analyze a dream of a relative stranger (let alone any piece of behavior), without first appreciating where that particular dream (or behavior) fits into the person's entire life. Unfortunately, however, as we have seen earlier, many students are invariably tempted to remove a sentence or paragraph from its context in the Course, and then declare *A Course in Miracles* to mean what the *words* say, while in reality they have contradicted the very message of the Course itself. This would be no different, for example, from taking the famous opening four notes of Beethoven's Fifth Symphony and proclaiming that the three Gs and E-flat constitute the symphony, rather than understanding the incredible development of that simple motif over four movements that truly *is* the symphony. Beethoven's genius did not rest so much in his melodies or themes, but rather in their development throughout the music, which reflected his own inner development as an artist and person. In like fashion, one would not wish to judge *Hamlet* or *Macbeth* by their comic relief scenes of the graveyard digger and drunken porter respectively, the purpose of which is simply to relieve the tension as the dramas race to their tragic end. It would be a quite a mistake to take these scenes as representative of the plays themselves.

My point, once again, is that removing a musical passage or scene from the works of genius, proclaiming they are the whole, is equivalent to wrenching passages in *A Course in Miracles* from their context and thinking that they reflect Jesus' true message to us. The short-term effects of good feelings are hardly worth the loss of the long-term benefits of studying *A Course in Miracles* as it is. Instead, students should always strive to understand the Course's teachings in the light of their growing personal experience of letting go of guilt through forgiveness. As less guilt remains to distort perception, the light of *A Course in Miracles*' truth will shine through more and more, allowing the student to understand Jesus' teachings with much greater clarity.

An Uncompromising Non-Dualism

We can summarize this and the previous chapter with the following statement, slightly modified from the manual for teachers. In its original form, the subject of the passage is death, "the central dream from which all illusions stem" (M-27.1:1), yet the principle applies as well to our theme of recognizing duality for what it is. Here is the passage, with the word *duality* substituted for *death*:

> Teacher of God, your one assignment could be stated thus: *Accept no compromise in which **duality** plays a part.* Do not believe in cruelty, nor let attack conceal the truth from you. What seems to die has but been misperceived and carried to illusion. Now it becomes your task to let the illusion be carried to the truth. *Be steadfast but in this; be not deceived by the "reality" of any changing form.* Truth neither moves nor wavers nor sinks down to death and dissolution (M-27.7:1-6; italics and bold mine).

A similar idea is more succinctly stated in the text:

> Yet the truth is you and your brother were both created by a loving Father, Who created you together and as one. *See what "proves" otherwise, and you deny your whole reality* (T-21.II.13:1-2; italics mine).

The message of *A Course in Miracles* is effectively sum-marized in these passages. The uncompromising principle of not accepting as true any form that duality takes can serve as the criterion by which to know where the meaning of Jesus' words in *A Course in Miracles* should be taken literally and where metaphorically.* *Any* statement, without exception, that suggests God, the Holy Spirit, or Jesus as being a person *outside* ourselves, let alone as an actual *person* who interacts with our separated selves and the world, is expressing a dual-istic dimension that is meant only as a metaphor to teach the meaning of God's non-dualistic Love to dualistic minds. Sim-ilarly, statements that would seem to suggest that we need to forgive someone perceived as external to us follow the same metaphoric principle. In truth, there *is* no person outside us, since we all are—including, we may add, the person we iden-tify as ourselves—projected images of a split mind. While our experience is that we forgive others, in reality we are really forgiving split-off parts of our self, as I described in great detail in Chapter Five in *All Are Called*. That is why the pen-ultimate meaning of forgiveness is that, through the Holy Spirit's help, we learn to forgive ourselves. Only then can we take forgiveness' final step of realizing that there is nothing to forgive.

Therefore, as we have repeatedly seen in this chapter, to take these symbols literally is to confuse levels and compro-mise the truth. Only those statements that reflect the unified reality of Heaven and God and Christ should be understood as true and *should* be taken literally. To make the point one more time, Jesus' teachings come largely within a dualistic frame-work, since on the lower rungs of the ladder—where almost all of the Sonship typically are found—that framework is all

---

* In 1993 I conducted a workshop on this topic at the Foundation for *A Course in Miracles*. The workshop was recorded and then published as an audio-tape album, *Duality As Metaphor in A COURSE IN MIRACLES*. See Related Material at the back of this book.

that can be understood. However, Jesus also holds out to his students where the ladder is leading. And it is the non-dualistic statements, interspersed throughout the three books, that point the way we are to go when we are ready. A wonderful passage from the workbook expresses this range of the ladder that represents our journey back to God:

> Our Love awaits us as we go to Him, and walks beside us showing us the way. He fails in nothing. He the end we seek, and He the Means by which we go to Him (W-pII.302.2).

Imagine Jesus, therefore, as the symbol of this Love. His reality (and our own) as God's Love is at the top of the ladder ("the end we seek"), at the same time we experience his love guiding us from the bottom as we make our way up the ladder ("the means by which we go to Him").

To confuse *means* and *end*, duality and non-duality, will ensure that students of *A Course in Miracles* will never move beyond the lower rungs of the ladder to complete the journey home. In these two chapters we have seen how often in the Course Jesus refers to the inherent limitation of language in not being able to express truth directly. It is clear from these many references that Jesus most certainly wishes his students to understand this essential idea. Rather than bringing him down to our level, the ego's perennial ploy, students of the Course are asked by Jesus to allow him to raise them up to his. Only then can the goal of *A Course in Miracles*—complete forgiveness for what never happened—be achieved. We shall return to this important theme at the conclusion of the book.

As a way of summarizing this discussion of the differences between duality and non-duality, we present portions from the first part of the supplement, *The Song of Prayer*. Here the image of a ladder is introduced to describe the process of forgiveness or prayer. Though, as with *A Course in Miracles* itself, the terms *duality* and *non-duality* are not used, the description of the ladder's rungs extending from form to formlessness serve the same purpose of expressing the student's movement from the illusory world of perception and form (duality) to the upper rungs where the world of separation gradually disappears into the unity of God's creation (non-duality). This summary is, in effect, a wonderful portrait of the Course's path of forgiving the arrogant world of guilt, illusion, and specificity through looking at the ego with humility and without fear. Thus God's world of knowledge and oneness is allowed at last to dawn on the Son's pure and unsullied mind. Here, then, is the ladder of duality, ultimately reaching beyond itself to the non-dualistic truth of Heaven. Part of what is presented here, the reader may recall, was discussed in Chapter Seven of *All Are Called* (pp. 312-16):

> Prayer has no beginning and no end. It is a part of life. But it does change in form, and grow with learning until it reaches its formless state, and fuses into total communication with God. In its asking form it need not, and often does not, make appeal to God, or even involve belief in Him. At these levels prayer is merely wanting, out of a sense of scarcity and lack....
>
> Prayer is a ladder reaching up to Heaven.... Prayer in its earlier forms is an illusion, because there is no need for a ladder to reach what one has never left. Yet prayer is part of forgiveness as long as forgiveness, itself an illusion, remains unattained. Prayer is tied up with learning until the goal of learning has been reached.... The stages necessary to its attainment, however, need to be understood, if peace is to be restored to God's Son, who lives now with the illusion of death and the fear of God....
>
> The earlier forms of prayer, at the bottom of the ladder, will not be free from envy and malice. They call for vengeance, not for love....
>
> At these levels, then, the learning goal must be to recognize that prayer will bring an answer only in the form in which the prayer was made. This is enough. From here it will be an easy step to the next levels....
>
> Guilt must be given up, and not concealed. Nor can this

be done without some pain, and a glimpse of the merciful nature of this step may for some time be followed by a deep retreat into fear....

Even the joining [in prayer of two brothers], then, is not enough, if those who pray together do not ask, before all else, what is the Will of God. From this Cause only can the answer come in which are all specifics satisfied; all separate wishes unified in one. Prayer for specifics always asks to have the past repeated in some way....

Prayer is a way to true humility. And here again it rises slowly up, and grows in strength and love and holiness. Let it but leave the ground where it begins to rise to God, and true humility will come at last to grace the mind that thought it was alone and stood against the world. Humility brings peace because it does not claim that you must rule the universe, nor judge all things as you would have them be. All little gods it gladly lays aside, not in resentment, but in honesty and recognition that they do not serve....

Now prayer is lifted from the world of things, of bodies, and of gods of every kind, and you can rest in holiness at last. Humility has come to teach you how to understand your glory as God's Son, and recognize the arrogance of sin. A dream has veiled the face of Christ from you. Now can you look upon His sinlessness. High has the ladder risen. You have come almost to Heaven. There is little more to learn before the journey is complete. Now can you say to everyone who comes to join in prayer with you:

I cannot go without you, for you are a part of me.

And so he is in truth. Now can you pray only for what you truly share with him. For you have understood he never left, and you, who seemed alone, are one with him.

The ladder ends with this, for learning is no longer needed. Now you stand before the gate of Heaven, and your brother stands beside you there. The lawns are deep and still, for here the place appointed for the time when you should come has waited long for you. Here will time end forever. At this gate eternity itself will join with you. Prayer has become what it was meant to be, for you have recognized the Christ in you (S-1.II.1; 7:1; 8:3-5,8; S-1.III.2:1-2; 3:1-3; 4:1-2; S-1.IV.3:1-3; S-1.V.1; 3-4).

Finally, we conclude this chapter with a lovely and prayerful passage from the end of workbook Lesson 167, summarizing the goal of using the reflections of truth to lead beyond all reflections to the Oneness of Truth Itself. It can be read as a meditation:

> Let us today be children of the truth, and not deny our holy heritage. Our life is not as we imagine it. Who changes life because he shuts his eyes, or makes himself what he is not because he sleeps, and sees in dreams an opposite to what he is? *We will not ask for death in any form today. Nor will we let imagined opposites to life abide even an instant where the Thought of life eternal has been set by God Himself.*
>
> His holy home we strive to keep today as He established it, and wills it be forever and forever. He is Lord of what we think today. And in His Thoughts, which have no opposite, we understand there is one life, and that we share with Him, with all creation, with their thoughts as well, whom He created in a unity of life that cannot separate in death and leave the Source of life from where it came.
>
> We share one life because we have one Source, a Source from which perfection comes to us, remaining always in the holy minds which He created perfect. As we were, so are we now and will forever be. *A sleeping mind must waken, as it sees its own perfection mirroring the Lord of life so perfectly it fades into what is reflected there.* And now it is no more a mere reflection. It becomes the thing reflected, and the light which makes reflection possible. No vision now is needed. For the wakened mind is one that knows its Source, its Self, its Holiness (W-pI.167.10-12; italics mine).

Chapter 4

THE ROLES OF JESUS AND THE HOLY SPIRIT – I
MAKING THE INNER VOICE SPECIAL

Introduction

While many aspects of *A Course in Miracles* are difficult to understand and are subject to widespread misinterpretations and distortions, perhaps none is so flagrant an area of confusion as the role of Jesus or the Holy Spirit in the Atonement process. We have touched on many of the important variables in this issue earlier in this book, not to mention in *All Are Called*, but Jesus and the Holy Spirit are important enough figures, to say the very least, to warrant a more complete treatment, which this and the next chapters provide. We begin, however, with some general observations about the nature of humility as understood in the Course, before continuing on with the very special relationship students of *A Course in Miracles* develop with what they believe in all sincerity to be their inner voice.

The Ladder of Humility

Frequently in *A Course in Miracles* Jesus contrasts the attitude of humility with arrogance. In my *Glossary-Index for A COURSE IN MIRACLES* the two terms are defined this way:

> *Humility* is of the right mind, which recognizes its dependence on God, while *arrogance* is of the wrong mind, which feels it is in competition with Him; spirit rests in the grandeur of God, from Whom it derives its power, while the ego's grandiosity comes from believing that *it* is God, with the power to determine our function in God's plan; in this way the ego confuses *humility* with *arrogance*, telling

> us we are unworthy to be God's instruments of salvation
> (*Glossary-Index*, fourth edition, p. 106; italics added,
> except for *it*).

The issue of humility can be summarized in this wonderful statement from the text: "Be humble before Him, and yet great *in* Him" (T-15.IV.3:1). Students are thus urged by Jesus to recognize their gratitude to God for their creation—*without thoughts of competition or usurpation*—wherein lies their true greatness. It is in letting go of all thoughts of independence and individuality that students are able to replace the arrogance of the ego's thought system of specialness with the humility of identifying with the Holy Spirit's forgiveness. This ultimately reminds them that their true Identity is the abstract and non-personal spirit that is Christ. At this point, then, one no longer wishes to be on one's own, demanding that the ego self be atop the throne of creation. As the workbook lesson says: "I choose the second place to gain the first" (W-pII.328).

In the context of studying *A Course in Miracles*, arrogance takes the form of believing that one has "mastered" the Course by a simple reading or two, without really recognizing what is involved in its ongoing study and constant practice. As we discussed in Chapter One, such an attitude effectively seals off any further learning that can occur, since students already believe that they have learned all that *A Course in Miracles* can teach them. A limit thus has been placed on learning, but without the students being aware that this is what they have done. What remains in their consciousness is the belief that they have understood the Course, mastered its principles, and are now full-fledged teachers of God who are "sent" by Jesus or the Holy Spirit on the important mission of saving the world in Their names. We return to this spiritual specialness at the end of the chapter.

Humility, on the other hand, seeks *only* to learn, which comes from students' recognition of how dependent on their egos they have truly made themselves to be. They therefore become grateful for the opportunity the Course offers them to let go—finally and truly—of their investment in uniqueness, self-importance, and specialness, the core of the problem that maintains the separation from God. We can then say that students' progress in their study of *A Course in Miracles* can be measured by the degree to which they are able to grow through their egos' arrogance and become truly humble. *The Song of Prayer* speaks of the "ladder of prayer" as a symbol for the process of forgiveness, as we indicated in the last chapter. We can just as easily rename this process the "ladder of humility."

A safe rule of thumb to follow is that anytime students feel that they have "learned" the Course, this feeling should serve as a red flag that signals the intrusion of the ego's arrogance. As we have seen in the Introduction, Jesus cautions his students that "to learn this course requires willingness to question every value that you hold" (T-24.in.2:1), and it would be the height of arrogance to believe that one had truly brought to light and examined *all* the values that are present in one's mind. And, yet, not fulfilling this requirement, Jesus continues, "will jeopardize your learning" (T-24.in.2:2). *A Course in Miracles* makes no compromises in asking its students to give up all ego thoughts of specialness and guilt. As Jesus says in the final vision that provides the text with its inspiring conclusion: "Not one illusion is accorded faith, and not one spot of darkness still remains to hide the face of Christ from anyone" (T-31.VIII.12:5).

There are always exceptions of course (and it is the usual temptation for students to believe that *they* are the exceptions), but students of *A Course in Miracles* should be encouraged at least to approach its study with this humble attitude that accepts their place on the bottom of the ladder (the clear assumption Jesus is making in the Course), so that they can be gently, lovingly, and with great wisdom led up the ladder to return home. With such an attitude of humility—being like a little child who wishes more than anything else in the world to be taught by its older brother Jesus—the student is ensured of the learning that is *A Course in Miracles*' aim and its only goal. In the Course, Jesus uses the symbols of the eagle and the sparrow to contrast his wisdom with our own little knowledge and strength. This reflects the point here about students not asking the ego's specialness (the sparrow) to teach them what *A Course in Miracles* says (the eagle), for then they will certainly learn its teachings through the eyes of this specialness, unaware that they have changed around Jesus' message to fit their own unconscious needs. Here are Jesus' words:

> Ask not the sparrow how the eagle soars, for those with little wings have not accepted for themselves the power to share with you (T-20.IV.4:7).

> When this power has once been experienced, it is impossible to trust one's own petty strength again. Who would attempt to fly with the tiny wings of a sparrow when the mighty power of an eagle has been given him? And who would place his faith in the shabby offerings of the ego when the gifts of God are laid before him? (M-4.I.2:1-3)

It is therefore arrogance that would have students think that they know what *A Course in Miracles* is saying simply because many of the words and concepts seem similar to what they are accustomed to and familiar with. Humility, on the other hand, would have students recognize that *A Course in Miracles* is *unlike* any other spirituality they have seen, and therefore what is required of them is the openness to being taught by *it*, rather than *their* unconsciously teaching the Course what it is saying.

In light of the arrogance of youth in believing it can understand something that is so clearly beyond its little wisdom, I am reminded of an experience I had while in college. I was taking a comparative literature course in Western literature, which was taught by Dr. W. Edward Brown, perhaps the finest teacher I ever had throughout my student years. He was a brilliant scholar, and as humble in his wisdom as he was demanding of his students, though always holding to his high standards with a quiet and gentle kindness.

We were reading Goethe's two-part masterpiece *Faust*, the most accomplished version of this great myth of a man selling his soul to the devil in exchange for the fulfillment of his life's dreams and ambitions. Part One is by far the more accessible of the two, and I remember being quite moved the first time I read it. However, Part Two's wisdom was clearly far beyond my twenty years, and I could not really appreciate the profundity of this fruit of the last period of Goethe's long and rich life. At the time, moreover, it seemed to me to be wordy and needlessly abstruse, not to mention relatively boring. And so with all of my youthful arrogance I went up to Dr. Brown after class one morning and offered him my "considered" opinion as to the superiority of *Faust,* Part One. I shall never forget my esteemed professor's response. He let me finish my "learned" critique about the failings of Part Two, and simply replied: "Read it again." It took me some eight years or so until I did in fact read Part Two again. And only then could I see how truly blind I had been to this great and wise expression of creative genius.

I have often thought of Dr. Brown's words when confronted by students of *A Course in Miracles* who claim to be understanding it, when their responses make it very clear that they really do not understand at all what is contained in this thought system. To these students I wish to say, *Read it again.* If you think you have mastered in such a short period of time what Jesus is teaching, *Read it again.* If you are so certain the Course is saying how the Holy Spirit will magically answer all of your needs in the unreal world, thereby making duality real as we have seen in the previous chapter, *Read it again.* If your experience is that the Holy Spirit is guiding you to do very important work in the world on His behalf, *Read it again.* Indeed, *A Course in Miracles* should be read again, again, and still again.

My purpose in this chapter, therefore, is to consider in more depth the specific example of the ego's arrogance of specialness exemplified by so many students of *A Course in Miracles*: misunderstanding the role of Jesus or the Holy Spirit. Our discussion here will follow directly from the previous chapter's explanation of the difference between duality and non-duality, and students' almost inevitable confusion between these two levels. Discussing the role of internal guidance will provide a concrete example of how this confusion has expressed itself, and why. However, since we are speaking of the need students have to make Jesus and the Holy Spirit special, and obviously themselves as well, I must first present a brief overview of the dynamics of specialness so that we can then better understand just how and why this phenomenon inevitably occurs.

The Dynamics of Specialness: Jesus and the Holy Spirit

The most important aspect to consider about specialness is that it is virtually synonymous with duality. The very term *special* directly implies comparison with another (i.e., one is more or less special than someone else), which of course is impossible in a state of oneness or non-duality. We have seen that in this state there is, and always will be, no differentiations at all. Therefore, specialness cannot exist in Heaven. And since Heaven is the only reality, it must logically follow that specialness is inherently illusory, just as duality is. This fact becomes crucial to our discussion of the Holy Spirit as fact and symbol, as we shall see presently.

Once duality is accorded the status of truth, and by this we mean that two distinct and separate entities are made to be real, one inevitably has made the concept of differences real as well. How else could two entities be distinct and separate if they be not different? At this point, before going any further into the ego dynamics, the reader can see how far we have come from the perfect Oneness and undifferentiated unity of Heaven, the non-dualistic state that was described in Chapter Two, as well as in Chapter One of *All Are Called.* We have also discussed that the *language* of *A Course in Miracles*— which is certainly dualistic and seems to reflect the existence of a differentiated Heaven where the three aspects of the Trinity are clearly separate from each other—is merely meta-phoric, and is not meant to suggest that the *form* of the dualis-tic words has changed the *content* of non-dualistic truth that is the Course's metaphysical foundation.

From the perspective of the ego's dream of duality, where all students of *A Course in Miracles* believe they are, it is im-portant to understand how a concept of a differentiated God or Holy Spirit originated, since in truth, of course, they could not and have not changed Their undifferentiated reality of One-ness. Therefore, if a differentiated and dualistic God, aware of His Son's separation from Him, could not have come from the true God, then the only remaining alternative is that such a God came from the ego itself. There is no other possibility. In other words, a benevolent, loving, and giving God, concerned over His Son's alien state of separation, must be a split-off part of the already split mind of the Son himself, what in *All Are Called* was termed self C split off from self A.*

Unable to accept the Presence of God's Love as part of him —a fact that is anathema to the unloving ego—the Son projects this Presence outside of him, thereby effecting a com-promise with the ego in this form: God's Presence is not denied entirely, but is placed *outside* the Son's mind where it becomes recognized and experienced in the special "person" of the Holy Spirit, now perceived as the idealization of the dualistic *homo sapiens.* Stated another way, the non-human and non-dualistic love that is the Son's true Identity has not been accepted within himself, but can be accepted in distorted

---

* A more detailed treatment of the dynamic of splitting off is found in *All Are Called*, Chapters Two, Three, and Four.

form when experienced outside the Son as a dualistic and personal, quasi-human presence, and one no longer a part of his self.

Thus, in truth, the figures of Jesus or the Holy Spirit are really the projections (reflections) of the memory of a nondualistic God within our dualistic minds. The problem, however, is that this projected split-off part of our self is actually *believed* and *experienced* to be real, and the dynamic of projection is so quickly forgotten that for all intents and purposes God's true inner Presence—since *ideas leave not their source*—is hidden behind the veil of denial and the belief that there can be an "inner" presence of truth that is still outside of us.

What has occurred in the long run, therefore, is that the god of specialness has once more triumphed over love by becoming the substitute for it. This can be understood when the student recalls that love is perfect and undifferentiated unity. The Holy Spirit, in becoming an external entity that is perceived and experienced as outside the Son—even though He is *thought of* as being internal—now has become the expression of the god of specialness by substituting for the Presence of God's Love that in truth, once again, *is* the Son's Identity. This mistake can be avoided through students of *A Course in Miracles* remembering not to confuse a dualistic symbol for the non-dualistic reality, and to use more properly the metaphor of the Holy Spirit as the means for ultimately moving beyond the symbol to the truth of oneness that is *within* them and *is* them as Christ.

If I may return to the extremely important point discussed in the previous chapter, we can recall that the Course's dualistic treatment of Jesus and the Holy Spirit is purposive. Only by using such symbols and terminology can the student of *A Course in Miracles*—so identified with the body and the concept of a dualistic self—be led through the symbol to the truth of the real and non-dualistic Self that is beyond it. And so, once again, this lovely bi-level passage from the work-book, which cannot be quoted often enough:

> Our Love awaits us as we go to Him, and walks beside us showing us the way. He fails in nothing. He the End we seek, and He the Means by which we go to Him (W-pII.302.2).

In this way the symbol of an external Jesus—"our Love"—whose "hand" we take as we slowly and gently make our way to him, disappears as a separate entity, as do we, and the memory of Who we are *as one Son*—the true Christ—dawns in our minds as we approach Heaven's gate. What was two has become one again, as we disappear into the "Presence beyond the veil, not to be lost but found; not to be seen but known" (T 19.IV-D.19:1).

There is an even more subtle aspect to this dynamic of making Jesus (or the Holy Spirit) a separate and distinct entity, and it goes right to the heart of the dynamics of specialness. It helps to explain the great ambivalence any sincere and honest student of *A Course in Miracles* would have to feel about Jesus. It also helps to explain Jesus' several references in the Course about the need to forgive him. We thus return to our brief overview of the dynamics of specialness.

We have seen that the principal premise of the thought system of specialness is the reality of duality and differences, the origin of which rests with the original (*and ongoing*) separation thought. This is the belief that the Son of God can actually be outside the perfect unity of creation, separate from and independent of the Oneness of God; in other words, that ideas *can leave*, and indeed *have already left* their source. This apparent act of accomplishing the impossible is what the ego calls sin, which encompasses the belief that the Son has stolen his individuality from God, at a cost of destroying his Creator and usurping His role and function. The plot now thickens, and becomes even worse as the ego grows increasingly vicious and insane.

The Son, having believed that he has indeed stolen from God, now believes in the guilt that demands that God steal back the "priceless pearl" (T-23.II.11:2)—the power, life, and Love of Heaven—that was originally stolen from Him. And so now the Son "knows for certain" that he has a deadly enemy, one who is hell-bent on his destruction. He "knows" this because the projection of his guilt has made that hateful figure real—made literally in his own image and likeness of sin— and seemingly beyond any capacity of the mind to question its existence. The reader no doubt recalls the graphic passage I presented in *All Are Called* from the manual for teachers (M 17.5:3-9; 7:10-13) which describes this insane mentality of "kill or be killed." Therefore, the Son's world has become a battleground, in which each combatant can survive only by the elimination of the other, the expression of the ego's principle of *one or the other*. War is now not only justified but essential to survival, and so the Son must always remain on his guard lest his enemy, to state this fearful belief once again, steal back from him what he—in the deepest recesses of his dreaming mind—believes he first stole from him. What is here reflected, in summary, is the ego's "unholy trinity" of sin, guilt, and fear: *sin*—the belief that the separation, usurpation, and death of God actually occurred; *guilt*—the experience of self-hatred that "proves" that the impossible occurred; and *fear*—the "certain knowledge" that punishment and vengeance are inevitably forthcoming.

The reader will also remember our discussion in *All Are Called* (pp. 52-59) wherein the Son, through the dynamic of denial (or repression), is "saved" from his guilt by not remembering its source in his mind (self A). What remains is only the awareness of the need to protect himself (self B) from *unjustified* attack from outside himself (self C), warranting his *justified* attack in self-defense. Since the "other" person is simply a projection of the Son's unconscious ego (there always remains but one Son—whether in Heaven or on earth), he must be thinking and doing the same thing as the Son is.

And thus does every seeming fragment of the seemingly separated Sonship walk this earth in mortal terror, lest the insane enemy—who can be anyone—do to him what he secretly believes he has first done to him.

The prototype of this insanity, once again, is our relationship with our strange and projected image of God; a God from Whom we believe we have stolen life and power. And now we wait in terror—like Chicken Little in the children's story—before the inevitable occurs and

> God becomes impatient, splits the world apart, and relegates attack unto Himself. Thus has He lost His Mind, proclaiming sin has taken His reality from Him and brought His Love at last to vengeance's heels (T-26.VII.7:4-5).

It is thus certain that this made-up ego-God will one day steal back the "life" the Son had stolen from Him, and regain His proper place in Heaven, while the Son, his life now taken from him, will inevitably die. That is why—from the ego's perspective—it is correctly stated in the Adam and Eve myth in *Genesis* that God has invented death as a punishment for sin (Genesis 3:14-19).

And so it is this strange belief that becomes the prototype for all special relationships—since all relationships are reflections of the one relationship—and is at the heart of the five laws of chaos that reflect the true insanity of the ego thought system. This insanity culminates in these statements taken from the third, fourth, and fifth laws, which should be familiar to readers of *All Are Called*:

> And now is conflict made inevitable, beyond the help of God. For now salvation must remain impossible, because the Savior has become the enemy.
>
> There can be no release and no escape. Atonement thus becomes a myth, and vengeance, not forgiveness, is the Will of God.... Only destruction can be the outcome....
>
> The ego values only what it takes. This leads to the *fourth* law of chaos, which.... is the belief you have what you have taken. By this, another's loss becomes your gain, and.

...enemies do not give willingly to one another.... And what your enemies would keep from you must be worth having, because they keep it hidden from your sight.

All of the mechanisms of madness are seen emerging here: the "enemy" made strong by keeping hidden the valuable inheritance that should be yours; your justified position and attack for what has been withheld; and the inevitable loss the enemy must suffer to save yourself. Thus do the guilty ones protest their "innocence." Were they not forced into this foul attack by the unscrupulous behavior of the enemy, they would respond with only kindness. But in a savage world the kind cannot survive, so they must take or else be taken from.

What is stolen and defended, so that it will not be stolen back, is the "priceless pearl" of our specialness, the seemingly innate quality of our individuality and uniqueness that makes us separate, different, and therefore more special than any living thing. And it is this we believe our brother stole from us, just as we had first stolen from him. Thus must we find this pearl of specialness' hiding place in his body and "wrest [it] in righteous wrath" from him in justified murder:

And now you "understand" the reason why you found it not. For it was taken from you by this enemy, and hidden where you would not think to look. He hid it in his body, making it the cover for his guilt, the hiding place for what belongs to you. Now must his body be destroyed and sacrificed, that you may have that which belongs to you. His treachery demands his death, that you may live. And you attack only in self-defense (T-23.II.7:5–8:2,4; 9:1-4,6–10:4; 11:4-9).

Therefore, returning now to the original premise with which we began—the belief in the reality of separation and differences—we can understand why a Jesus that is perceived to be different from us, would *have* to be perceived by the ego as the enemy who has what we have not. According to Christianity, he is the only-begotten Son of God, the innocent and holy one who is beloved of the Father. And since we must be different—our individuality "proves" that to us—what he has we lack, according to the ego's "immutable" laws of chaos. And so, our insane egos conclude, the love and innocence that is Jesus' was first stolen from us. Therefore, we are justified in hating him for his sin against us, and justified in killing him to recapture what is rightfully ours. That is the meaning of those passages in the text in "The Obstacles to Peace"—which also explain the strange and insane theology of the Christian Churches, and the cannibalistic eucharistic theology of the various Catholic Churches—that the reader may recall our discussing in depth in Chapter Seven of *All Are Called*. I briefly re-present the passages here:

> I am made welcome in the state of grace, which means you have at last forgiven me. For I became the symbol of your sin, and so I had to die instead of you. To the ego sin means death, and so atonement is achieved through murder. Salvation is looked upon as a way by which the Son of God was killed instead of you. Yet would I offer you my body, you whom I love, *knowing* its littleness? Or would I teach that bodies cannot keep us apart? Mine was of no greater value than yours; no better means for communication of salvation, but not its Source. No one can die for anyone, and death does not atone for sin (T-19.IV-A.17:1-8).

But death *does* atone for sin in the ego's theology, since that is the only just and deserved punishment for the other's sin against us of having stolen our life. It is thus clear that it was not the Christian churches that invented these strange doctrines. They merely reflected in one specific form what the ego thought system was from the beginning.

Jesus continues the same theme in the following obstacle, pleading with his brothers to rethink their view of him and therefore of themselves:

> Let me be to you the symbol of the end of guilt, and look upon your brother as you would look on me. Forgive me all the sins you think the Son of God committed. And in the light of your forgiveness he will remember who he is, and

113

forget what never was. I ask for your forgiveness, for if you are guilty, so must I be. But if I surmounted guilt and overcame the world, you were with me. Would you see in me the symbol of guilt or of the end of guilt, remembering that what I signify to you you see within yourself?...

Forgive me your illusions, and release me from punishment for what I have not done. So will you learn the freedom that I taught by teaching freedom to your brother, and so releasing me. I am within your holy relationship, yet you would imprison me behind the obstacles you raise to freedom, and bar my way to you (T-19.IV-B.6; 8:1-3).

Thus we can see that believing Jesus to be different from us becomes a two-edged sword. While extremely helpful and necessary on the bottom rungs of the ladder, continuing to believe in him *only* as an elder brother will ultimately reinforce the very thought system of specialness that Jesus is attempting to help us undo. This mistake inevitably follows from the failure to understand that the dualistic language in *A Course in Miracles*—that involving Jesus, for example—is not meant literally. Rather, Jesus provides that dualistic form to help his students *begin* their journey up the ladder of humility.

On the other hand, it is extremely important that students of the Course do not throw out the dualistic baby with the non-dualistic bathwater. Students should be humble and take Jesus' hand *because* they are at the bottom of the ladder. It is only near the top that students can truly know that he is an illusion, along with themselves. As one of Helen's poems, "A Brother's Prayer," concludes:

> The flicker of an instant stands between
> Us and complete salvation. Need we do
> More than God asks? The face of Christ is seen
> And then unseen forever. Sorrow too
> Has disappeared, and I along with you.
> (*The Gifts of God*, p. 63)

But until that blessed moment comes, the non-dualistic truth of Jesus' message must come in the form that his students can understand without fear. Thus he teaches near the beginning of the text, in the context of taking magic in the form of medical treatment:

> The value of the Atonement does not lie in the manner in which it is expressed. In fact, if it is used truly, it will inevitably be expressed in whatever way is most helpful to the receiver. This means that a miracle, to attain its full efficacy, must be expressed in a language that the recipient can understand without fear. This does not necessarily mean that this is the highest level of communication of which he is capable. It does mean, however, that it is the highest level of communication of which he is capable *now*. The whole aim of the miracle is to raise the level of communication, not to lower it by increasing fear (T-2.IV.5).

Jesus' own Course thus becomes the perfect example of the principles he was teaching his students; his words not being "the highest level of communication" of which his students are capable of understanding, but certainly the highest level that they can tolerate in their fearful state.

The next section will elaborate on the nature of this two-edged sword of developing a relationship with Jesus, perceived and experienced to be a dualistic presence within the mind.

The Two-edged Sword of a Dualistic Jesus

To be sure, a beginning student of *A Course in Miracles* would wonder: can asking Jesus for help be wrong? And is not that one of the things he insists on in the Course, that we go to him (or the Holy Spirit) for all help, regardless of the littleness or magnitude of our concerns? Indeed, a knowledgeable student of the history of the scribing of *A Course in Miracles* might continue such an argument: Is not that what Helen Schucman herself did in asking Jesus for very specific advice regarding just about everything, including where to go to shop for particular items, what street corner to stand on for a taxi, etc.?

The answers to these questions, of course, is "Yes." Jesus does teach this process, and Helen did ask his help for all kinds of things. However, as we have seen, Jesus speaks on a dualistic level to meet his students where they are, in order to lift them up the ladder's rungs to a more proper appreciation and awareness of the truth of their relationship with him. This process has been chronicled in my *Absence from Felicity: The Story of Helen Schucman and Her Scribing of A COURSE IN MIRACLES*, and I draw upon the discussion there for this section.

As discussed in that book, Helen had been asking Jesus for specifics as a defense against acknowledging and accepting her deeper relationship with him. She let the specific, dualistic questions define their relationship, camouflaging the non-specific love that truly gave her lifelong relationship with Jesus its meaning, and in fact gave her very life its center. This issue of asking Jesus came to its climax during Helen's final years, the period when she and I were very close and discussed this issue together many, many times. As frequently occurred, my conversations with Helen stimulated her to write down a message from Jesus. One of those conversations about receiving specific guidance from Jesus resulted in Helen's receiving the following message (one of what Helen, Bill, and I referred to in those years as "special messages") in the early fall of 1975, after *A Course in Miracles* had been initially distributed to 300 people by photo-offsetting the entire manuscript.

The message was a plea from Jesus that Helen move beyond asking him for specifics, to an acceptance of him and his love for her. It was the beginning of a deeper teaching of the real meaning of prayer and of asking for help. Here is this first message, dated October 5, 1975. It begins with the famous quotation from Matthew 19:26, its meaning here shifted from the biblical emphasis on God's involvement with externals to the Course's focus on the mind's choice for His Love:

To God all things are possible, but you must ask His answer only of Himself.

Perhaps you think you do, but be you sure that if you did you would be quiet now and wholly undismayed by anything. Do not attempt to guess His Will for you. Do not assume that you are right because an answer *seems* to come from Him. Be sure you ask, and then be still and let Him speak. There is no problem He cannot resolve, for it is never He Who keeps apart some questions to be solved by someone else. You cannot share the world with Him and make half of it His while half belongs to you. Truth make no compromise. To keep apart a little is to keep all separate. Your life, complete and whole, belongs to God or none of it is His. There is no thought in all the world that seems more terrible.

Yet it is only when this thought appears in perfect clarity that there is hope in peace and safety for the mind so long kept dark and twisted to avoid the light. This *is* the light. Step back and do not dwell upon the forms that seem to keep you bound. You.... will have whatever you will need. God does not fail. But lay no limits on what you would give to Him to be resolved. *For He can not offer a thousand answers when but one is all there is. Accept this one of Him, and not one question will remain to ask.*

Do not forget if you attempt to solve a problem, you have judged it for yourself and so you have betrayed your proper role (*Absence from Felicity*, pp. 395-96; italics mine, except for *is* in the third paragraph).

The reader familiar with *The Song of Prayer* will recognize these thoughts, which reappear in the supplement's opening pages and to which we shall return in a later chapter. Sufficient for now is mention of the important idea that God's true answer is *one*: the non-specific memory of His Love. Focusing on the many answers—the specific answers to specific needs, demands, and problems—ends up, once again, as the defense against the experience of this love. This experience develops only as the students begin the ascent up the ladder of prayer. To return now to the 1975 message:

> Remember you need nothing, but you have an endless store of loving gifts to give. But teach this lesson only to yourself. Your brother will not learn it from your words or from the judgments you have laid on him. You need not even speak a word to him. You cannot ask, "What shall I say to him?" and hear God's answer. Rather ask instead, "Help me to see this brother through the eyes of truth and not of judgment," and the help of God all His angels will respond.
>
> For only here we rest. *We cast away our little judgments and our petty words; our tiny problems and our false concerns.* We have attempted to be master of our destiny and thought that peace lay there. Freedom and judgment *is* impossible. But by your side is One Who knows the way. Step back for Him and let Him lead you to the rest and silence of the Word of God (*Absence from Felicity*, p. 396; italics mine, except for *is* in the last paragraph).

In these final two paragraphs of the message, to paraphrase some of the discussion in *Absence*, we find that Jesus is urging Helen to focus not on the dualistic answers to specific requests for guidance or information, but rather to step back from the little concerns that interfere with the experience of his love. As he teaches in the text's Introduction, repeated from before:

> This course does not aim at teaching the meaning of love, for that is beyond what can be taught. It does aim, however, at removing the blocks to the awareness of love's presence, which is your natural inheritance (T-in.1:6-7).

It is thus the dwelling on specific answers to dualistic concerns, using Jesus for that purpose, that will end up ensuring that the student never passes beyond the early stages of the Course's long-term process of letting go of the ego thought system through forgiveness. And it is the turning to Jesus for help in removing these interferences that constitutes the Course's purpose, not the granting of specific answers to specific questions—"our little judgments and our petty words;

our tiny problems and our false concerns." But before we can learn of Jesus' true role in this process of forgiveness—the principal burden of the next chapter—we must first learn more about the ego's tactic of having substituted a false role instead.

My point here, once again, is that the ego has taken the helpful experience at the ladder's beginning—a very personal Jesus with a definite personality who speaks to us and specifically guides our lives—and used it for its own purposes. For in the ego's vicious and subtle hands, this experience of Jesus now acts as a block and interference to recognizing him for who he really is: the symbol within our separated minds of the abstract and universal Love of Christ, which is our reality as well. Thus, the learning is inhibited that would help us to understand that Jesus is a loving symbol within our separated dream of guilt and hatred, the symbol that reminds us of Who we truly are. The personal love we feel from Jesus, often expressed in specific forms within our dualistic experience, becomes the means whereby we grow to joining him where *we*—he and all of us—truly are in the Oneness of Christ's Love.

We continue now with Jesus' messages to Helen that will help us better understand this substitute of a dualistic specialness for a true experience of his presence and love, which is the non-dualistic response to our calls for help.

In 1977 Helen and I were discussing this issue of asking for specifics again, and Jesus' personal response to Helen soon gave way to a more general discussion that ended up as the supplement *The Song of Prayer*. In the context of the issue of asking specific help of Jesus on behalf of others, Jesus' response was to reassert the importance of not seeing differences between people, but rather to reflect the true unity, which alone is prayer and which

> is the same for yourself or for another. There is no difference. If only you received the answers for another, there would be a difference.

119

Jesus then continued by presaging his dictation of what would later emerge as the supplement:

> You have not been wrong in the past about how you have asked, but you are ready for a step ahead now....
>
> Asking is the way to God because it offers you His Will as He would have you hear it. We will have a series of lessons [the supplement] on asking because you have not understood it. But do not think because of that, that you have been mistaken in your attempts. You have done well and will do better (*Absence from Felicity*, p. 464).

What is so clearly reflected in these excerpts is Jesus' recognition of what he would later refer to in *The Song of Prayer* as the "ladder of prayer" (S-1.II): the *process* that students must undergo in their journey through the world of duality that they made, back home to the non-dualistic world they believe they had abandoned forever. And so there is the importance of beginning with experiences of a dualistic Jesus meeting one's needs and answering one's questions—"You have not been wrong in the past about how you have asked" and "You have done well." But a student must not rest with that, and must be prepared to be led still further up the ladder—"you are ready for a step ahead now," "We will have a series of lessons on asking because you have not understood it," and "You...will do better." This ladder leads beyond the initial experiences of God being present in the dualistic dream, to the growing recognition that He is not. Therefore, to make this important point once again, students should not mistake the reflections or symbols of truth for the truth itself. And this teaching now becomes the focus of Jesus' message to Helen and to all the students of *A Course in Miracles*. The subject here is that asking *specific* questions inevitably places limitations on God:

> Any specific question involves a large number of assumptions which inevitably limit the answer. A specific question is actually a decision about the kind of answer that is acceptable. The purpose of words is to limit, and by limiting, to make a vast area of experience more manageable.

But that means manageable by *you* (*Absence from Felicity*, p. 466).

The reader may recall this statement previously quoted from the manual for teachers:

God does not understand words, for they were made by separated minds to keep them in the illusion of separation (M-21.1:7).

The statement in the message about managing a "vast area" is an important point, for it emphasizes Helen's underlying ego purpose in continuing to ask for specifics ("the purpose of words"), which was to place a limit ("make...more manageable") on Jesus and the experience of his love. We shall return to this phenomenon later.

The message continues:

For many aspects of living in this world that [making "more manageable"] is necessary. But not for asking. God does not use words, and does not answer in words. *He can only "speak" to the Christ in you, Who translates His Answer into whatever language you can understand and accept* (*Absence from Felicity*, p. 466).

The message of October 5, 1975, referred to above (p. 117), made the same point, and we briefly recall it here:

Step back and do not dwell upon the forms that seem to keep you bound....lay no limits on what you would give to Him to be resolved. For He can not offer a thousand answers when but one is all there is. Accept this one of Him, and not one question will remain to ask.

To understand this very important teaching, let us consider again the abstract and formless nature of God's Love, which alone is reality, and which is a reality we truly share as God's Son. As the Course states: "Complete abstraction is the natural condition of the mind" (W-pI.161.2:1). This reality as Christ, however, is beyond our limited and separated ego self, to which we give a name, a history, and an anticipated future. It is therefore impossible for us to *know* God in this world, because as Jesus explains in the Course, this world in general, and bodies and brains in particular, were made to fulfill the ego's purpose of keeping knowledge of God, Christ, and Their unity away from us ("Thus were specifics made" [W-pI.161.3:1]).* When we call upon the Love of God, turning to Him as our Self, we are in effect able to transcend our ego identification, if only for an instant. In that holy instant which transcends time and the entire ego thought system, we remember our reality and Identity as God's Son. Thus we become that Identity, abstract and formless as our Creator. Love has rejoined itself, and that Love is One.

The part of our minds that chooses to return to the "place" we never truly left is "where" God "speaks" to us. However, when our minds return to their belief in separation, and we once again experience ourselves as a personal self in relation to our Creator—as opposed to being one *with* Him—the "speaking" is mediated through our separate minds and comes out as words, which our minds, and therefore brains *can* understand. It is thus *our* separated minds that structure the unstructured, shape the shapeless, and form the formless. It is not God Who does this, because He does not know of structure, shape, or form. His Love, which simply is, supplies the content; our minds supply the shape or words. An image of a glass of water might help clarify this very important idea. For the purposes of this example, we shall think of water as abstract and formless, thereby having the properties of spirit. Thus, water will here symbolize for us the non-specific unity of Self, love at one with Love, while the glass will symbolize the separated and specific mind. When the glass is filled with water it shapes the "formless" liquid. Even more to the point, when the filled glass is placed in a freezer and the water

---

* A full discussion of this purposive dynamic of the ego's body is beyond the scope of this book, but the interested reader may consult *Love Does Not Condemn*, pp. 425-37, as well as *All Are Called*, Chapter Four.

freezes, the water assumes a solid shape—the cylindrical form of the glass. Thus the shape of the glass has determined the form the water has taken, and in fact, has limited its free flow. Similarly, the Love of God is shaped and contained by the split mind, thus limiting accessibility to the amount of love that the Son's fear can tolerate.

To restate this, in the holy instant, our minds have chosen to become one with God's Love, which is not a state in which our egos allow us to continue, since it means the end of the ego itself. As the Course explains:

> Sometimes a teacher of God may have a brief experience of direct union with God. In this world, it is almost impossible that this endure.... All worldly states must be illusory. If God were reached directly in sustained awareness, the body would not be long maintained (M-26.3:1-2,7-8).

And so the mind chooses to return to the ego identification, yet it brings the Love of God with it. To the extent to which fear remains in the mind, however, the body's words will obscure and distort the purity of the love, limiting its free extension; the less fear, the more transparent are the words, which then but serve to express the love in a form that can be accepted without fear. Using the analogy of a picture of light and its frame, the Course speaks of the Holy Spirit's purpose (content) for relationships (the form) in the world:

> [The Holy Spirit's picture of light] is framed for perfect clarity.... [It is] lightly framed, for time cannot contain eternity.... The picture of light, in clear-cut and unmistakable contrast [to the ego's dark picture], is transformed into what lies beyond the picture. As you look on this, you realize that it is not a picture, but a reality. This is no figured representation of a thought system, but the Thought itself. What it represents is there. The frame fades gently and God rises to your remembrance, offering you the whole of creation in exchange for your little picture, wholly without value and entirely deprived of meaning (T-17.IV.13:3; 14:1; 15).

Thus, it is not the frame that is important, but the picture of light that it contains; likewise, it is not our words that are important, but the content of love that they express. And so it is not really the person of Jesus that we seek and yearn for, but the love that he expresses, and even more to the point, the love in us as Christ that he reflects back to us. As more and more love shines through our minds, the specific frame of Jesus or the Holy Spirit recedes into the abstract and formless light of God, as do we as separated individuals: "The frame fades gently and God rises to your remembrance."

The Holy Spirit is *A Course in Miracles'* symbol of that choice within our minds. He is spoken of—dualistically—as if He were a person, since that is the only way we could relate to the Correction in our minds that is not our ego selves. Again, it is essential that the Course student recognize that while in *A Course in Miracles* the role of the Holy Spirit is absolutely crucial, He remains nonetheless a symbol and not reality. Thus Jesus explains near the very end of the Course, in important lines quoted as well in *All Are Called*:

> His [the Holy Spirit] is the Voice for God, and has therefore taken form. This form is not His reality, which God alone knows along with Christ.... For in its place ["death's thin melody"] the hymn to God is heard a little while. And then the Voice is gone, no longer to take form but to return to the eternal formlessness of God (C-6.1:4-5; 5:7-8).

Moreover, the Holy Spirit's function of symbolizing the truth in our minds should not be confused with the non-dualistic reality of Heaven's Love. This distinction is vital as a help to students who might otherwise be tempted to make the Holy Spirit literally real, and thus His "words" and "actions" real as well. We shall return to this important issue in a later chapter.

For us in the Western world, however, and certainly as it was for Helen, Jesus is the greatest *symbol* of God's Love:

> The Name of Jesus Christ as such is but a symbol. But it stands for love that is not of this world.... It becomes the

shining symbol for the Word of God, so close to what it
stands for that the little space between the two is lost, the
moment that the name is called to mind (M-23.4:1-2,4).

Jesus then, and the specific ways we experience him for ourselves, is the framing glass which allows us to experience
God's Love in a form that we can grow to accept. The form is
not God's Love, yet it will ultimately blend into that Love, as
one day we all shall once again.

Returning now to the special message to Helen, the Love
of God—the only answer to any of our problems, concerns, or
questions—is beyond all words or thoughts. The reader may
recall from Chapter Two my citing of this important line from
the workbook: "We say 'God is,' and then we cease to speak,
for in that knowledge words are meaningless" (W-pI.169.5:4).
Yet does this Love of God reflect itself to us in the form that
we can accept, a form that we, to state it again, establish for
ourselves. In metaphoric language, the process is explained to
Helen in the message as Christ translating for us: "Christ...
translates His [God's] Answer." In *A Course in Miracles* itself, this "translation" is a function usually accorded to the
Holy Spirit. It is stated metaphorically to correspond to what
our experience is, not because it is reality itself.

Another useful analogy that can help our understanding is
our perception of sunrises and sunsets, brief mention of which
was made in *All Are Called* (p. 37). We all, to a person,
observe the sun seeming to rise and set each day. Many
people, in fact, report profound spiritual or aesthetic experiences surrounding these perceptions. Yet, almost all of us
have been taught that it is not the sun that rises or sets. Rather,
it is the earth's rotation on its axis that causes the sun to "rise"
and "set," while the planet's revolution around the sun causes
the change of seasons. Thus, the *appearance* of the sun's
movement is really an illusion that belies the *reality* of its relatively fixed position.

The ancient world believed that the earth was the center of
the cosmos, a belief that was "verified" by the 2nd-century

Greek mathematician Ptolemy's theory of astronomy (which then spilled over to theology), in which the sun revolved around the earth. Clearly, people's uninformed *experience* gave rise to what was thought to be objective and empirical truth. It was not until the 16th century that the error was corrected when the Polish astronomer Copernicus realized that experience lied, and that the astronomical truth was rather that the earth and other planets revolved around the sun. About a century later the great Italian Renaissance man Galileo was tried and convicted by the court of the Inquisition for upholding the Copernican astronomy against the "theologically correct" Ptolemaic view. The illusion of experience had again promoted an illusory theology that was granted supremacy over common sense and truth.

Likewise, we find that students' experience of Jesus or the Holy Spirit doing things *for* them, or saying things *to* them, is the illusion that belies the reality that *they*, the students, are the true sources of their lives and the agents that make possible what they hear. It is essential that students of *A Course in Miracles* realize that they are the ones who choose to move away from the presence of love and light in their minds, referred to as the Holy Spirit or Jesus. Thus they are the ones who must choose to return to this *stationary* source of light. The mind's movement—wandering off from love and then returning to it—is *their* responsibility, not Jesus'. In the end, it is their own dream from which they awaken, and it is only their decision to awake that ends the dream. The next section will address the actual role that Jesus plays in this awakening.

Therefore, all of our specific questions and needs arise from the state of dualism, and have their origin in our having chosen to move away from the non-dualistic Source in our minds. That is why the Course teaches that all questions are of the ego (T-27.IV; C-in.3-4; C-2.2). Therefore, these questions can only find their true answer in our return to the mind's decision to separate, choosing now for God instead of against Him. Focusing on specific needs or questions thus becomes the reinforcer of what the ego would have us believe: that we have *in fact* left God to inhabit a dualistic world of separation and differences. A response from outside our minds and selves, which is how we usually experience Jesus, simply then continues the illusion of our separation.

And so in his message to Helen, Jesus urged his scribe to return to the Love of God for her answer, as he similarly urges students of *A Course in Miracles* in this very beautiful lesson: "I call upon God's Name and on my own." We find here once again, in a passage we have partially cited before, Jesus' plea to his students to abandon the illusions of duality ("the little things and sounds of the world") and turn back instead to the Name of God, the great symbol of our non-dualistic Self:

> Think not He [God] hears the little prayers of those who call on Him with [dualistic] names of idols cherished by the world. They cannot reach Him thus. He cannot hear requests that He be not Himself [a non-dualistic Self], or that His Son receive another name than His....
>
> Turn to the Name of God for your release, and it is given you. No prayer but this is necessary, for it holds them all within it. *Words are insignificant, and all requests unneeded when God's Son calls on his Father's Name....*
>
> All little things are silent. Little sounds are soundless now. The little things of earth have disappeared. The universe consists of nothing but the Son of God, who calls upon his Father. And his Father's Voice gives answer in his Father's holy Name. In this eternal, still relationship, in which communication far transcends all words, and yet exceeds in depth and height whatever words could possibly convey, is peace eternal. In our Father's Name, we would experience this peace today. And in His Name, it shall be given us (W-pI.183.7:3-5; 10:1-3; 11; italics mine).

We continue now with the balance of Jesus' special message, picking up with the idea I discussed earlier; namely, that words can serve either the ego's fear or Jesus' love. Once again, it is not the form that is important, which emphasis always leads to arrogance, but the underlying content that reflects the humility of a real relationship with Jesus. God's "Voice," without form and words, is truly silent, as we shall see.

> Sometimes words will limit fear; sometimes not. That is why some people hear words, some receive feelings of inner conviction, and some do not become aware of anything. Yet God has answered, and His Answer will reach you when you are ready.
>
> Answers are not up to you. Any limit you place on them interferes with hearing. *God's Voice is silent and speaks in silence. That means that you do not phrase the question and you do not restrict the answer* [meaning that it is best for us not to do so].
>
> Asking is a form of prayer. It is not a demand. It is not questioning. It is not limitation. The only real request is for God's Answer. This needs the *humility* of trust, not the *arrogance* of false certainty. Trust cannot lie in idols, for that is merely faith in magic. Trust requires faith that God understands, knows, and will answer. It means a state of peace. For this you can safely ask. In fact, if you do not feel that you have it, asking for it is the only real request that you can make (*Absence from Felicity*, pp. 470-71; italics mine).

Another expression of the same idea is the oft-quoted statement in *A Course in Miracles* that our one and only function is to accept the Atonement for ourselves. We do not ask or demand; we simply *accept* the peace and truth that is already present in us. Thus we find clearly stated what will be presently reiterated, that our true requests should be for inner peace, and that is the only prayer that makes sense.

This ends Jesus' special message to Helen, after which came the notes that belong more properly to *The Song of Prayer* itself, and which we shall consider next.

The Two Levels of Our Relationship with Jesus

For our discussion of Jesus—the illusion and the reality—and his proper role in our Atonement path, we refer again to *Absence from Felicity*, beginning with the section that discusses the opening pages of *The Song of Prayer*. They deal with the all-important subject we have previously looked at—praying for specifics—and our discussion here begins with this statement from the supplement:

> Prayer is the greatest gift with which God blessed His Son at his creation. It was then what it is to become; the single voice Creator and creation share; the song the Son sings to the Father, Who returns the thanks it offers Him unto the Son (S-1.in.1:1-2).

Prayer thus is used as a synonym for the state of perfect non-dualistic and undifferentiated unity between God and Christ, Creator and creation. It is the memory of that unity in our split minds that *A Course in Miracles* refers to as the Holy Spirit, that memory manifested for us in the world's dream by Jesus. The symbol Jesus is *not* the Love of God, but again, since we are not ready to set aside our fear to accept the Love Who created us and Who we are, we need to accept love in the forms we can accept for now:

> To you who are in time a little while, prayer takes the form that best will suit your need. You have but one (S-1.in.2:1-2).

However, as we have seen, once students confuse the symbol with the reality, and believe that the dualistic symbol is *real* and does *real* things in the dualistic world, the temptation becomes very great to entreat this symbol for special favors to meet special needs, thereby reinforcing the belief in its reality. It is this dynamic of asking God for help that has gone under the name of prayer in most of the world's religions, and one of the principal purposes of *The Song of Prayer,* as discussed before, was to correct this misconception of the relationship between the spiritual seeker and God (or Jesus) that has crept into the minds of students of *A Course in Miracles*. As Jesus continues:

> [Prayer] is not merely a question or an entreaty. It cannot succeed until you realize that it asks for nothing....True prayer must avoid the pitfall of asking to entreat. Ask, rather, to receive what is already given; to accept what is already there (S-1.I.1:2-3,6-7).

Then, too, we should not forget that such asking is illusory, and therefore it can be tempting to forget that the truth is already present within us and need only be accepted by our choosing again.

The supplement then continues:

> You have been told to ask the Holy Spirit for the answer to any specific problem, and that you will receive a specific answer if such is your need. You have also been told that there is only one problem and one answer. In prayer this is not contradictory....it is not the form of the question that matters, nor how it is asked. The form of the answer, if given by God, will suit your need as you see it. This is merely an echo of the reply of His Voice. The real sound is always a song of thanksgiving and of Love (S-1.I.2:1-3,6-9).

Here we find the same teaching of reflecting the difference between form and content that we found in the special message discussed in the previous chapter. However, now this teaching is presented in a more generalized manner, allowing us also to understand better the principle that would explain the form in which *A Course in Miracles* comes. In other words, the form of the teaching adapts, just as Jesus has been explaining above, to the specific teaching need of the section in question. When addressing his students on the lower rungs of the ladder, Jesus speaks dualistically (many problems; many solutions); when addressing students well along their way, his words reflect the uncompromising truth of Heaven (one problem; one solution).

Thus we see that Jesus' words throughout *A Course in Miracles* and the two supplements reflect the idea that prayer is a *process*. Again, the end of the last paragraph reflects the end of the process where we understand that there is only one problem—the separation—and one solution—the acceptance of the Atonement. However, at other times Jesus is reflecting the early stages of the process, where we *experience* the Holy Spirit as solving problems for us. The true solution to our problems, however, always rests in the one Answer that is God's Love, that is the "real sound" of the song of prayer. As Jesus will now explain to us, it is the experience of the song that we truly want—his love—not the illusory forms in which we may experience its reflection:

> You cannot then, ask for the echo. It is the song that is the gift. Along with it come the overtones, the harmonics, the echoes, but these are secondary. In true prayer you hear only the song. All the rest is merely added. You have sought first the Kingdom of Heaven, and all else has indeed been given you (S-1.I.3).

In other words, in continuing the theme of his special message to Helen, which we examined in the previous chapter, Jesus is here cautioning all students of his Course to remember that what they truly want is the peace of God, not its specific reflections in the dualistic world of perception. The reality of love is our heart's desire, not the illusory manifestations of the ego's thought system; it is the wondrous song of God's Love that is what we yearn to recall, not the various echoes that deflect through our fearful minds.

The purpose of Jesus in our lives is thus not to grant our specific requests nor to answer specific questions, but rather to *remind* us of the one Answer to all these concerns that rests quietly within our minds, patiently awaiting our welcome. As the Course states: "Love waits on welcome...and the real world is but your welcome of what always was" (T-13.VII.9:7). The goal is *not* the satisfaction of specific requests or needs.

131

Therefore, once we have reunited with this love, have taken the hand of Jesus which reminds us of Who we truly are, all our concerns inevitably disappear. Since the content of our problems was the separation from love, their undoing simply lies in joining with this love again. That is the meaning of the allusion to the biblical statement (Matthew 6:33) that when we have sought the love of the Kingdom of Heaven, all else "has indeed been given [us]," and by this is *not* meant, again, the specific toys our ego demands for our happiness. We will have remembered the peace and Love of God that is our only Answer, and in that Answer we know that we already have all that we need, for we both *have* and *are* the gift of the Kingdom.

The Song of Prayer continues, with Jesus becoming even more specific now about our dependence on specifics:

> The secret of true prayer is to forget the things you think you need. To ask for the specific is much the same as to look on sin and then forgive it (S-1.I.4:1-2).

"True prayer" is Jesus' term here for the upper reaches of the process of prayer, the real meaning of joining with the Love of God. A bit later in the supplement, as we have seen, he compares the process of prayer with a ladder. Praying for specifics, or seeking guidance for specific answers, reflects the lower rungs of the ladder. This is referred to as "asking-out-of-need," and always involves "feelings of weakness and inadequacy, and could never be made by a Son of God who knows Who he is" (S-1.II.2:1). Therefore, students uncertain of their Identity cannot help praying in these forms (S-1.II.2:3).

Jesus' purpose here clearly is not to make people feel guilty as they lapse into this magical form of prayer, but simply to remind them of what they truly want. One must always begin at the beginning, and *A Course in Miracles* would never suggest that its students should skip over the steps necessary to reach their goal of true peace. It is these steps that allow God to take

His "final step" of lifting His children back unto Heaven—"God will take this final step Himself. Do not deny the little steps He asks you take to Him" (W-pI.193.13:6-7). However, here in the early pages of the supplement, Jesus is attempting to correct the errors that his students, as well as Helen,* were making right at the beginning of the Course's public life. He is reminding people that they are tempted to be content with the little crumbs the ego holds out to them, when they can have instead the beautiful song of their Identity as Christ. As he reminds his students in the Course, a line I cited in the Introduction: "The Son of God ask[s] not too much, but far too little" (T-26.VII.11:7).

This point becomes clearer in the next passage from the supplement:

> Also in the same way, in prayer you overlook your specific needs as you see them, and let them go into God's Hands. There they become your gifts to Him, for they tell Him that you would have no gods before Him; no Love but His. What could His answer be but your remembrance of Him? Can this be traded for a bit of trifling advice about a problem of an instant's duration? God answers only for eternity. But still all little answers are contained in this.... There is nothing to ask because there is nothing left to want (S-1.I.4:3-8; 5:6).

Thus, when we feel indecisive or unsure of a situation, unknowing about what we are to do, we are asked to lift our mind's attention from the battleground below in which we believe we exist, and where we continually seek and demand "a bit of trifling advice about a problem of an instant's duration." Leaving the battleground, we rejoin the loving presence of Jesus or the Holy Spirit, and are thus reminded that all we want is the peace of God. From that ego-free place of peace

---

* However, as I discuss in *Absence from Felicity* (pp. 461-65), there was always a part of Helen's mind that knew better and was aware of her use of specifics as a defense against Jesus.

and love within our minds, we then return our attention to the situation confronting us. Once more on the battleground, but now carrying the memory of our true goal, we shall inevitably recognize what we should do. We have done our part by removing the fear of joining—the interference to our awareness of love's presence—and the Answer will then flow through our minds in the form we need to hear: "There is nothing to ask because there is nothing left to want."

A lovely passage in the text, cited in *All Are Called*, nicely summarizes this process of how one lives in the world, and yet knows that one is not of it. Jesus asks his students to return to his love in their minds, what he has called the "place of refuge, where you can be yourself in peace" (T-18.VI.14:5). It is the place of rest

> to which you can return. And you will be more aware of this quiet center of the storm than all its raging activity. This quiet center, in which you do nothing, will remain with you, giving you rest in the midst of every busy doing on which you are sent. For from this center will you be directed how to use the body sinlessly. It is this center, from which the body is absent, that will keep it so in your awareness of it (T-18.VII.8).

It is clear that Jesus has posed this question to all his students: Is the little answer you receive to a specific question what you really want, when in its place you can have the peace of God, *and* the certainty of your next steps in this illusory world? The little answers are contained in the one Answer, but not vice versa; we bring illusions to the truth, not truth to the illusions.

This teaching, then, comprises the "series of lessons" that Jesus mentioned to Helen in his preliminary message to her. He was reminding her, again in this final period of her life, to recall who she was, and that it was no longer necessary to pretend she was someone she was not. Her life as Helen could then express her reality as love. And Jesus' message to her clearly is meant for all his students.

We come back now to the supplement, where Jesus returns to people's experiences on the ladder's lower rungs, and their need for help:

> This is not a level of prayer that everyone can attain as yet. Those who have not reached it still need your help in prayer because their asking is not yet based upon acceptance. Help in prayer does not mean that another mediates between you and God. But it does mean that another stands beside you and helps to raise you up to Him (S-1.I.6:1-4).

The true teacher of God therefore is not one with a *special* mission, nor a *special* gift to give others *special* messages of wisdom. Rather, it is to remind others of the choice they may make to separate finally from the ego's specialness and to join Jesus' love. Thus Jesus is reinforcing for his students the idea that no one is more special than any other, a fact he states early in the text: "All my brothers are special" (T-1.V.3:6).

Commenting once more on the different levels of prayer, we can extrapolate this principle to the different levels of understanding Jesus, including what it means to have a relationship with him. We must therefore speak of Jesus on two basic levels: the first is the metaphysical, wherein his love and presence are abstract and non-specific, and which can be symbolized by the water in our example of the glass; the second reflects our experience within the dream, where Jesus is known by us as a body with a personality, since we believe our identity as a personal self is rooted in the corporeal. Jesus' love and presence are therefore mediated through our separated minds that believe we are in bodies, and so our experience of him as a person is determined by the particular shape of the glass that represents our own learning needs. These two levels were succinctly summarized by me in a workshop held at the Foundation for *A Course in Miracles*, in response to a question about who or what Jesus really was. My answer is presented here in slightly edited form:

Jesus is both a "who" and a "what." The "what" is the symbol of the Holy Spirit's Love. He is now that same abstract presence of Love in your mind that the Holy Spirit is. At the very end, when you are in the real world, then you will know that. Until that point is reached, however, he is a "who" for you, and an extremely important one at that.

As long as you believe that you are a "who," then you need a "what" that looks like a "who"—you need another specific symbol that will represent for you that abstract presence of God's Love that is the Holy Spirit. And by the way, you are making a big mistake if you do not think you need a "who." If, however, Jesus is a difficult symbol for you, then choose another one. However, for most people in the Western world, Jesus is it. Almost all people here would recognize that they have unresolved issues with him, if they are truly honest with themselves.

So in the end, yes, Jesus is abstract—a "what." But as long as you believe you are a specific and distinct individual—a "who"—then you need someone who can speak to you on that specific level.

Correspondingly, the bottom rung of the ladder described in *The Song of Prayer* consists of asking for things of this "who," because we believe we are a specific "who" as well. We believe our reality is here in the world:

At these levels prayer is merely wanting, out of a sense of scarcity and lack (S-1.II.1:5).

As we grow in forgiveness and ascend the ladder of prayer, however, we become increasingly aware of the abstract and formless nature of love's presence, "until it [prayer] reaches its formless state, and fuses into total communication with God" (S-1.II.1:3). At this point the "who" becomes a "What."

This concludes our discussion of the supplement *The Song of Prayer.* Our focus more specifically was on the consideration of the nature of prayer and the nature of Jesus, highlighting the contrast between the illusion and reality. Our final section of this chapter provides a preliminary view of spiritual specialness, the problem that is inevitably connected to a student's confusion between the role the ego assigns to Jesus and what more properly belongs to him.

A Preliminary Note on Spiritual Specialness

We begin this section by recalling that given the profound identification people in this world have with their physical and psychological selves—and students of *A Course in Miracles* are certainly no exception—it is almost impossible for Course students to avoid getting trapped in this web of specialness. Being aware of its pitfalls, however, will ensure that the web will lose its venomous power. On the other hand, being unconscious of one's need for specialness, and believing instead in the reality of receiving special attention and favor from God, Jesus, or the Holy Spirit, will simply ensnare the student more and more in this web. This makes it ever more difficult to become extricated from the insidiousness of spiritual specialness. The trap works in this way:

Once one chooses to be special—the basic choice to be in a body and living in a world that is the body's home—there is the need to defend that specialness and prove it real. Otherwise, one's very own existence as a special and individual being is called into question. Therefore, if one is to exist as this special person, teaches the humble arrogance of the ego, what better way to witness to its reality than to be specially chosen to do *holy, special, and very important work* in this world. This obviously necessitates there being a special Someone to do the choosing, for of course without that *special* Someone for whom one does the *special* assignments for His *special* work, one's ego would cease to be special and consequently have no importance.

The terrible ego trap then becomes inevitable: If students decide that they have been *called* to do important work, then, again, there must be One Who calls. Therefore, there must be a Holy Spirit, made in the image and likeness of its "creator," *homo sapiens*, Who thinks out, plans, and then selects His *special* ones for His *special* plan. It is almost as if the Holy Spirit were sitting in front of a giant chessboard manipulating people like pieces on the board. And all this because the ego insists—in its exaggerated sense of self-importance born of its need to ensure its own existence—on having it this way.

Therefore, this student of specialness first decides—usually unconsciously—on a *special* form of importance, and then this *special* vision is projected onto an abstract Presence, Who then becomes the specific Person He is needed to be. In this way, the true Presence of God's Love has been transformed into the true presence of the ego's special love. This occurs even though, unbeknownst to the student whose mind has been veiled by thoughts of being special, the spirit and meaning of *A Course in Miracles* have been violated and distorted. Such making up of a God or Holy Spirit of specialness also serves to neutralize—through the dynamic of denial—the ego's dream of an angry and vengeful God that is the cornerstone of its delusional thought system. For now He is perceived and experienced to be the benevolent opposite of the ego's "truth." Moreover, this hideous and terrifying "truth" can seemingly never be undone, for it has been covered over by these insidious veils of specialness.

The results are psychologically devastating, for now this maniacal God forever lurks in the deeper and darker recesses of the mind, casting His cruel and vicious shadow on everything that is seen and experienced—a cruel and vicious world—but the source of which in the mind is never known and therefore never questioned. The reader may recall the telling passage from "The Two Worlds" in Chapter 18 of the text that was quoted in *All Are Called* (pp. 85-86). There Jesus depicted the ego's projection of its guilt onto the world, so that its shadow could conceal the presence of the hated "enemy" lurking within the mind.

Thus all people, like Don Quixote, tilt the windmills of the ego God's shadow world, actually believing their enemy is really there and outside themselves. It is from this enemy that the God of specialness will save them. This is the dualistic God that acts in the dualistic world, demanding payment for His deeds of charity and mercy, including such payment that comes in the form of presumed faithfulness to *A Course in Miracles.*

One of the sources of this mistake that reinforces the underlying ego need to be special, is that so many students of *A Course in Miracles* do not recognize the great differences that exist between the non-dualistic Course and the dualistic Judaeo-Christian (or biblical) tradition as spiritual paths. *A Course in Miracles* can never be truly understood—in theory or practice—while it is placed within a context, such as the biblical tradition, that is inherently alien to its teaching and message. Since the premises of non-duality and duality are mutually exclusive, the conclusions deduced from them inevitably share in their mutually exclusive nature. *Ideas leave not their source,* and so, following the rigorous logic of *A Course in Miracles'* thought system, if the sources are different, then the ideas which are an inherent part of them must be different too. Therefore, no one is really called by Jesus or the Holy Spirit to do anything, although this is an essential as well as a promised aspect of the biblical God's dualistic activity in the world. This strange kind of anthropomorphism is but one more example of the human ego's insane arrogance in believing that God, or His representatives, think, feel, and act like *it* does. This mistake becomes even more understandable when one recalls the line from the Course, quoted in the previous chapter: "You cannot even think of God without a body, or in some form you think you recognize" (T-18.VIII.1:7).

To state this important point once again, the mistake of spiritual specialness comes from the ego's attempts to assume an importance it does not have. This should obviously come as no surprise, since the origin of the ego is found in its attempt to be more special (and therefore more important) than God. We have already discussed the belief that is at the core of the dualistic thought system that *is* the ego: that the Son in truth is in competition with his Creator and Source. And so how like the ego to bring the non-dualistic truth of Heaven down to its dualistic substitute for Heaven, thereby changing it to its own distorted version of specialness. Yet how real its truth seems, because the ego has convinced the Son of God to pay attention to *form* (always an aspect of duality) at the expense of *content*.

Thus, it is imperative for students of *A Course in Miracles* to recognize this crucial distinction between form and content, as we pointed out earlier in Chapter Two. In this way they will not fall into the trap of believing that the Holy Spirit operates in a world of form. The short twenty-two-year history of *A Course in Miracles'* life in the world has already begun to repeat the almost 3,000-year-old Judaeo-Christian pattern of believing that certain people are specially *chosen* by God to do very important work in the world, even if it means murder, as in the Crusades and other "holy wars." While I do not know of Course students actually killing other people in the name of *A Course in Miracles*, at least not yet, the dynamics of specialness and judgment that *are* already manifest certainly *reflect* the ego's desire to kill in order to preserve its own specialness. The spiritual specialness in almost all of Western spirituality should be apparent not only from a reading of the Bible, let alone the history of Western religious life, but also unfortunately in *A Course in Miracles'* brief history and in the published writings already surrounding it.

The Course's emphasis remains always, if you read it correctly, on undoing the interferences in the *individual* student's mind, and not on form, structures, and *very important work*. That is why, as we shall see in Chapter Six of this book, there is absolutely nothing in *A Course in Miracles* on groups or organizations. They are totally irrelevant to the Course's curriculum, and reflect the anthropomorphic projections onto a God Who now thinks like a dualistic ego, believing in external joining, amassing ever-increasing numbers of students and followers, etc. This is no different from the thought system reflected in the various Christian churches, that believed that God was concerned with the number of true believers that could be converted and totaled. The second and third laws of chaos, described in Chapter 23 of the text, deal very directly with this form of ego insanity of making God into our own image and likeness, sharing in the insane thought system of specialness that made Him.

Everyone wants to be special, some even want to be specially special by being judgmental of other people's presumed specialness, or else to be the lowest of the low because of their rampant and unredeemable specialness. Therefore, it is almost inevitable that *A Course in Miracles* will be read and understood through the lens of this specialness. This also explains, as we observed in an earlier chapter (p. 24), why so many students these days are channeling "holy words," whether coming from Jesus or some other advanced being. These *special* ones then proceed, "under instructions" of course, to give these *special* messages to *special* people who then use these *special* words as the basis for constructing their *special* and very important visionary castles in the sky under the umbrella of *A Course in Miracles.* And all the time their ego's ugly specialness is concealed beneath the "Holy Spirit's" *very important work.* Jesus not only does not want martyrs (T-6.I.16:3), he does not want missionaries. His *love* in our minds is the missionary, which then becomes expressed through us. But that expression is not our concern, nor should it be our identification, as he emphasizes in three pointed passages, here referring to the extension of holiness, forgiveness, and the miracle respectively:

> Concern yourself not with the extension of holiness, for the nature of miracles you do not understand. Nor do you do them. It is their extension, far beyond the limits you perceive, that demonstrates you do not do them. Why should

> you worry how the miracle extends to all the Sonship when you do not understand the miracle itself? (T-16.II.1:3-6)

> Extension of forgiveness is the Holy Spirit's function. Leave this to Him. Let your concern be only that you give to Him that which can be extended. Save no dark secrets that He cannot use, but offer Him the tiny gifts He can extend forever. He will take each one and make of it a potent force for peace (T-22.VI.9:2-6).

> The miracle extends without your help, but you are needed that it can begin. Accept the miracle of healing, and it will go forth because of what it is. It is its nature to extend itself the instant it is born. And it is born the instant it is offered and received.... Leave, then, the transfer of your learning to the One Who really understands its laws, and Who will guarantee that they remain unviolated and unlimited. Your part is merely to apply what He has taught you to yourself, and He will do the rest (T-27.V.1:2-5; 10:1-2).

It is our humility that "allows" Jesus or the Holy Spirit to extend Their love and peace through us, and our arrogance that takes that function for itself, certain that it is God-given.

All people have their special illusions and special needs, the denial of the pain of their guilt over this specialness being very high on the list. Rather then looking with Jesus at their guilt— saving from him "no dark secrets"—students of *A Course in Miracles* would often much rather tell him the wonderfully special words that he would then conveniently tell them. Therefore, to make this chapter's point one final time, focusing on hearing Jesus or the Holy Spirit is clearly setting oneself up for a painful fall, for such a practice grossly underestimates the unconscious investment in the reality of the ego's thought system of specialness. It is the Course's emphasis on undoing the ego, and *not* on hearing the Voice of the Holy Spirit, that makes it so unique in the world's spiritual literature. For it is the undoing of the ego by accepting Jesus' true role in the Atonement that paves the way for an authentic experience of his love, the process that is the subject of the next chapter.

Chapter 5

THE ROLES OF JESUS AND THE HOLY SPIRIT – II
LOOKING AT THE EGO: BRINGING DARKNESS TO LIGHT

Introduction

What then is the protection against spiritual specialness creeping in and rearing its ugly though oftimes subtle head? *A Course in Miracles'* clear and unequivocal answer to the problem is that students' work must reflect an ongoing commitment to look at their guilt, with the love of Jesus or the Holy Spirit by their side. As Jesus says in the text, in the context of the perceived problem of being hopelessly trapped in life's prison that *is* suffering, a paragraph I quoted in *All Are Called*:

> Now you are being shown you *can* escape. *All that is needed is you look upon the problem as it is, and not the way that you have set it up.* How could there be another way to solve a problem that is very simple, but has been obscured by heavy clouds of complication, which were made to keep the problem unresolved? Without the clouds the problem will emerge in all its primitive simplicity [the choice for the dualistic ego, rather than for the Holy Spirit, the reflection of the non-dualistic God]. The choice will not be difficult, because the problem is absurd *when clearly seen.* No one has difficulty in making up his mind to let a simple problem be resolved *if it is seen* as hurting him, and also very easily removed (T-27.VII.2; italics mine, except for 2:1).

Thus, the student of *A Course in Miracles* should focus, *and focus only*, on bringing the guilt and investment in specialness to Jesus' love, that the ego be looked upon for the silly choice it is. One turns to Jesus for this help in looking, rather than speaking to him about the holy work one is to do with and for others. In doing the latter, as we have already discussed, students inevitably end up dictating to Jesus (or the Holy Spirit) how They should be operating within their own particular dream of specialness. Chapter Six of this book is devoted to further exploration of the subject of spiritual specialness, specifically regarding its expression in students of *A Course in Miracles* "joining together" in groups, networks, communities, etc., and so we leave this subject until then.

We turn now to examining the true role of Jesus or the Holy Spirit in one's spiritual life, and specifically how this role is to be understood in following the spiritual path of *A Course in Miracles*. We begin our discussion with Helen Schucman, scribe of the Course, and her relationship with Jesus, focusing on its implications for students of *A Course in Miracles*. Helen's experiences provide a wonderful example of both levels—the specific and abstract—that can well serve those seeking to emulate this holy woman by taking her experiences with Jesus as a model for the *process* of developing their own relationship with Jesus.

Helen Schucman's Relationship with Jesus
The Illusion and the Reality

Helen Schucman's relationship with Jesus provides all students of *A Course in Miracles* with an instructive example of the right-minded and wrong-minded ways of thinking about their own relationship with the Course's source. And so in this first section we look at Helen and her scribing of *A Course in Miracles*, focusing on her experience of Jesus. Our point of departure, however, is not so much Helen's specific experiences of Jesus—which are discussed at great length in *Absence from Felicity*—but rather on the meaning of these experiences: the content rather than the form. This, I hope, will help Course students to deepen their understanding of the true nature of the scribing of *A Course in Miracles*, not to mention their own personal experiences of Jesus or the Holy Spirit.

About a year or so after the Course was published, an obviously sincere woman approached Helen and asked how Jesus could have possibly written *A Course in Miracles*, as he did not know English. While, on the one hand, the question might appear to be a simplistic one, on the other hand, the woman's question helps us to focus the inquiry on the role Jesus actually played in the scribing of *A Course in Miracles*. At first blush, and as the story of the scribing is usually told, it would seem as if the person of Jesus stood within Helen's mind with a microphone, dictating to her—word for word, in English!—the three books of the Course. It must be remembered certainly that, on one level, this process of internal dictation was Helen's experience (though without the microphone!). But similar to the misperception of the experience of the sun's rising and setting that we discussed in the previous chapter, this experience, though valid for the individual, nonetheless should not be taken for the actual truth, let alone taken to serve as a model in specific form for other people's experience.

Before continuing my comments on the Course's scribing, I should like to relate a relevant incident involving Helen and Jesus. This incident, perhaps more than any other, illustrates the two levels with which one can describe a relationship with Jesus: the appearance and the reality, the experience and the truth, the form and the content. I shall first relate the circumstances as they occurred, and then discuss them in the context of what it truly meant for Helen, and therefore for all students, to have an ongoing relationship with Jesus.

One afternoon during a trip to San Francisco in the summer of 1975, Helen and I visited a lovely chapel that had been built by the brother of a Maryknoll Sister who was a dear friend of ours. As Helen and I sat quietly, preparing to pray to Jesus, an eyelash fell into Helen's eye. She related to me how this was not an uncommon experience for her, as her eyelashes were long and frequently fell into her eyes. However, she continued, this never presented a problem for her because Jesus always removed the eyelashes. Helen then described to me how she would close her eyes and pray to Jesus, and when she opened them the eyelash would always be out. And so sitting in the chapel, we proceeded to close our eyes and pray together. Sure enough, moments later, there was the eyelash, plain as day, resting comfortably on Helen's cheek.

Clearly, Helen's *experience* was that Jesus took the eyelash out of her eye, but this really makes no sense unless one is prepared to believe that the non-physical Jesus literally plucked the very tangible eyelash from Helen's eye with his finger, or some variations thereof. What I believe really happened with the eyelash, however, is as follows:

Consider again that Jesus literally does not do anything. He remains an abstract presence of love in our minds, analogous to a lighthouse that simply shines its light into the dark night. Those ships that are lost at sea perceive the light and sail towards it. The lighthouse itself does not actively call *to them*, but its passive though constant presence reminds them of where their ship's safety truly lies. Similarly, the "passive though constant presence" of Jesus (and the Holy Spirit) serves as a reminder that our safety lies in going towards Their light that is in the mind, not in the rough seas of the ego's thought system.

As I documented in *Absence from Felicity*, Helen spent a lifetime attempting to run away from Jesus, continually turning from his light and using the darkness of her ego concerns and judgments as a hiding place from his truth. That is why early in the dictation Jesus told her, relative to the two stages involved in escaping from darkness: "First, the recognition that darkness cannot hide.... Second, the recognition that there is nothing you want to hide even if you could." Incidentally, this statement is currently found in "The Escape from Darkness" in Chapter 1 of the text (T-1.IV.1:1,3).

One of the ways Helen expressed this running away from Jesus was by attacking her eyes. Vision has always been a major symbol in spiritual thought systems, and *A Course in*

Miracles is no exception. It would therefore stand to reason that Helen's ego would attack her eyes as symbolic of her attempts not to see the truth that Jesus was teaching her. In fact, while Helen was taking down the Course, she went through a period when she was sure she was losing her eyesight. Panic-stricken, she checked into the Eye Institute that was part of the Columbia-Presbyterian Medical Center in New York City where she worked. But she was released after a couple of days when all the tests came back negative. Soon afterwards, her eyesight returned. Moreover, for many, many years Helen was "meditating" on developing a detached retina, since her fear of this was so great. *Fear* of something always reflects the ego's underlying *attraction* for it, and, indeed, near the end of her life Helen did "succeed" finally in detaching her retina.

Another example of Helen's resistance to sharing in Jesus' vision came in the context of a series of efforts he asked her to make to *look* at him on the cross, presumably so that she would be able to *see* that he was not suffering. Very often I would try to help Helen in this, praying with her as she "saw" an image of the crucifix. But she would always—without any seeming control over the shift—move Jesus to the lower left-hand corner of her visual field, thereby avoiding having to see him full face. She was thus never able to *see* him as he asked.

On a much smaller scale, then, Helen's "detached eyelashes" also can be understood as reflecting her resistance to looking at what Jesus would have her see. Thus, on a level she was not in touch with, she would make a decision to separate from his love and therefore be apart from the vision of Christ that is the goal of the Course. This decision, coming from fear, was essentially as non-specific as the love that Jesus represented, even though it manifested in specific forms. In this case, the eyelash in the eye was the inevitable *effect* of the *cause*: Helen's decision to separate from Jesus' love. When Helen decided to let Jesus help her with the eyelash, she was reflecting on this bodily level the decision made in her mind to move closer to him and to join with his love. Thus she undid the cause of the eyelash in the eye—being separate from Jesus—by choosing to join him once again. At this point, with the cause undone, the effect was undone as well, and so the eyelash ended up on Helen's cheek.

The point in all this is that Jesus in reality did nothing. Helen did all the work; first in moving away from Jesus (symbolically leading to *her* putting the eyelash in her eye), and then in moving back to him (symbolically leading to *her* removing the eyelash from her eye). Yet her experience, similar to our example of the sun rising and setting, was that Jesus helped her. In reality, just as the sun remains stationary relative to the earth, which revolves around it, Jesus' love and light remained still—"passive and constant"—while Helen first moved away from him, and then returned.

Resuming our discussion of Helen and her scribing of *A Course in Miracles*, and recalling a similar discussion in Chapter Six of *All Are Called*, we can see that while her experience most definitely was of Jesus—a person *outside* herself —who related to her and dictated to her, in truth the reality was much different. Helen was able to return her mind to that memory of God's Love—her true Identity—symbolized by her as Jesus. By uniting with him, she united with love. That union has no form or specifics, for love, as we have seen, is abstract and beyond all divisions of the ego. This love, of which Jesus was the manifestation, flowed through the separated mind we know as Helen (the water taking shape in the glass) and came out to the world as the three books we know as *A Course in Miracles*. It was therefore Helen's mind that gave the Course its *form*; the *content* came from *outside* her ego (or wrong) mind, from a love that nonetheless is *within* her right mind, as indeed it is in all of us.

Thus, Helen's own description of *A Course in Miracles'* scribing was that Jesus had made use of her "educational background, interests and experience, but that was in matters of style [i.e., form] rather than content" (*Absence from Felicity*,

p. 211). As one looks at the particulars of the Course's form and structure, one can find almost exact parallels with Helen's own life:

Helen was *American* and obviously *English speaking*, the idiom and language of the Course.

She was a *Freudian psychologist* and *educator*, and the Course contains a sophisticated psychodynamic study of the ego, coming within a curricular format: text, workbook for students, and manual for teachers. Its goal, moreover, is that we learn from our inner Teacher, the Holy Spirit, so as to become teachers of God.

Despite her clear and lifelong ambivalence with organized Christianity, Helen nonetheless identified with the Christian tradition, more specifically *Roman Catholicism*, and was very well versed in the *Bible's beautiful King James language* (biblical theology left her cold at best, and enraged at worst). The language of *A Course in Miracles* falls within the traditional Christian framework, but corrects the distortions and misunderstandings of this two-thousand-year-old tradition, and indeed, as these two books make clear, overturns the basic premises upon which biblical Judaism and Christianity rest. In addition, the Course contains over eight hundred biblical quotations and allusions.

Helen was a lover of *Shakespeare* as well as the great English poets, and the writing of *A Course in Miracles* is quite Shakespearean in form, with large portions of the material coming in blank verse and iambic pentameter, the poetic meter of Shakespeare.

Helen possessed a *keenly logical mind*—her love if not worship of logic was manifest as far back as her college years —and the Course's theory is presented with a rigorous logic, that once its basic premises are accepted, cannot be argued with.

Finally, Helen had great respect and love for *Plato*, and a number of specific allusions to Plato's work can be found in the Course. In addition, as I pointed out in *Love Does Not*

Condemn, A Course in Miracles comes within the philosophical tradition that, even though it traces its beginnings to the pre-Socratics, more properly begins with Plato, the true father of Western philosophy, along with Socrates, his teacher.

The one seeming exception to this list, in terms of the formal characteristics of the Course, is the strong Gnostic theme that runs throughout the material, not to mention usage of specific Gnostic terminology.* Helen and I never discussed the subject—my interest in Gnosticism did not really begin until after her death—but, to the best of my knowledge, she had no conscious awareness of this important philosophical and religious movement. However, since Platonists were among the leading Gnostic teachers, and Platonic Gnosticism is reflected in much of the Course's teachings, there must certainly have been part of Helen's mind that was familiar with this tradition.

Therefore, to state the point again, Helen was responsible for the Course's specific form; the abstract love of Jesus—the Course's source—for its content. To a question raised by *A Course in Miracles* group that we had once visited, Helen responded that naturally *A Course in Miracles* was psychological and set up as a curriculum, since she was a psychologist and educator. I reminded her afterwards, however, that she became a psychologist and teacher because of a decision she had made prior *to*, and on a level different *from* her conscious existence as Helen Schucman. This was similar to the fact that the three people closest to the Course—Helen, William Thetford, and I —all had Ph.D.'s in Clinical Psychology. *A Course in Miracles* teaches that time is not linear, and choices are made on the level of the mind—outside time and space—independent of the brain and body with which we identify.† Thus our choices to become psychologists, and Helen's to become an educator as

---

* Gnosticism and its relationship to *A Course in Miracles* is discussed at length in *Love Does Not Condemn*.
† The interested reader may consult my *A Vast Illusion: Time According to A COURSE IN MIRACLES* for an in-depth treatment of the Course's understanding of time.

well, were hardly accidental or serendipitous. Helen's professional life as a psychologist and teacher was necessary so that her brain could accept the Course's teachings in that form. The difficulty in understanding this atemporal phenomenon comes from our linear-programmed brains which cannot go beyond their own temporal programming, and so cannot understand the mind's non-linearity.

However, Helen's experience, as we have seen, was that Jesus *used* her particular talents and abilities, just as she experienced him as helping her solve specific problems. In fact, in the original dictation, omitted in the published Course, Jesus said to Helen:

> You must have noticed how often I have used your own ideas to help *you*.

And then in the context of how the Holy Spirit teaches us "to use what the ego has made to *teach* the opposite of what the ego has *learned*" (found in slightly modified form in the published text, T-7.IV.3:3) Jesus said to Helen:

> You could not have a better example of the Holy Spirit's unified purpose than this course. The Holy Spirit has taken very diversified areas of your past learning, and has applied them to a *unified* curriculum.

In truth, once again, it was really the mind beyond Helen—called here the Holy Spirit—that took the "diversified areas" of her life and "applied them to a unified curriculum."

Therefore, we can now better understand, on a more sophisticated level, the true nature of Helen's relationship with Jesus. An abstract and non-specific presence, Jesus remains a thought of perfect love within the right minds of all people who still believe in the reality of the dream. The thought we know as Helen rejoined the thought we know as Jesus. Within the dream of the world, this union of love manifested itself as *A Course in Miracles*. Moreover, the real Self of Helen that was this love was expressed in some of her visions in which she appeared as a perfectly objective and impersonal priestess; the more complete expression of this union of love, as it more directly reflected the abstract impersonal nature of this Love of Christ.

Given this reality, we can now also understand the motivation behind the supplement *The Song of Prayer*, and the more personal message that preceded it. By focusing on the specifics of her ego's concerns, Helen was virtually able to bury the love of her Self. The miracle of this abstract love became sacrificed for the magic contained in the demands for specific answers to her specific questions. Returning to our earlier analogy, instead of holding an almost infinite container to the flowing and love-laden waters of Jesus, Helen presented him with the narrow thimble of her ego needs, that he might fill only that. In this sense, again, the love of Jesus was made more "manageable." To repeat part of his all-important message to her:

> A specific question is actually a decision about the kind of answer that is acceptable. The purpose of words is to limit, and by limiting, to make a vast area more manageable.... Answers are not up to you. Any limit you place on them interferes with hearing.

All the questions about specifics thus came to symbolize for Helen the limitation placed on love by fear. In *A Course in Miracles* Jesus urges his students to recognize and choose against this price, which must inevitably be paid when one focuses on specifics. At first, at the lower rungs of the ladder of prayer, the asking for specifics can represent our attempts to join with Jesus in an acceptable way that would minimize our fear of uniting with his love. However, it is an easy temptation to become seduced by the specialness of the "answers," thereby avoiding the true Answer. Helping her to move beyond this temptation, again, was the purpose of Jesus' message to Helen. It is always helpful, to restate this important point still one more time, to be reminded of the difference between symbol and reality, appearance and truth: the specific *forms* of the world only have meaning to the extent that they help us to move beyond them to the abstract *content* of God's Love that is our sole desire and goal. We can now proceed to discussing even more directly the help that Jesus offers us on our pathway home to God.

Looking with Jesus at the Specificity of Illusions

We begin by restating this important caution: When tempted to believe in the "rightness" and "helpfulness" of their inner and often specific experiences, students of *A Course in Miracles* should remind themselves of these familiar and cautionary words from the text:

> Trust not your good intentions. They are not enough. But trust implicitly your willingness, whatever else may enter (T-18.IV.2:1-3).

This last sentence of course, is a reference to the little willingness we are asked to give to the Holy Spirit to abandon our belief that we are correct in our perceptions and values. So often, when people ask for specific answers to specific questions—to expand our discussion from the previous section of this clever ego tactic—they are really asking the Holy Spirit or Jesus to provide them with the answers for which they have already unconsciously wished. In the third rule for decision at the beginning of Chapter 30, Jesus makes the same point in asking students to understand why they are not having the kind of day they really want:

> ...realize that you have asked a question by yourself, and must have set an answer in your terms. Then say:
>
> *I have no question. I forgot what to decide.*
>
> This cancels out the terms that you have set, and lets the answer show you what the question must have really been.
>
> Try to observe this rule without delay, despite your opposition. For you have already gotten angry. And your fear of being answered in a different way from what your

version of the question asks will gain momentum, until you believe the day you want is one in which you get *your* answer to *your* question. And you will not get it, for it would destroy the day by robbing you of what you really want (T-30.I.6:2–7:4).

Thus, by really asking Jesus to answer *their* question, always some aspect of the specific, students are bringing truth to illusion, rather than illusion to the truth as they are repeatedly asked to do in the Course. Since the Sonship made the world (the illusion) *specifically* to exclude the Love of God (the truth), it is the height of the ego's arrogance to ask God (or His symbolic manifestations) to enter the illusory dream to help solve a problem made up especially to keep Him away, and, moreover, one that He knows nothing about. That is why, again, in *A Course in Miracles* Jesus asks us instead to bring our mistaken beliefs and perceptions to the truth that is within our minds, where, in the presence of its light, the darkness of our fears and concerns simply disappears.

Since the ego thought system is almost completely unconscious to us, we are unaware, for the most part, of the silent investments we have in the outcome of events. This is the advantage to moving beyond specifics: there is far less likelihood of one's hearing being "contaminated." In the section on Helen's "Special Messages" in *Absence from Felicity*, I discuss that even Helen, whose "hearing" was so pure and ego-free when it came to taking down *A Course in Miracles*, could be most unreliable when it came to specifics related to personal concerns of herself or others. To re-state what we have already discussed, unconscious ego conflicts and demands most easily surface when one's attention is riveted on specific questions, needs, and outcomes. When one is at rest in the peace of God, however, there is no serious concern with outcomes, and the answer is always known and understood. This does not mean, certainly, that specific decisions are not necessary. As Jesus states in *The Song of Prayer*:

> There are decisions to make here, and they must be made
> whether they be illusions or not (S-1.I.2:4).

And in the *Psychotherapy* supplement, Jesus reminds us that

> Even an advanced therapist has some earthly needs while
> he is here (P-3.III.1:3).

This means that some attention needs to be given to earning
money to supply these needs. The point, however, is not that
students of *A Course in Miracles* should not involve themselves in the specifics of the world—that would be hardly
practical, let alone possible—but rather that the problem lies
in their placing undue emphasis on *hearing* the Holy Spirit
give them the specific answer to a specific question or need.
Such continuing concern and focus will ultimately draw away
from the real Answer. Part of the special message to Helen of
October 5, 1975 is deserving of repeat quotation here:

> To God all things are possible, but you must ask His answer
> only of Himself.
> Perhaps you think you do, but be you sure that if you did
> you would be quiet now and wholly undismayed by any-
> thing. Do not attempt to guess His Will for you. Do not
> assume that you are right because an answer seems to come
> from Him. Be sure you ask, and then be still and let Him
> speak.

This extremely important warning against believing that the
inner voice is God's simply because one experiences it as
such, is underscored by this very humbling statement from the
manual for teachers, cited earlier: "Only very few can hear
God's Voice at all" (M-12.3:3).

Before continuing, I should like to digress to tell a story
that points up the mistake of holding up Helen, or anyone else
for that matter, as an example of impeccable hearing regarding
specifics. A number of years ago I received a telephone call
from a very distraught man, who related to me how he had
been receiving specific guidance from the Holy Spirit over the
past few years. I do not recall most of the details of our

conversation, but I do remember that he was being "told" very specific things regarding places, dates, etc. One piece of this guidance stated that he was going to die on a specific date, *which was due now in three days.* And this man was calling me the day before he was supposed to enter the hospital for minor surgery, which was to take place on the very day the Holy Spirit "told" him would be his last on earth. I explained to him the confusion of form and content, and provided some specific examples for him of Helen's hearing mistakes. Fortunately, he understood, and feeling greatly relieved, entered the hospital for his surgery. A week or so later he called to tell me that he was safely home, the operation a success, and he was obviously still very much alive.

I frequently caution students of *A Course in Miracles* about this kind of mistake, urging them to be suspicious of any specific guidance they receive, even more so when Jesus and the Holy Spirit sound urgent or demanding. Love is always patient, since it knows not of time. The *content* of authentic guidance is always from the Holy Spirit, but the *form* is the product of the individual's separated mind and therefore should not be treated as special.

There are many passages in *A Course in Miracles* which specifically address how Jesus sees his (or the Holy Spirit's) role of looking with us at the ego's darkness, and we shall examine a few of these now, even though some were discussed in *All Are Called.* We begin with perhaps the clearest statement in the entire Course about this process, which essentially defines healing as the result of looking together with Jesus at the illusions of the ego:

> No one can escape illusions unless he looks at them, for not looking is the way they are protected. There is no need to shrink from illusions, for they cannot be dangerous. We are ready to look more closely at the ego's thought system because together we have the lamp that will dispel it, and since you realize you do not want it, you must be ready. Let us be very calm in doing this, for we are merely looking

honestly for truth. The "dynamics" of the ego will be our lesson for a while, for we must look first at this to see beyond it, since you have made it real. We will undo this error quietly together, and then look beyond it to truth.

What is healing but the removal of all that stands in the way of knowledge? And how else can one dispel illusions except by looking at them directly, without protecting them? Be not afraid, therefore, for what you will be looking at is the source of fear, and you are beginning to learn that fear is not real.... Do not be afraid, then, to look upon fear, for it cannot be seen. Clarity undoes confusion by definition, and to look upon darkness through light must dispel it (T-11.V.1:1–2:3,8-9).

Earlier in the text Jesus makes a similar plea to his students:

Watch carefully and see what it is you are really asking for. Be very honest with yourself in this, for we must hide nothing from each other (T-4.III.8:1-2).

Think honestly what you have thought that God would not have thought, and what you have not thought that God would have you think. Search sincerely for what you have done and left undone accordingly, and then change your mind to think with God's. This may seem hard to do, but it is much easier than trying to think against it.... As a loving brother I am deeply concerned with your mind, and urge you to follow my example as you look at yourself and at your brother ... (T-4.IV.2:4-6,9).

Passages like these make no real sense, and cannot truly be understood by students *unless* they first recognize the total unreality of all they perceive and experience. And because perception is unreal and reflects the ego's attempts to make up false problems to distract us from the truth, how could Jesus possibly be directly involved in them? He *is* involved with us, but only insofar as his presence *in our minds* reminds the decision maker *in our minds* that our problems are in fact made up. Therefore, we can choose to look at them for the illusions they truly are. The honesty he calls for thus involves

157

our being able to see our problems for what they are—to "look upon the problem as it is, and not the way that you have set it up." We cannot do this looking without him, for to do so means we have again forsworn his love and chosen the eyes of the ego's specialness to look through instead. Moreover, looking at our ego's choices with Jesus expresses our having rejoined him, thus undoing the very foundation of the ego's thought system of separation that had given rise to the perceived problem in the first place.

Similar passages can be found in the Course that describe the same healing function of bringing the darkness of the ego thought system to the light of truth, gently looking without fear, a function equally ascribed to the Holy Spirit. Here are two examples:

> The Holy Spirit's function is entirely communication. He therefore must remove whatever interferes with communication in order to restore it. *Therefore, keep no source of interference from His sight, for He will not attack your sentinels. But bring them to Him and let His gentleness teach you that, in the light, they are not fearful, and cannot serve to guard the dark doors behind which nothing at all is carefully concealed.* We must open all doors and let the light come streaming through. There are no hidden chambers in God's temple. Its gates are open wide to greet His Son. No one can fail to come where God has called him, if he close not the door himself upon his Father's welcome (T-14.VI.8; italics mine).

> *The Holy Spirit asks of you but this; bring to Him every secret you have locked away from Him. Open every door to Him, and bid Him enter the darkness and lighten it away.* At your request He enters gladly. He brings the light to darkness if you make the darkness open to Him. But what you hide He cannot look upon. He sees for you, and unless you look with Him He cannot see. The vision of Christ is not for Him alone, but for Him with you. *Bring, therefore, all your dark and secret thoughts to Him, and look upon them with Him.* He holds the light, and you the darkness.

They cannot coexist when both of You together look on
them. His judgment must prevail, and He will give it to you
as you join your perception to His (T-14.VII.6; italics
mine).

The reader can certainly note that nothing is said in any of
these passages about what Jesus or the Holy Spirit will do for
us. Rather, the emphasis is consistently placed upon our bringing our illusions to Their Love, so that its light can dispel the
darkness of the ego. That is Their and Their light's *only* function. Also, the closing lines of the last passage reflect the undoing of the ego's attempts at *dissociating* the two mutually
exclusive thought systems belonging to itself and the Holy
Spirit. Our next section discusses this crucial dynamic in more
detail.

Finally, we have this passage from the end of Chapter 27,
which also nicely summarizes the Holy Spirit's role in looking
with us at the cause of our pain: the decision to take seriously
the "tiny, mad idea" of the ego's separation. By bringing the
darkness of our suffering to His light, we learn to laugh at the
silliness of believing that the Son, Whom God created perfect,
could ever be separate from Perfection. The point is reflected
here that the Holy Spirit (or Jesus) would have to be as insane
as we, if He were truly to address these illusory problems and
concerns. Thus we would find again how the subtle ego would
attempt to bring the truth of the Holy Spirit to its illusions to
solve them. The reader may recall one more time our example
of the insanity of attempting to correct the poor image on a
movie screen by going to the screen, rather than to the source
of the problem in the projection booth. Therefore, Jesus is
once again in this passage reminding his students to focus not
on the perceived problem, but rather on *looking* at what we
believe to be our problem with his or the Holy Spirit's Love as
the source of our vision:

In gentle laughter does the Holy Spirit perceive the
cause, and looks not to effects. How else could He correct
your error, who have overlooked the cause entirely? *He*

> *bids you bring each terrible effect to Him that you may look*
> *together on its foolish cause and laugh with Him a while.*
> *You* judge effects, but *He* has judged their cause. And by
> His judgment are effects removed. Perhaps you come in
> tears. But hear Him say, "My brother, holy Son of God,
> behold your idle dream, in which this could occur." And
> you will leave the holy instant with your laughter and your
> brother's joined with His (T-27.VIII.9; italics mine in
> sentence 3).

And yet the ego is hellbent—literally—on keeping the
Holy Spirit's memory of Heaven away from itself. The psychological term we give to this particular form of its strategy
is *dissociation*, and we briefly turn to an examination of this
dynamic now.

The Undoing of Dissociation

Frequently in *A Course in Miracles*, Jesus discusses the
psychological defenses that Helen and Bill were so familiar
with as psychologists in order to clarify or expand upon his
teaching. *Dissociation* is one such term, and an understanding
of it is extremely important to appreciate the dynamics of the
ego's strategy in excluding Jesus or the Holy Spirit from our
minds. Likewise, it is extremely important to understand this
dynamic in order to better appreciate the role that Jesus and
the Holy Spirit play in undoing the ego: bringing the darkness
of its illusions to the light of Their truth.

We begin with a definition: dissociation is the ego's
attempt to separate two conflicting thought systems—its own
and the Holy Spirit's—which yet keeps them both in our
minds in such a way that *its* illusory thought system of darkness is safe from undoing by the light of truth that Jesus represents for us. The ego is not able to abolish or destroy the
Holy Spirit, but it can conceal His Presence through this
defense mechanism. It knows that once these two mutually

exclusive thought systems are brought together—the meaning of Jesus' emphasis in *A Course in Miracles* on bringing the darkness to the light, the illusion to the truth—the ego must disappear. Thus, dissociation comes to the ego's rescue by ensuring that the reason of the right mind remain split off and made inaccessible to meaningful choice by our decision maker.

And this then is why the ego blesses all attempts on the part of students of *A Course in Miracles* to persist in bringing the Holy Spirit's light to the darkness, which they invariably do whenever they ask the light of Jesus to solve a problem—which means *any* problem—that is outside the mind. By so seducing students, the ego is able to keep the darkness of its guilt away from the light of forgiveness, which exists *only* in the mind. Dragging Jesus into the dream that is the world, making him the great problem solver of all that concerns us, simply keeps us out of our minds—literally and figuratively! —which is where he truly is, and which is the only place he *can* be. However, calling on Jesus to help us look at our mind's decision to be separate from him (and therefore from God) is the way, indeed *the only way,* he can help us. Only by bringing our attention back to our minds—the true meaning and purpose of the miracle—can the ego's dissociation be rendered null and void. This is the exact meaning behind Jesus' words to Helen early in the Course's scribing—retained in the published edition—when she complained to him that he was not helping her more to overcome her fears. The reader may recall Jesus' answer from our discussion of this same point in *All Are Called* (p. 210), as well as from the Introduction to this book (pp. 6-7):

> The correction of fear *is* your responsibility. When you ask for release from fear [i.e., bringing the truth to the illusion], you are implying that it is not. *You should ask, instead, for help in the conditions that have brought the fear about.* These conditions always entail a willingness to be separate. At that level you *can* help it....

161

You may still complain about fear [Helen still was, obviously], but you nevertheless persist in making yourself fearful. I have already indicated that you cannot ask me to release you from fear. I know it does not exist, but you do not. If I intervened between your thoughts [mind] and their results [what appears to be in the world], I would be tampering with a basic law of cause and effect; the most fundamental law there is. *I would hardly help you if I depreciated the power of your own thinking. This would be in direct opposition to the purpose of this course* [to bring the illusions that the world and our problems are real back to the truth that is the Holy Spirit's presence in our minds]. It is much more helpful to remind you that you do not guard your thoughts carefully enough....I cannot let you leave your mind unguarded... (T-2.VI.4:1-5; T-2.VII.1:1-7; 2:1; italics mine).

In this next passage we find a very clear statement about the nature of the ego's use of dissociation, and its undoing:

Our emphasis has been on bringing what is undesirable to the desirable; what you do not want to what you do. You will realize that salvation must come to you this way, if you consider what dissociation is. Dissociation is a distorted process of thinking whereby two systems of belief which cannot coexist are both maintained. If they are brought together, their joint acceptance becomes impossible. But if one is kept in darkness from the other, their separation seems to keep them both alive and equal in their reality. Their joining thus becomes the source of fear, for if they meet, acceptance must be withdrawn from one of them. You cannot have them both, for each denies the other. Apart, this fact is lost from sight, for each in a separate place can be endowed with firm belief. Bring them together, and the fact of their complete incompatibility is instantly apparent. One will go, because the other is seen in the same place (T-14.VII.4).

Therefore, we can now understand and summarize exactly what part Jesus wants to play in our Atonement path. We have seen from our discussion of *The Song of Prayer* how Jesus does *not* wish to unduly encourage his students in the practice of asking him for specific information for specific questions—what I have termed "asking to destroy" in *All Are Called* (p. 310)—or to indulge them by the granting of special favors to satisfy certain special needs. Rather, Jesus wishes his students to develop the practice of recognizing how *all* their concerns—without exception—stem from their having separated from his love and wisdom, having joined instead with their ego's distortions of love and wisdom that parody the real thing. The specific *forms* that constitute the focus of students' attention exist solely to cloud the *content* of separation over which students feel so guilty, and to mask the dissociation which keeps Jesus' love split off from their awareness.

And so to truly find an answer to their problems, Jesus asks his students to join with him again, a reflection of the *greater joining* (T-28.IV) which will undo the actual cause of the suffering and distress. This joining takes the form of looking with him at the ego's strategy of dissociation and projection, and how all external concerns have been unconsciously designed to keep his presence in their minds hidden from any access. Joining with Jesus in understanding this undoes the very dissociation that was the ego's defense against him. The defense gone, nothing remains but the love of Jesus, which is, of course, the only answer to all problems. To accept anything less is to fall into the ego's trap of making the error real, thus ensuring that the student will continue to remain mired in the web of duality, instead of rising above the trap and being gently led through the ego's world of dualistic illusion, eventually to return to the non-dualistic world of God's truth.

Chapter 6

GROUPS: FALSE VERSUS TRUE JOINING

Introduction

Throughout this book we have seen how so much of the misunderstanding that students of *A Course in Miracles* have with its teachings relate to their not recognizing how Jesus uses language in presenting his message. Thus, we have spoken of the different levels on the spiritual ladder that Jesus reflects in his presentation. To return to a point made in the Introduction, students of *A Course in Miracles*—at varying times in their lifetime's work with the Course, not to mention their own inherent spiritual awareness—will understand the Course differently, based upon their own progress in the process of forgiveness. However, problems enter in, as has been discussed in previous chapters, when students are not aware of these differing levels in the Course. In this chapter we focus on the particular mistake of not understanding what Jesus means by joining. We begin with a discussion of the more general problem of level confusion as a means for introducing this theme.

Level Confusion: The Meaning of Joining

I have spoken often of the crucial distinction Jesus makes in *A Course in Miracles* between *form* and *content*. This translates into the distinction between behavior (the body) and thought (the mind). Stated still another way, we are dealing with the distinction between *effect* and *cause*; the cause always resting in the mind's decision to join with the ego or the Holy Spirit, while the effect refers to the behavioral or external results of the mind's choosing: the shadows of guilt or reflections of love that are cast upon the world from the mind.

165

The problem is that many students think *A Course in Miracles* is about joining on this behavioral level, and so they focus much of their attention on joining together with other Course students in groups, organizations, conferences, cyberspace interactions, etc. Yet those they believe they are joining with are but representations in form of the original ego thought of fragmentation, and how can you join with others unless you first believe they are separate from you? And since fragmentation is the opposite of oneness, how would it ever be truly possible then to join with them? Indeed, such "joining" would be the very antithesis of what Jesus is really teaching us in *A Course in Miracles* about what it means to experience communion with another. The reader may recall this important sentence from the text: "Minds are joined; bodies are not" (T-18.VI.3:1). This crucial distinction between the mind and the body is underscored in the following passages from the text on the true meaning of communion with others, which lies in our *first* being in communion with Jesus or the Holy Spirit:

> *Come therefore unto me, and learn of the truth in you. The mind we share is shared by all our brothers, and as we see them truly they will be healed. Let your mind shine with mine upon their minds, and by our gratitude to them make them aware of the light in them.* This light will shine back upon you and on the whole Sonship, because this is your proper gift to God. He will accept it and give it to the Sonship, because it is acceptable to Him and therefore to His Sons. *This is true communion with the Holy Spirit,* Who sees the altar of God in everyone, and by bringing it to your appreciation, He calls upon you to love God and His creation. You can appreciate the Sonship only as one. This is part of the law of creation, and therefore governs all thought (T-7.V.11; italics mine).

I am within your holy relationship, yet you would imprison me behind the obstacles you raise to freedom, and bar my way to you. Yet it is not possible to keep away One Who is there already. And in Him it *is* possible that our communion, where we are joined already, will be the focus of the new perception that will bring light to all the world, contained in you (T-19.IV-B.8:3-5).

And yet this communion is not possible on the physical level, since, again, "Minds are joined; bodies are not":

> Communion is another kind of completion, which goes beyond guilt, *because it goes beyond the body* (T-19.IV-A. 17:15; italics mine).

> *The Holy Spirit's messengers are sent far beyond the body, calling the mind to join in holy communion and be at peace.* Such is the message that I gave them for you (T-19.IV-B.3:1-2; italics mine).

> The body could not separate your mind from your brother's unless you wanted it to be a cause of separation and of distance seen between you and him. *Thus do you endow it with a power that lies not within itself.* And herein lies its power over you. For now you think that it determines when your brother and you meet, and limits your ability to make communion with your brother's mind. And now it tells you where to go and how to go there, what is feasible for you to undertake, and what you cannot do. It dictates what its health can tolerate, and what will tire it and make it sick. And its "inherent" weaknesses set up the limitations on what you would do, and keep your purpose limited and weak (T-29.I.5; italics mine).

These well-intentioned students of *A Course in Miracles* have thus failed to understand that Jesus' words about joining with our brothers are metaphors for the greater joining in the *mind*, without which external joining is meaningless and potentially destructive. This potential danger results from their thinking that they have fulfilled the forgiveness requirements of the Course, when indeed all they have accomplished is to barricade themselves still further from the problem of guilt in the *mind*. Of the guilt and hate inherent in the special relationship, which is always focused on the body, Jesus states:

> The special love relationship is an attempt to limit the
> destructive effects of hate by finding a haven in the storm
> of guilt. It makes no attempt to rise above the storm, into
> the sunlight. On the contrary, it emphasizes the guilt out-
> side the haven by attempting to build barricades against it,
> and keep within them. The special love relationship is not
> perceived as a value in itself, but as a place of safety from
> which hatred is split off and kept apart (T-16.IV.3:1-4).

And so the underlying guilt remains safely hidden in the mind,
from which it is continually projected out onto others *without
the student recognizing what is truly happening.* We can
briefly note the two specific forms of special hate and special
love that this projected guilt takes, which are relevant to our
discussion here. The following section presents these in more
depth.

In *special hate,* others are continually being judged against,
for they are not as special as we are. Indeed, groups are groups
because they have been judged as different from others; e.g.,
the statement "I need a group I can talk to" clearly implies that
there are "other groups that do not understand me." In this
way, the individuality of our specialness is reinforced, as is the
belief that differences are important. And so the Sonship is inevitably conceived of as split, the ego's secret goal.

In *special love,* the unknowing ones believe they are hearing an inner and special Voice, the Voice for God, when all
that is really coming through is the ego's voice that speaks
only for specialness. This error is reminiscent of the specialness that has passed for Christianity for two thousand years.
As noted earlier, otherwise well-meaning Christians "joined
together" in their specific Churches, yet continued to demonstrate the shadowy and oftimes vicious projections of their
submerged guilt, all the while thinking they were following
their Lord of love and Prince of peace. We have seen before
that when guilt is denied it must be projected out, inevitably
giving rise to a *special* world of good and bad, holy and unholy, victim and victimizer—all the while the true and unified

Love of Christ is kept safely hidden by the ego's thought system and by its world.

In summary, it cannot be said too often that the only true joining—and the real focus of Jesus' teachings in *A Course in Miracles*—is the joining with him or the Holy Spirit in our minds. Only then can the ego's thought system of separation be undone and replaced by the *greater joining* (T-28.IV) of Christ with Christ that joining with Jesus allows us to remember. And it is this joining (the *cause*) that automatically becomes reflected in our experiencing a joining with others (the *effect*).

An example of what it truly means to join is found in *Psychotherapy: Purpose, Process and Practice*. In this passage we can see how joining means looking without judgment at *one's own belief in sin* projected onto another, the operational definition of looking with Jesus or the Holy Spirit. This is in contrast to the ego's meaning which is simply joining with another who is believed to be external to oneself. The final sentence offers a clear statement that this joining, while occurring within the context of two separate people—therapist and patient—really occurs in the mind:

> This realization [that only forgiveness heals an unforgiveness] is the final goal of psychotherapy. How is it reached? *The therapist sees in the patient all that he has not forgiven in himself, and is thus given another chance to look at it, open it to re-evaluation and forgive it.* When this occurs, he sees his sins as gone into a past that is no longer here. Until he does this, he must think of evil as besetting him here and now. *The patient is his screen for the projection of his sins, enabling him to let them go.* Let him retain one spot of sin in what he looks upon, and his release is partial and will not be sure.
>
> No one is healed alone. This is the joyous song salvation sings to all who hear its Voice. This statement cannot be too often remembered by all who see themselves as therapists. Their patients can but be seen as the bringers of forgiveness, for it is they who come to demonstrate their

169

sinlessness to eyes that still believe that sin is there to look upon. *Yet will the proof of sinlessness, seen in the patient and accepted in the therapist, offer the mind of both a covenant in which they meet and join and are as one* (P-2.VI.6-7; italics mine).

Spiritual Specialness and Joining

As we discussed at the end of Chapter Four, spiritual specialness refers to people acting out their egos' specialness, but disguising it in spiritual dress. This frequently comes in the form of their believing that they have received *special* instructions, *special* favors, or *special* commissions from *special* divine persons such as Jesus or the Holy Spirit, all of which serves to make these people spiritually different from others and therefore more *special*.

The religious and spiritual history of Western civilization is replete with such examples, up to and including the present day. Even a cursory examination of the past two millennia would reveal the fact that Christians believed that they were ontologically better than others. This has been discussed in my *Love Does Not Condemn*, where the early history of the conflict between the Christian Churches and the Gnostic schools was perceived as a particularly pernicious example of this specialness. The bulk of this section is excerpted from that book (pp. 287-88,296,539-43), somewhat edited for inclusion here:

Indeed, there can be no more insidious nor contradictory characteristic of religious groups than the belief that they are somehow "special"—i.e., better, holier, and more beloved of God than other groups. The paradox of such belief in a movement that purports to be rooted in God and His revelation is obvious, when one recalls the unity that *is* the condition of the creation of Christ. It is but another example of what, in a discussion of religion and *formal* religion in the *Psychotherapy* supplement, Jesus refers to as the attempt to reconcile the irreconcilable and unite mutually exclusive ideas (P-2.II.2:1-3).

If one can point to a common element in all religious forms and institutions that has contributed to their descent from a truly authentic spirituality, it would be this belief in specialness. In our Western tradition, we see it right from the beginning of the two biblical religions, and it has continued on to the present day. Since many students see *A Course in Miracles* as the "third testament," following along the Old and New Testaments in a continuum of divine revelation, some brief observations about the history of the Judaeo-Christian biblical tradition might be instructive.

The 1st-century Christian teaching cannot be understood apart from its historical roots in Judaism, where the concept of the "chosen people" finds a prominent place. While it is true that this notion of "chosenness" can be interpreted in ways other than the obvious, it nonetheless remains as a concept of separation—*which originates in the divine*—that is based upon a spiritual arrogance that places oneself and one's group somehow closer to the Creator than others. This is a conclusion that can be reached only by interpretations of data mediated through the narrow eyes (and mind) of one's personal and special universe.

The "chosenness" of the Children of Israel was taken over by Christianity, which unabashedly saw itself as the heir to the throne of the erstwhile beloved people, the throne vacated by the recalcitrant Jews. St. Paul, himself a Jew, arrogantly provided the foundation for this belief in his famous image of the olive tree and its branches, written to the Romans in the middle of the 1st century A.D.:

> ...have the Jews fallen for ever, or have they just stumbled? Obviously they have not fallen for ever: their fall, though, has saved the pagans in a way the Jews may now well emulate....all the branches are holy if the root is holy. No doubt some of the branches [the Jews] have been cut off, and, like shoots of wild olive, you [non-Jewish Roman Christians] have been grafted among the rest to

share with them the rich sap provided by the olive tree
itself... (Romans 11:11,16-17).

They—first the Jews who accepted Jesus as the promised
Messiah, joined later by the Gentiles—were now God's
chosen, witnessed to by their confession of faith in the risen
Lord Jesus, perceived, of course, to have been Jewish and thus
automatically part of God's original chosen race. This group
became more rigorously (if not rigidly) defined as the decades
and centuries passed, and emerged finally as a narrowing and
exclusive Church which self-righteously proclaimed itself as
the true heir to the Jewish Jesus and the apostles. A small
hierarchy defined this Church and became the arbiter of those
who belonged within its special circle and those who did not.
Moreover, without this Church, the hierarchy claimed, salvation was impossible.

The Gnostic Christians were excluded from this circle and
so, in true ego fashion, many of these "heretics" set up their
own criteria for membership in the eschatological circles of
the saved and the damned. This membership was born out of
these Gnostics' own sense of spiritual specialness. They believed that they were the special recipients of *gnosis* (knowledge or revelation), which set them apart from the rest of
humanity who clearly were not as privileged as they. In some
Christian forms of Gnosticism this specialness obviously was
meant, at least in part, as a defensive position against the specialness of the more orthodox Church. Thus we find that many
Gnostics also proclaimed *themselves* to be chosen by God—
as opposed to the orthodox who now have fallen from grace—
to fulfill the special mission of bringing the light of truth to the
world of darkness. Unfortunately, the categories of special
love and special hate clearly remained intact, with only the
names belonging to each group having changed.

The great 3rd-century Neoplatonist philosopher Plotinus,
who had no use for either Christians or Gnostics as his profound Platonic spirituality was without form or ritual, provided us with a telling criticism of the Gnostics' "spiritual

specialness." In the second book of his *Enneads,* he addresses those Gnostics who managed to talk themselves and others into believing that they were better than all other people, including the gods (the greater cosmos) themselves, and the gods' creation, "the blessed Soul":

> But stupid men believe this sort of talk as soon as they hear "you shall be better than all, not only men, but gods"—for there is a great deal of arrogance among men—and the man who was once meek and modest, an ordinary private person, if he hears "you are the son of God, and the others whom you used to admire are not, nor the beings they venerate according to the tradition received from their fathers; but you are better than the heaven without having taken any trouble to become so"—then are other people really going to join in the chorus? It is just as if, in a great crowd of people who did not know how to count, someone who did not know how to count heard that he was a thousand cubits tall; what would happen if he thought he was a thousand cubits, and heard that the others were five cubits? He would only imagine that the "thousand" was a big number (Enneads.II.9.9).

What Plotinus is describing is the common occurrence of the blind leading the blind. If you have no standards by which to judge another's "revelatory" proclamations and claims, then you accept anything if it feeds your *special* needs that others be *special,* which then automatically makes you *special* for simply being in their *special* presence. Not only that, the persons making the special claims for themselves usually end up believing in their "truth," because they now receive validation from others, the culmination of this very circular process. To state it again, having been told by those around them that they, the special ones, are spiritual giants ("a thousand cubits tall") and above the others (who are only "five cubits"), the audience accepts this and reinforces it in the proclaimers. Thus, a vicious circle of deception is set up that becomes extremely difficult to break, for the reinforcement of the

173

specialness is so very strong. As we shall see presently, one can observe this phenomenon of spiritual specialness in many students and followers of *A Course in Miracles*.

While what we are calling "spiritual specialness" appears in the members of almost all spiritual or religious movements, very often it is inherent in the theologies themselves of these religions. This usually comes in the form of believing that the group or Church members have been singled out by God or the Holy Spirit to perform some holy function that will benefit humanity and contribute towards the saving of the world. Visitations by God (or His agents), special writings that have been "given," divinely inspired messages about one's mission, are only three of the many and varied justifications people give for the satisfaction of their ego's specialness. Once specialness has been made an inherent part of any theology or spirituality, spiritual specialness among its followers is not only reasonable and understandable, but logically inevitable as well.

However, such intrinsic specialness is clearly not the case with the teachings of *A Course in Miracles*, the whole message of which specifically addresses the ego's investment in specialness, differences, and exclusion. Inherent, then, within the Course's theology is the correction of the form of the ego's thought system we have been calling spiritual specialness. Nonetheless, many of the Course's students have not entirely escaped this subtle trap. The battlefield that usually ends up as the home of religious and spiritual movements—both *within* the movement itself, as well as *between* itself and other spiritualities—is also finding its way into the "community" that is already beginning to sprout up around the Course. Thus students of *A Course in Miracles* often confuse form with content, and forget Jesus' earlier cited statements that "All my brothers are special" (T-1.V.3:6), and that the Course is only one path among "many thousands" (M-1.4:2).

This is certainly not to say that students should not join with each other in groups and events in what are authentic experiences that reflect forgiveness; nor that people should not feel the presence of Jesus or the Holy Spirit, and that these abstract and non-specific experiences cannot be meaningfully translated by the mind to specifics. Helen's experiences of Jesus and the scribing of *A Course in Miracles* certainly attest to the legitimacy of that phenomenon. But it does say that the ego can very easily jump into what could otherwise be valid experiences of forgiveness or of Jesus, and then turn them into something special and important. They then join together *as if* they were a group unto themselves, part of a distinctive family or network, this groupiness somehow making them and the Course itself special. And it is these distortions, born of the ego's really joining with itself, that need to be understood and addressed, lest one's spiritual progress be sidetracked or even aborted.

The mistake, of course, lies in failing to realize that what truly unites people as a family is their common Source, which is only of spirit. Our worldly families—biological, marital, ethnic, religious, local community, country, sports allegiances, etc.—are nothing more than classes we have chosen to attend, in which we hope ultimately—through turning to Jesus as our inner teacher instead of the ego—to learn that there is in truth but one Family: Christ. Contrasting our worldly names with the one true Name, which we share with God our Creator, Jesus states in the workbook Lesson "The Name of God is my inheritance," a passage from which I have extensively quoted in Chapter Three:

> You live by symbols. You have made up names for everything you see. Each one becomes a separate entity, identified by its own name. By this you carve it out of unity. By this you designate its special attributes, and set it off from other things by emphasizing space surrounding it. This space you lay between all things to which you give a different name; all happenings in terms of place and time; all bodies which are greeted by a name.

Rather, we are asked to

accept the Name for all reality, and realize the many names
... [we] gave its aspects have distorted what ... [we] see, but
have not interfered with truth at all. One Name we bring
into our practicing. One Name we use to unify our sight.

And though we use a different name for each awareness
of an aspect of God's Son, we understand that they have but
one Name, Which He has given them.

And so we pray:

Father, our Name is Yours. In It we are united with all
living things, and You Who are their one Creator. What we
made and call by many different names is but a shadow we
have tried to cast across Your Own reality.... Your Name
unites us in the oneness which is our inheritance and peace.
Amen. (W-pI.184.1; 13:3–14:1; 15:1-3,8-9; italics omitted).

However, we are certainly not asked by Jesus to deny our
specific affiliations in this world. Instead, we are urged *not* to
take them seriously as realities to be upheld, justified, and
defended, but simply to be used for the Holy Spirit's teaching
purpose. Recall that passage from the same workbook lesson
just cited:

You have need to use the symbols of the world a while. But
be you not deceived by them as well. They do not stand for
anything at all.... They become but means by which you
can communicate in ways the world can understand, but
which you recognize is not the unity where true communication can be found (W-pI.184.9:2-5).

Another form of spiritual specialness we need to explore is
that involving *A Course in Miracles* itself. Although *A Course
in Miracles* is obviously not the first spiritual thought system
to have explored the metaphysical issues of truth and illusion,
it *is* the first to have integrated psychology and spirituality in
the powerful way I have discussed throughout these two
books. For example, to underscore this important point, its
seminal statement "The world was made as an attack on God"
(W-pII.3.2:1) cannot be understood without a grasp of both

the Course's metaphysical *and* psychological principles. Nonetheless, it is important to understand that this uniqueness does not make its teachings nor its students ultimately any better or more deserving of Heaven's blessing than others. Jesus is quite clear in *A Course in Miracles* about the dangers of believing that a certain group is a more special recipient of the Holy Spirit's Love:

> Salvation cannot seek to help God's Son be more unfair than he has sought to be. If miracles, the Holy Spirit's gift, were given specially to an elect and special group, and kept apart from others as less deserving, then is He ally to specialness. What He cannot perceive He bears no witness to. And everyone is equally entitled to His gift of healing and deliverance and peace (T-25.IX.7:1-4).

The biblical text "For many are called, but few are chosen" (Matthew 22:14) provides a clear statement of specialness on the part of a God Who chooses only certain of His children for salvation. As we have seen, Jesus corrects this egregious ego interpretation—a correction that serves as the basis for the titles of these two books—so that the responsibility for salvation is clearly placed on his *students*: "All are called, but few choose to listen" (T-3.IV.7:12).

Once a special group is formed, it is almost inevitable that it will seek to justify its specialness by turning against other groups. Thus, as did the early churches, students of the Course factionalize among themselves. Opposing camps of interpretation arise, arguing with each other over whose understanding of the Course is more correct, or more faithful to Jesus' teachings, etc. The point here again is not to deny that differences among students do in fact exist, nor that healthy debate of these differing points of view cannot be valuable, but rather to avoid making the differences into an issue that divides and attacks. Gloria and I so often counsel those who attend our workshops and classes that one of the most meaningful lessons a student of *A Course in Miracles* can have is learning how to disagree with others without it being an attack. The early history of Christianity, filled with theological finger pointings, *ad hominem* diatribes, and persecutions, should serve as a model for how differences in interpretation or theology should *not* be handled. It is silly for students to use *A Course in Miracles*, clearly based on principles of forgiveness and unity, as a weapon against other students, simply because of differing interpretations or practices.

In general, these inter- and intra-mural divisions rest on the confusion of form with content, the same confusion we explored several times before. Such confusion, in fact, is the heart of the ego's defensive system of protecting its special relationships, as we see in these excerpts from passages cited earlier:

> Whenever any form of special relationship tempts you to seek for love in ritual, remember *love is content, and not form of any kind.* The special relationship is a ritual of form, aimed at raising the form to take the place of God at the expense of content (T-16.V.12:1-2; italics mine).

And of the ego's laws of chaos, grouped around the belief in specialness, Jesus adds:

> And yet, how can it be that laws like these can be believed? There is a strange device that makes it possible. Nor is it unfamiliar; we have seen how it appears to function many times before.... No law of chaos could compel belief but for *the emphasis on form and disregard of content* (T-23.II.16:1-3,5; italics mine).

Differences are inevitable in a world of form that was founded on differences, the world originating with the thought that there was a difference between God and His Son. In the physical universe of perception such differences are the norm, and in *A Course in Miracles*, again, Jesus does not ask us to deny our physical experience in this world, nor our awareness of differences. It is the underlying *investment* in maintaining the thought of separation that is the issue. Similarly, judgments are unavoidable here; for example, I must have made a judgment to write this book and not some other; you, the reader, likewise have made a judgment to read this book and not some other. When Jesus tells his Course students not to judge, he really means not to condemn.

Therefore, while on the one hand we must inevitably identify with our groups of preference (the *form*), we must on the other hand be vigilant against the special love and/or hate judgments (*content*) that almost as inevitably creep into our group identifications and behavior. In other words, differences in understanding and presentation of the Course's teachings will, without question, almost always arise, and this does not mean that others' comments on *A Course in Miracles* should necessarily be agreed with nor supported on the level of form, if the form be mistaken. After all, once again, differences do exist in the world that we believe is real and is our home, and so it would be, to cite a passage quoted before, "a particularly unworthy form of denial" (T-2.IV.3:11) for Course students to deny any experience in the world of form. As Jesus teaches regarding healing and the perceptions of sickness:

> The body's eyes will continue to see differences. But the mind that has let itself be healed will no longer acknowledge them (M-8.6:1-2).

By this Jesus means that the healed mind acknowledges differences on the level of form, but does not acknowledge these differences as meaningful or as having any effect on reality. And so we can see differences in Course teachers and students, and even seek to correct mistakes if so guided, but without this affecting the awareness of our shared reality as God's one Son.

We can thus conclude that despite these perceived differences in the world, students need not carry with them an emotional investment of judgment, which could only mean that the differences have been eagerly sought after and therefore welcomed. In that case the differences have been taken seriously, to be exposed as sins and then justifiably opposed in the name of truth. And as has been discussed in *All Are Called* (e.g., pp. 159-62), this is due to the strong unconscious need to have other people be wrong so that we can be right, in clear opposition to the right-minded perception of the Holy Spirit:

> When you *react* at all to errors, you are not listening to the Holy Spirit. He has merely disregarded them, and if you attend to them you are not hearing Him.... To perceive errors in anyone, and *to react to them as if they were real, is to make them real to you.* You will not escape paying the price for this, not because you are being punished for it, but because you are following the wrong guide and will therefore lose your way (T-9.III.4:1-2; 6:7-8; italics mine).

Instead of these misperceptions, Jesus would urge his students to "remember...to laugh" at the silliness of making differences ultimately important. Again, it can very often be a helpful experience to learn how to differ with another *without* becoming upset, and without letting the ego make the difference into a major symbol of separation and sin, therefore justifying attack. In "The Correction of Error" in Chapter 9 of the text, just quoted from, Jesus provides us with guidelines for correcting the *form* of someone's mistake, yet honoring and respecting the *content* of his correctness as God's Son:

> To the ego it is kind and right and good to point out errors and "correct" them. This makes perfect sense to the ego, which is unaware of what errors are and what correction is. Errors are of the ego, and correction of errors lies in the relinquishment of the ego. When you correct a brother, you are telling him that he is wrong. He may be making no sense at the time, and it is certain that, if he is speaking from the ego, he will not be making sense. But your task is still to tell him he is right. You do not tell him this verbally, if he is speaking foolishly. *He needs correction at another level, because his error is at another level.* He is still right, because he is a Son of God. His ego is always wrong, no matter what it says or does (T-9.III.2; italics mine).

The key here is learning to be appropriate to one's role of correcting form (as with a school teacher instructing third graders
in the rudiments of arithmetic), without *overreacting* to mistakes. Clearly Jesus is talking about *our* responses or interpretations of mistakes, and not to the form of the mistake itself,
which many times it is loving to correct, and most *un*loving
not to.

An error that frequently arises from this underlying belief
in specialness is making certain people (or even places) associated with *A Course in Miracles*, historically or currently,
special or more holy than others. This inevitably places these
special love objects on a pedestal, with the outcome of mur-
derous hate both obvious and predictable. The only "special"
person of the Course is Jesus or the Holy Spirit; that is, the
internal presence of God's Love that, again, leads Jesus in the
Course to state that all his "brothers are special."

One final point regarding groups centering on *A Course in
Miracles*: The central process of studying the Course and following its particular spiritual path is an individualized one.
There can be no escaping the hard work and dedication involved in *individually* studying and re-studying the text, as
well as doing the workbook exercises during the one-year
training program that is integral to the Course's educational
process. All too often, joining a group or class can subtly
interfere with this responsibility of the student, substituting
the form of joining with the group for the content of joining
with the Holy Spirit *within one's own mind*. Sometimes even,
leaders or teachers of groups seek to set up guides for their students, almost legislating how they should study *A Course in
Miracles*. They thus have forgotten Jesus' addressing this
issue at the end of the manual for teachers, in a passage we
cited briefly in Chapter One. We are told by Jesus that "the
curriculum is highly individualized, and all aspects are under
the Holy Spirit's particular care and guidance" (M-29.2:6).
Since all students of *A Course in Miracles* are capable of being
guided specifically by the Holy Spirit, it would certainly be

presumptuous for someone to tell them how they should approach the Course, let alone set up formal or informal guides in how to study it. Moreover, as the Course is set up to be studied *as is*, such attempts at restructuring its study for others would be typical of the ego's arrogant efforts to prove that it knows better than God, Jesus, or the Holy Spirit.

To summarize this chapter, then, we can recognize the error of mistaking form for content that has characterized people's experiences of joining together. The joining with each other emphasized by *A Course in Miracles* comes from undoing the barriers of separation that exist within our *minds*. This process can occur regardless of whether we are in the physical presence of others, or whether they are even aware of our unforgiveness. External joining is an example of *magic*, if the value of salvation is placed upon it; the joining in our minds through forgiveness, on the other hand, is the *miracle*. Our problems cannot be solved through the magical use of external situations, but only through the use of the miracle's ability to heal our thoughts. Only on the level of the mind can true joining occur, because it was only on the mind's level that the thought of separation seemed to occur. In an important passage discussing the world of perception, Jesus emphasizes this distinction between correcting the errors of differences in the mind, *where the problem is*, or outside the mind in the world where the differences only *appear* to be. Incidentally, the first paragraph of this passage does not appear in the first edition of the Course, as the reader may recall from our discussion in *All Are Called* (p. 187).

> *Where do all these differences come from? Certainly they seem to be in the world outside. Yet it is surely the mind that judges what the eyes behold. It is the mind that interprets the eyes' messages and gives them "meaning." And this meaning does not exist in the world outside at all. What is seen as "reality" is simply what the mind prefers. Its hierarchy of values is projected outward, and its sends*

the body's eyes to find it. The body's eyes will never see
except through differences. Yet it is not the messages they
bring on which perception rests. Only the mind evaluates
their messages, and so only the mind is responsible for seeing. It alone decides whether what is seen is real or illusory,
desirable or undesirable, pleasurable or painful.

*It is in the sorting out and categorizing activities of the
mind that errors in perception enter. And it is here correction must be made.* The mind classifies what the body's
eyes bring to it according to its preconceived values, judging where each sense datum fits best (M-8.3:1–4:3; italics
mine).

It is thus only a short step from the magical belief in the
efficacy of Course groups meeting together, to the investment
in *A Course in Miracles* organizations and networks. And
before you know it, we are on the familiar road that leads to
religious institutionalization and churches, factionalism, judgments, and persecutions. To state the central point again, the
issue is not that groups in and of themselves are mistakes, but
rather that investment in their form as necessary, meaningful,
or salvific is the error. As we have observed, the history of
Christianity serves as a glaring example of the unfortunate
consequences of *not* recognizing the great potential for specialness inherent in forming groups, cloaking the ego's hidden
specialness in spiritual clothing.

Finally, it should be apparent by now that *A Course in
Miracles* is a spiritual *teaching*, set up and given to be practiced on an *individual* basis in the context of developing a personal relationship with Jesus or the Holy Spirit. It was *never*
conceived by Jesus (nor understood by Helen, who scribed the
Course from him) as a movement, or something that was to be
followed in groups. This is in marked distinction from how
organized religions view themselves, with rituals, special
prayers, specially ordained and prepared people as an intrinsic
part of their religious path. *A Course in Miracles* has none of
these. While it goes without saying, once again, that students

should practice the Course any way they choose, with anyone they choose, it should never be forgotten that nothing of group practice, or groups joining together in networks is *inherent* in the Course itself.

Chapter 7

ERROR AND THE EGO

Introduction

I have emphasized throughout how important it is for students of *A Course in Miracles not* to allow the metaphysics that underlie all of Jesus' teachings in the Course to get too far away from them. The two errors that are our principal focus in this chapter are the direct and inevitable result of forgetting the fundamental unreality of *everything* that exists in the material universe, *without exception*. The process of looking at the ego with the Holy Spirit or Jesus—the essence of forgiveness—ceases to be what it is without its vision being based upon Their presence that is *outside the dream of time and space*.

The first error we will be considering is *making the error real*. Here, we establish the world and the body as real by assigning them negative or positive values; forms of this mistake involve spiritualizing matter, developing ethical or moral systems of asceticism, libertinism, or moderation and advocating passivity or activism as a response to socio-political situations, and believing that spiritual practices have meaning and power in and of themselves.

The second error is *minimizing our investment in the ego's thought system*. One of the principal characteristics of this mistake is believing that a spiritual path is easy and requires little or no effort, for one need only "turn problems over" to the Holy Spirit, hear His Voice, and then He does the rest.

Making the Error Real

We have discussed at length the tremendous investment the ego has in maintaining its thought system of separation, individuality, and specialness, protected by the belief in the reality of the physical world. This world's origin is usually ascribed to God or, in secular systems, to cosmic forces outside the mind. To doubt these cosmogonies, however, is to raise the question: If God (or other forces) did not create the world, who did? The answer strikes sheer terror in our minds, for to recall the world's origin in the ego mind, and its purpose as a defense against God, is to confront our own guilt and accept responsibility for the separation. The reader may remember that it was precisely to *avoid* this terror that the ego, having first been chosen by the Son of God over the Holy Spirit, virtually compelled the Son to make the world and individual bodies in the first place. Therefore, since the ego has convinced us that this acceptance of responsibility brings us face to face with our own destruction at the hands of the vengeful Creator, it should come as no surprise that many students of *A Course in Miracles* strongly resist accepting completely what the Course is teaching. Thus, what creeps into these students' understanding and practice of the Course are subtle ways of making the world and the body real, thereby "protecting" the ego's existence. Let us examine some of these now.

There are many, many passages in *A Course in Miracles*—some of which we have presented in earlier chapters—that clearly state that God did not and could not have created the physical world. Believing He did, directly contradicts the integrity of the Course's thought system, a basic premise of which is that God could not create a being (or anything) unlike Himself. Nonetheless, students of *A Course in Miracles* are often tempted to change its teachings to read that God did not create a world of pain, but did create a world of physical beauty, not to mention a body that can be improved upon and even made immortal. In this regard one familiar with classical philosophy will immediately see the close parallels—psychologically if not always philosophically—with the Platonic tradition, wherein the physical beauty and majesty of the universe is extolled, while the pain and sufferings of the body are abhorred.

One of the purposes of my book *Love Does Not Condemn* was to help students recognize, on the one hand, the Platonic soil in which *A Course in Miracles* has its philosophical roots, and, on the other, to distinguish the Course's teachings from those that incorporate the paradox of a perfect and absolute Oneness somehow creating an imperfect physical universe, a paradox that is inherent within this Platonic tradition. Understanding this background could then, it was hoped, alert the student of the Course to this error.

As has been emphasized, it is the Course's uncompromising metaphysical absoluteness that is so deeply problematic for many people. Indeed, one of its stated goals is to effect a *total* transfer of learning, for "the impairment of the ability to generalize is a crucial learning failure" (T-12.V.6:4). As the workbook states in its Introduction:

> The purpose of the workbook is to train your mind in a systematic way to a different perception of *everyone and everything* in the world. The exercises are planned to help you generalize the lessons.... [If] Transfer of training in true perception.... has been achieved in connection with any person, situation or event, *total transfer to everyone and everything* is certain (W-in.4:1-2; 5:1-2; italics mine).

Because of this ego investment in our maintaining belief in the reality of the illusory, it is difficult to accept the full implications of Jesus' statements in *A Course in Miracles* about God not creating the world. These implications include not according reality *at all* to any aspect of the physical and/or psychological world (truly one and the same, since the outer world is but a shadow of the inner), including perceptions of "pain and loss...sickness and...grief...poverty, starvation and...death" (W-pI.187.6:4). These implications likewise include not according efficacy to any of the world's methods of healing or alleviating pain, traditional and non-traditional alike. Certain New Age practices of visualizing healing, or sending light to diseased bodies or to conflicted situations in the world, also fall into the same trap of making the error real.

Why would you send light or visualize healing unless you first believed there were a real darkness *outside you* that needed healing? As I have continually stressed, the only problem is the darkness of guilt in *our* minds that believe that darkness is real outside. To restate this important teaching: "...seek not to change the world, but choose to change your *mind* about the world" (T-21.in.1:7, italics mine).

What heals my pain or sickness is not the "healing energies" of another or of the universe itself, nor the arousal of the energy within my body (kundalini), but rather the only true "healing energy" which is the undoing of my thoughts of guilt through acceptance of the Holy Spirit's correction of forgiveness. Physical or mental energies can certainly affect the body's electromagnetic field, thereby bringing physical or mental relief, but these changes nonetheless occur within the domain of the ego/body world. Thus, we are dealing with effects (the body), not the true cause (the mind). Imputing spiritual properties to matter, be it Mother Earth or certain minerals such as crystals, likewise reflects the same error.

One would not think, it would seem, that study of *A Course in Miracles* would lend itself to rituals, given its clear statements about form and content. However, as mentioned in Chapter Seven of *All Are Called* and Chapter One of this book, a student's practice of the workbook can easily turn into a ritual that *must* be performed, and performed properly with the "required" amount of repetitions of the day's idea successfully carried out. Moreover, the truth and beauty of the Course's teaching, the loving gentleness of Jesus that comes through its words, can also lead to a transfer of these *thoughts* to the actual books themselves. Thus people may believe that the mere touch of the blue cover (formerly green in the United Kingdom), or the running of one's hands over its pages, promotes healing, or that the simple repetition of its words magically infuses the message into one's self, *without the necessity of challenging one's thought system* and allowing it to be changed by accepting the Holy Spirit's thought system as a replacement. In addition, once groups form, it is quite easy to fall into informal rituals that soon evolve into practices that, when not performed, lead to anxiety and discomfort, if not feelings of deprivation and anger.

Once again, the relevant issue here is not the use of, or belief in such practices, but the attempt to combine them with the teachings of *A Course in Miracles*. Such attempts, conscious or otherwise, are subtle ego ploys to minimize the radicalness of the Course and blur its distinctiveness from other systems. This leads us to another important way in which the ego attempts to dilute the clarity of the Course's message: claiming that the Course is "just like" other spiritualities. To discuss this at any length is beyond the scope of this book, but a few words should suffice to make the point.

Very few contemporary or even ancient spiritualities have been exempt from inclusion in such attempts. These have included the following: Classical Hinduism and Buddhism, traditional or biblical Christianity (Roman Catholic and mainstream Protestantism), Judaism, Gnosticism, Christian Science, Science of Mind, Unity, Alcoholics Anonymous and the other twelve-step programs, the Urantia material, the Seth material, Edgar Cayce, Joel Goldsmith, C. G. Jung, transpersonal psychology, and an absolute plethora of contemporary channeled writings. To be sure, as we have already observed, many other spiritualities deal with forgiveness, the importance of our mind's power, and faith in a loving and non-punitive God. However, none presents these ideas in the metaphysical/psychological framework as does *A Course in Miracles*. Combining the Course with other paths also blurs its unique teaching. As discussed in the previous chapter of this book (pp. 178-79), many students of *A Course in Miracles* confuse Jesus' asking us not to judge with denying the differences that certainly do exist within the illusory world. Thus, one can recognize and accept differences among the many world spiritualities without judging against certain ones, or playing the game of spiritual specialness. Thus, to state it still once again, to teach that the Course is different from these other spiritualities is not to judge against them. Stating what Jesus once told Helen, "Don't take another's path as your own, but neither should you judge it."

Our final example of how students of the Course have made the body real falls under the three ethical categories I discussed in Chapter Seven in *All Are Called*: asceticism, libertinism, and the middle path of moderation. Again, despite the Course's strong and consistent teaching of the fundamental unreality of the body, many students cannot avoid the old Gnostic error of making the body psychologically real. This is done by seeing the body as the problem that has to be addressed through the development of certain ethical or behavioral norms. Let us take each category in turn, first the ascetic.

Asceticism is by far the most common form of this error into which students of *A Course in Miracles* fall. Passages in the Course, already quoted, that point out our investment in the body, or describe our guilty and fearful experience related to our bodies, are wrenched from their context to suggest that the body should be avoided or denied because it is sinful, evil, and the predominant obstacle to achieving unity with God. Sexuality, food, and money, not surprisingly, are the most widely used expressions of this belief that the body or materiality is the problem. Thus, a thought system that was given to help us learn how *not* to make the error real or, stated another way, how not to take the ego's world seriously, is transposed to say that the body is to be taken *very* seriously. Followers of the Course, therefore, are urged, among other things, to be celibate, thin, or vegetarian, not to drink coffee, smoke cigarettes, or earn large amounts of money, and not to charge money for activities relating to *A Course in Miracles*. The underlying premise here, not always stated and even unconscious, is that sexuality, certain foods, and money are inherently unspiritual. In one sense, to be sure, that is true, for *everything* in the physical realm is unspiritual, being made, as we have seen over and over again, to keep the spiritual out of our awareness and memory. However, to isolate certain bodily functions or aspects of the material world as being particularly unholy is to fall into the trap of the first law of chaos; namely, that there is a hierarchy of illusions (T-23.II.2), wherein some aspects of the illusory world are seen to be holier or better than others. Such differentiation, in and of itself, nicely serves the ego's purpose of establishing *its* miscreation as real, and God's undifferentiated creation as not real.

However, this certainly does not mean, as we have previously discussed, that one should not have preferences and make choices based on these preferences. It is the *imperative need* to have the preference satisfied that is the problem, not the simple preference itself, which is impossible to avoid in this dreamworld of multiplicity. I am reminded of a story from my childhood that well illustrates the difference between preference and imperative need. My mother always liked a piece of fruit before going to bed, and this almost never presented a problem. However, while on a vacation in Canada, my parents, brother and I arrived in Montreal very late Sunday evening. We had already checked into our motel, all of us very tired after a long day's travel, when my mother suddenly remembered that she did not have any fruit with her and therefore would not be able to go to sleep. And so, my father and I went out scouring the city for an open grocery store. However, this being before the days of 24-hour convenience stores, our attempts were in vain. I do not recall the end of the story, but I do not think my mother was very happy.

Another form of the same error of asceticism, though more subtle, is the notion that the body can be immortal. The underlying premise, of course, is that the body's death is somehow bad, and is a fate that can and should be overcome. By placing a value on eternal *physical* life, the body thus has been made real, for if the body can live forever it *must* be real. This error also results from the ego's effective use of denial, so that we forget that the body was made to keep the immortal hidden, immortality being a characteristic totally beyond the ego:

191

> Eternalness [immortality] is the one function the ego has
> tried to develop, but has systematically failed to achieve.
> The ego compromises with the issue of the eternal, just as
> it does with all issues touching on the real question in any
> way (T-4.V.6:2-3).

Still another form of making the error real comes through
detaching oneself from the world that is perceived as evil and
contaminating. Some of the forms taken by this error of deni-
grating the physical world are professing indifference to world
events by avoiding radio or television news, or newspapers
and news magazines, saying, in effect: "I shall not pollute my
mind with the world's negativity or violence by allowing the
news in. What goes on around me does not concern me
because it is too worldly and non-spiritual, and therefore
might disrupt my positive thinking and peace of mind."
Clearly, salvation does not depend on one's being kept abreast
of world affairs. However, the feeling of repulsion often
present in such "detachment" gives the ego away, for it has
first convinced us that the world is real by virtue of its negative valence, and then provides its own solution—separation
in the form of detachment—to a problem that *it* has established as deserving our attention.

If one is genuinely uninterested in the world news, so be it;
the lack of interest needs no justification. If one feels a sense
of abhorrence to the world or the body, so be it as well; this
abhorrence needs no justification either. What the latter does
need, however, is an absence of justification based upon so-
called spiritual ideals. This *justification* is the problem, a
shadow of the original problem of compounding the error by
witnessing to the separated world's reality and justifying the
defense against it. Feeling an abhorrence is a mistake, to be
sure, for one can only dislike something that has first been
judged as real. However, the mistake's *correction* is prevented
by 1) taking the mistake seriously and treating it as a sin, and
2) justifying its defense through projection and elevating the
feeling of abhorrence to a spiritual principle. It is much wiser

and healthier to accept the negative emotion without judgment of oneself. Then we are eventually able to bring its true cause —fear—to the Holy Spirit's Love, at which point the negative investment automatically disappears, as does darkness in the presence of light.

The second ethical form of the mistake of making the error real is *libertinism*. Here, students of *A Course in Miracles* take the teaching that the world and body are illusory as a justification for doing whatever they wish, especially in the areas of sexuality and aggression. I myself have been mistakenly quoted, totally out of context, as having said in workshops that if you have no guilt in your mind, then anything that you do will be loving. However, misapplication of this principle— rather than giving honor to the process of being an extension of the Holy Spirit's Love, unfettered by our thoughts of guilt—results in excusing the practice of sexual or sociopathic acting out, all done in the name of the spirituality of *A Course in Miracles*, to wit: "The illusory world has no meaning for me and therefore it does not matter what I do." A variation of this libertinism is the defiance of societal rules judged as being ego-based. Thus, one may practice the Course in a provocative manner, attempting to demonstrate one's freedom by not adhering to certain societal conventions. I can lie, steal, insult others, or even kill with impunity because, after all, it is all an illusion and my actions are the means the Holy Spirit has chosen to help me teach you this lofty spiritual principle. On rare occasions, one can even note a striking similarity of Course students, not only in content but in form, to the ancient Gnostic sect called the Adamites. These Gnostics removed their clothes (the encumbrance to the innocence of Eden— hence their name) when they prayed, so that they could manifest a pure spirituality that would take them closer to God. By removing the outer *form* (the layers of clothing), so students of *A Course in Miracles* may rationalize, one teaches the *content* of formlessness.

Similarly, it has not been unusual for students of *A Course in Miracles* to demonstrate their "spirituality" or advancement in the Course by divesting themselves of other symbols of society. Thus, they might refrain from locking cars or house doors, or carrying medical or life insurance, not because they are truly indifferent to the concerns that "normal" people have. Rather, their actions are often motivated by the need to force upon themselves the *form* of what they believe to be signs of spiritual advancement, magically hoping that the *content* of ego-freedom would infuse their minds through their behavior. Thus they can avoid the at times painful process of having to look within at the guilt and fear that is present, for now these have been covered over by a veneer of holiness. Thus, still again, we can see here the unconscious (and sometimes not so unconscious) flouting of the "evil and unspiritual society" through these defiant activities.

Finally, we find those students who assume a *moderate* ethical position so as to *avoid* the mistakes of either the ascetic or libertine extreme. While the *form* of this middle path appears consistent with what would be advocated by the Course, the underlying *content* of the fear of falling into a trap of either asceticism or libertinism reflects having *already* done so by making the body and behavior real.

Readers may remind themselves at this point of the psychoanalytic joke that suggests that one can never win, no matter what is done: Patients who come early for sessions are anxious, those who come late are resistant, while those who are on time are compulsive. However, as discussed in Chapter Seven of *All Are Called*, the Course's morality is not behavioral but is rather based on an *attitude* within the mind; i.e., the motivation for what we do—God or the ego.

Minimizing the Ego

One of the characteristics prominent in some Gnostic circles was the belief in the availability of the *gnosis* or revelation only to certain special people. This obviously meant that these Gnostics were beyond their egos—hence their self-designation as the "perfect ones." It was, of course, this boast that was a particular thorn in the side of the orthodox Church, for how can you rationally deal with someone claiming to have a special connection to Heaven? And of course, since the Church believed that *it* was the one with the special connection to Heaven, it certainly did not want anyone else to have it, too! Notably, one finds the same phenomenon existing today, where it seems that almost everyone, and his or her second cousin, is hearing or channeling the Holy Spirit or Jesus. In the phrase of one of the early Church Fathers, these "channelers" seem to be sprouting up like mushrooms.

This recent infusion of people experiencing an inner voice that is claimed to be the Holy Spirit has been widespread in the Pentecostal and Charismatic Renewal movements within the Protestant and Catholic Churches respectively. Almost as a rebellion against the hierarchical suppression of people's religious experience in the name of Church authority, the faithful now were allowed and encouraged by these movements to experience God for themselves, and to interpret scripture without the presence or at times even the blessing of a minister or priest. Clearly, the removal of the domain of spiritual experience from the sole proprietorship of the Church elite is a positive event; however, the point here is the mistake in believing that the easiest thing in the world is to set aside the ego and allow God's Voice to speak to you. This particular phenomenon has found an almost consummate expression in students of *A Course in Miracles.*

This error among Course students finds its justification by many lifting out of their context those passages, most often in the workbook, that suggest an ease in listening to the Holy Spirit. Thus, for example, Lesson 49 states: "God's Voice speaks to me all through the day," and begins:

> It is quite possible to listen to God's Voice all through the
> day without interrupting your regular activities in any way
> (W-pI.49.1:1).

A later lesson tells us:

> If you will lay aside the ego's voice, however loudly it
> may seem to call...then you will hear the mighty Voice of
> truth....Listen, and hear your Father speak to you through
> His appointed Voice....Hear and be silent. He would speak
> to you....Hear Him today, and listen to the Word which
> lifts the veil that lies upon the earth....Ask and expect an
> answer (W-pI.106.1:1; 2:1; 4:2-3; 5:1; 8:1).

And the reader may recall from Chapter One that the Lesson—
"Only God's plan for salvation will work" (W-pI.71)—even has
us address God Himself, asking Him to tell us His plans for us.

In view of passages such as these, torn from the fabric of the
entire curriculum of the Course, it is understandable that students spend their days believing that they are in constant communication with Heaven's Voice. Thus they are "told" when to
get up in the morning, what to wear, eat, and where to go; what
God's plan is, not only for themselves, but also for everyone
else ranging from world leaders to friends and family members,
fellow Course students and non-students alike. I frequently like
to remind students that although workbook Lesson 49 does say
that God's Voice speaks to us throughout the day, and that it is
"quite possible" to listen to It, nowhere does Jesus say that we
are in fact listening to It. The tremendous unconscious investment our minds have in holding on to the ego thought system,
and the remarkably ingenious ways in which we perpetuate the
world of specialness we have constructed make hearing the
Voice of forgiveness and love very, very difficult. Given the
weight accorded such passages by these students, *A Course in
Miracles'* overall thrust of undoing the ego so that we *can* hear
the Holy Spirit's Voice is inevitably lost. It should also be noted
that the above quotation from workbook Lesson 106 contains a
very important condition: "If you will lay aside the ego's voice,

however loudly it may seem to call..." (W-pI.106.1:1). The *if*, of course, is the key word. In this regard, one passage in particular from the manual for teachers, quoted twice before, is easily overlooked:

> Only very few can hear God's Voice at all.... Do not forget that truth can come only where it is welcomed without fear (M-12.3:3,7).

And how many walk this earth without fear?

As discussed in Chapter One, the workbook is meant to be a one-year training program; it is not meant to supply the theoretical substance of the curriculum, which is the purpose of any textbook. Part of the world's curriculum of specialness, the undoing of which is the goal of *A Course in Miracles*, is the belief that only a certain few—the religious elite—can be in communication with God. Only these few are seen to be worthy and chosen by their Creator, while the sinfulness and deserved guilt of the rest of the world's population prevent such an open and loving relationship with God. Such a belief clearly reinforces the ego's tale of sin, guilt, and fear of Heaven's retributive wrath. And so it is the reversal of this belief—inherent to all specialness—at which much of the workbook aims. It accomplishes this by beginning the process of training our minds to believe that the Love of God is not absent from us, at least not by His Will. Since it is *our* wills—in consort with the ego—to banish God from the kingdom of our minds, it is must also be *our* changed wills that welcome Him back in.

In many passages, therefore, the workbook, as well as the text, places this decision before us, emphasizing that the ego system can be changed in a single instant. Jesus helps us to understand that since there is no linear time—only the illusion of time that our guilt demands is required before our sin can be redeemed—there is in truth only *one* instant. However, such teachings can be very much misunderstood, to make this important point once again, when they are removed from the context of the overriding purpose of the Course: helping us to understand the enormity of the ego thought system in terms of its investment in proving the Holy Spirit wrong. For example, the manual for teachers discusses the apparent hopelessness of escaping the ego's battlefield of murder:

> There is a way in which escape is possible. It can be learned and taught, but it requires patience and *abundant* willingness (M-17.8:3-4, italics mine).

It is interesting to note Jesus' departure here from his usual use in *A Course in Miracles* of the adjective "little" to modify "willingness." Use of the word "abundant" here emphasizes to the reader the full extent of the ego thought system, and our need to exercise vigilance against our investment in it. Further, of the six stages in the development of trust, discussed in the opening pages of the manual, we find that four of them contain elements of discomfort. These are described with words such as "painful," "difficult," "It takes great learning," "enormous conflict," and "anticipated grief." In the fifth stage, the "period of unsettling," we are told that we must "attain a state [the anticipated sixth stage of the real world—"a period of achievement"] that may remain impossible to reach for a long, long time" (M-4.I-A.3:2; 4:2,5; 5:2,8; 7:1,7).

It is clear, if only from these brief excerpts, that the curriculum of *A Course in Miracles* is a lifelong one, helping its students to embark upon a journey that requires great diligence and consistent application. We are told by Jesus early in the text that we "are much too tolerant of mind wandering, and are passively condoning...[our] mind's miscreations" (T-2.VI.4:6). One of the important messages to be learned from the text is the respect we should accord our ego thought system, not because it is true, but because we believe in it. Thus we can also state that the process of learning the Course involves growing in the discernment of knowing to which voice we are listening. It is to help facilitate this discernment of the ego's voice, obviously based upon recognizing it, that in passage after passage in the text Jesus describes in graphic and sometimes painful detail the intricacies of the insane thought system we have elevated to the throne of reason and truth. The central teaching of *A Course in Miracles*, therefore, is not the love and unity that is our reality in Heaven, but rather the *identifying* and *undoing* of the guilt and fear—"protected" by our special relationships—that we believe to be our reality on earth:

> Be not afraid to look upon the special hate relationship, for freedom lies in looking at it.... In looking at the special relationship, it is necessary first to realize that it involves a great amount of pain. Anxiety, despair, guilt and attack all enter into it, broken into by periods in which they seem to be gone. All these must be understood for what they are. Whatever form they take, they are always an attack on the self to make the other guilty (T-16.IV.1:1; T-16.V.1:1-4).

And so, revisiting this important statement:

> The course does not aim at teaching the meaning of love, for that is beyond what can be taught. It does aim, however, at removing the blocks to the awareness of love's presence, which is your natural inheritance (T-in.1:6-7).

And later, again in the context of the special relationship, Jesus reiterates this central theme in a passage which was cited in the Introduction:

> Your task is not to seek for love, but merely to seek and find all of the barriers within yourself that you have built against it. It is not necessary to seek for what is true, but it *is* necessary to seek for what is false (T-16.IV.6:1-2).

Thus, we may fail to recognize that the essential teaching of *A Course in Miracles* is helping us to remember that the one problem of the world is guilt, as expressed through the special relationship, and that its undoing comes through forgiveness. This is very clearly and succinctly stated, using slightly different terms, in two successive workbook lessons, partially cited above: "Let me recognize the problem so it can be solved," and "Let me recognize my problems have been solved":

> The problem of separation, which is really the only problem, has already been solved [through the Holy Spirit].... Your one central problem has been answered, and you have no other.... Salvation thus depends on recognizing this one problem, and understanding that it has been solved. One problem, one solution (W-pI.79.1:4; W-pI.80.1:2,4-5).

Yet this problem cannot be easily recognized, let alone understood, because our whole existence in this physical world is predicated on *not* recognizing it.

Another unfortunate result of this process of denial is the confusion regarding the role of the Holy Spirit in our Atonement path. Coincident with the magical idea that all one need do to be free of the ego is have the wish that this be so (without dealing with the underlying attraction to its thought system), is the equally magical idea of the Holy Spirit as the Great Provider. We have discussed this in some detail above, and so only briefly mention it again here. Displacing our one need of undoing the belief in scarcity onto material lack, we also displace the solution for such lack onto the Holy Spirit. Rather than looking to His Love as the means for undoing our faulty belief system, He now becomes the one to magically solve our worldly problems by providing rent money, parking spaces, fulfilling relationships, good health, world peace, etc., etc., etc. The profound and truly healing message of *A Course in Miracles* thus becomes relegated to the trivial and superficial, much as the ancient spiritual wisdom of the *I Ching* has become reduced, in the hands of some, to a mere fortune-telling device.

Further, many followers of the Course unconsciously identify the Holy Spirit with the ego. Thus, they subtly replicate the original error of displacing God with their own self, and so exclude the Holy Spirit's true Presence from their awareness. Asking the Holy Spirit for solutions to our external concerns limits His role by defining it in our own terms, as we saw in Chapter Four, for such requests presuppose the understanding of what our needs are, without first consulting Heaven's wisdom. Again, we have taken His place by presuming to know by ourselves our problems and their solutions. As Jesus emphasizes at the end of the manual for teachers:

> There is another advantage,—and a very important one,—in referring decisions to the Holy Spirit with increasing frequency....To follow the Holy Spirit's guidance is to let yourself be absolved of guilt. It is the essence of the Atonement. It is the core of the curriculum. The imagined usurping of functions not your own is the basis of fear. The whole world you see reflects the illusion that you have done so, making fear inevitable. To return the function to the One to Whom it belongs is thus the escape from fear. And it is this that lets the memory of love return to you (M-29.3:1,3-9).

Thus, again, by believing—*on our own*—that we have real problems external to our minds that require solutions—*that we determine*—we fall into the trap of making the error real.

Finally, we may note that the errors we have been discussing inevitably lead to the previously mentioned lack of discernment between the voice of the ego and the Voice for God; for example, "Anything I hear is the Holy Spirit, because my intention is holy." Moreover, even if we do "hear" right— namely our guidance is not coming from the voice of guilt— the Holy Spirit's message is often meant for us personally, filtered through our own need system. The message itself need not necessarily apply to the whole world, let alone to certain individuals we may choose to single out as beneficiaries of our special revelation. Thus, we are reminded by Jesus, quoting again these important lines: "Trust not your good intentions. They are not enough. But trust implicitly your willingness..." (T-18.IV.2:1-3). This willingness reflects our truly giving to the Holy Spirit our investment in being holy, good, or helpful.

And so the overriding purpose of *A Course in Miracles* is *not only* to teach us that our true Identity is Christ and not the ego, but to help us understand the massive defensive structure we have built to defend against this truth. The Course thus provides us with the means of changing our minds and choosing again. Overly emphasizing the lovely truth about ourselves short circuits the process of undoing, by placing our sleeping guilt under the heavy blanket of denial, where it then can never be brought to the healing truth of forgiveness. To assert that the central teaching of *A Course in Miracles* is love and oneness is not only to fly in the face of the Course's own words, but also to deny ourselves access to the healing opportunity it offers us. In this regard, as we discussed before, students of *A Course in Miracles* may fall into the same category of *blissninnyhood* into which many well-intentioned contemporary spiritual seekers have unfortunately fallen. These otherwise sincere seekers end up hiding the pain of their own experience within a blissful cloud of denial, to no one's benefit, least of all their own. This cloud of denial then often leads a person to profess love and unity while really denying their unconscious guilt and projecting it onto others, never truly recognizing what is being done. Thus, one can observe the lack of peace and concord in individuals professing this very same peace and concord. Activists of any kind—be they for racial integration, world peace or inner peace, or anti-abortionists claiming to be pro-life—can easily end up witnessing to the underlying ego thought system of separation, attack, and death, which their conscious protestations appear to be against. Indeed, as the Queen observes in "Hamlet": "The lady doth protest too much, methinks" (III,ii).

To summarize, then, the errors that students of *A Course in Miracles* fall into are very similar in form to the errors to which many spiritual seekers fall prey. But despite the similarity in form, which is specifically relevant to this book, there is a similarity in content that underlies *all* spiritual errors: the ego's fear of our recognizing the insanity of its position, and accepting, finally, the sanity of the Holy Spirit's. With the fear of God's wrath finally examined and smiled at, the need for defenses against it disappears as well. And so the world will disappear at last, back into the nothingness from which it came (M-13.1:2).

Conclusion

RESPECTING THE MAGNITUDE OF
A COURSE IN MIRACLES

A Course in Miracles provides one of the most important statements ever witnessed to by mankind. It teaches us that not only is the world illusory—and therefore not created by God—but that the physical universe was indeed made as an attack on our Creator (W-pII.3.2:1). Thus Jesus explains the motivation for the world's seeming existence, not to mention the purpose behind the individual life of each of us who believe we walk this earth. Understanding the Course's unique contribution to world spirituality has been the principal burden of *All Are Called,* while *Few Choose to Listen* has accented the ego's attempts to diffuse this powerful teaching. Fearful of the implications of what *A Course in Miracles* truly teaches, the ego has tried to present the Course in its own image and likeness, substituting its littleness for the true magnitude of Jesus' vision. In fact, given the need of the ego to preserve itself by denying the truth that would extinguish its existence, it will probably take decades (if not centuries) for this gift to be understood and fully integrated. Correcting student errors early on in the Course's earthly life will help ensure that such integration will take place, and that the purity and power of its message will survive.

Two quotations from the world of music—from the 19th-century pianist-composer Franz Liszt and the 20th-century conductor Bruno Walter—provide us with a suitable framework within which we conclude this book's discussion of the ego's attempts to sabotage a student's study of *A Course in Miracles.* In their remarks, these two musical giants could well have been speaking of *A Course in Miracles* and its students.

In a 1870 letter—a reference I, unfortunately, cannot locate*—Liszt wrote regarding Richard Wagner's beautiful though lengthy music-drama, *Die Walküre*:

> Great works should be embraced entire, body and soul, form and thought, spirit and life. One ought not to carp at Wagner for his lengths—*it is better to expand one's scale to his* (italics mine).

Wagner's operas (or music dramas as he called his mature works) broke new ground in the musical and operatic world, not only for the composer's daring harmonies and integration of music and drama (Beethoven and Shakespeare were his models), but for the extraordinary expanse of his works. The third act of *Die Meistersinger* alone, for example, exceeds in length a considerable number of complete operas in the standard repertory. Wagner's was a flawed genius to be sure, but a genius nonetheless. And Liszt's comment relates to the fact that attempting to change the Master's work was not only disrespectful to Wagner's art, but was also depriving the listener of a powerful if not profound musical experience.

Our previous discussions of the ego's need to perpetuate its little self help us to understand what Liszt was saying, as true now as it was in the 19th-century musical world. Paraphrasing that great pianist, we may say that instead of expanding our little scale to the heights of *A Course in Miracles*, we scale the Course down to ourselves, finding all manner of justifications for doing so. As long as we prefer the ego's story over the Holy Spirit's, it will be the ego's fearful message that we hear, choosing *not* to listen to the Course's saving message of awakening from the dream of individuality and returning home. Thus, our statement to ourselves, "I do not *want* to see what this is saying," becomes: "The Course is *not* saying this." And so the

---

* It is quoted in Martin Bernheimer's article, "Die Walküre: The Chronology of a Music Drama," that accompanies the RCA Victor recording of that work (LD 6706).

204

message is given to our brains to change *A Course in Miracles* to mean something other than what it is truly teaching.

Inevitably then, instead of bringing our ego's illusions to Jesus' truth in *A Course in Miracles*, we end up dragging down the Course's truth to conform to our illusions. Examples on the level of form include attempts to change the masculine terminology on the grounds *A Course in Miracles* is unfair to women, or to remove the offensive Christian language because the Course seems to exclude members of other religions. Some even have tried to de-emphasize the religious language on the basis that the Course excludes practitioners of non-theistic spiritualities. Channeled writings have already appeared—some of which purport to be from Jesus—stating not only that their source is the author of *A Course in Miracles*, but also claiming to improve on the original by correcting, elucidating, simplifying, de-intellectualizing, or even transcending the Course. All of these, not surprisingly, de-emphasize, distort, or simply dismiss the Course's non-dualistic metaphysics as being irrelevant at best, or non-existent at worst.

This de-emphasis on the metaphysics of *A Course in Miracles* has given rise to a strong anti-intellectual movement regarding the Course, not too dissimilar from a more general movement that can be noted in our society today. This movement has also been associated with the overemphasis on experience and feelings that has overrun psychology and society at large, a movement whose contemporary roots date back to the post–World War II period of t-groups, sensitivity training, and the Gestalt psychology of Fritz Perls. Students of *A Course in Miracles* may therefore argue that understanding its theory is irrelevant, and that study of the text is a waste of time, clearly ignoring this previously cited caution at the end of the first chapter in the text:

> This is a course in mind training. All learning involves attention and study at some level. Some of the later parts of the course rest too heavily on these earlier sections *not to*

205

require their careful study. You will also need them for
preparation. Without this, you may become much too fearful of what is to come to make constructive use of it.
However, *as you study these earlier sections,* you will
begin to see some of the implications that will be amplified
later on (T-1.VII.4; italics mine).

In addition, as was covered in Chapter One, many students
emphasize the workbook at the expense of the text, rather than
viewing each book as a companion to the other. The mistake
here is similar to what we saw in the previous chapter. It reflects the same unconscious error of believing that our ego
identification is weak and can be easily discarded, leaving our
minds open to receive—instantaneously and joyously—the
Word of God. This anti-intellectual stance is thus in many
cases the expression of a fear of looking at the ego thought
system in all its ugliness. As we have commented before, no
one really wants to deal with the horrifying sin and guilt our
egos have convinced us is our reality.

Thus, rather than carefully reading the text—which lays
out the brutal nature of the ego thought system, necessitating
our dealing with it—a student may dismiss such discussions
of the ego as not important. Again, this misses the whole point
of *A Course in Miracles'* efficacy as a spiritual teaching, and
discounts the inherent unity of its curriculum, which does
depend on understanding and recognizing our investment in
perpetuating the ego's thought system, *precisely by not looking at it.* As we have already discussed, it is in *not* looking at
the ego that it is allowed to survive as a thought system in our
minds. To be sure, *A Course in Miracles* is not always easy to
understand, let alone practice. Yet the ultimate difficulty does
not really lie on a conceptual or intellectual level, but rather is
found within the teaching itself. This teaching, as we have discussed throughout the book, strikes terror in minds which still
identify with the ego self. And it is this very ego self that is so
threatened by what Jesus presents to us in his Course.

I should underscore that the attempt to dismiss as irrelevant the high intellectual level of the Course's teachings also reflects a denial of what *A Course in Miracles* is. It *is* an intellectual system, at least in form, and there already exist many fine spiritual systems—ancient and contemporary—that are non-intellectual. All these are as valid as the Course in their potential to lead their serious students to God. To deny *A Course in Miracles* its particular uniqueness is to diminish its contribution, just as forcing a non-intellectual approach into a Procrustean bed of the intellect would wreak equal havoc on that system. Moreover, it is important to realize that working through Jesus' intellectual presentation leads one to an *experience* of peace, and that experience, not a mere intellectual understanding, is the true goal of the Course.

Therefore, students should pay careful attention to *A Course in Miracles*' teachings on the ego, and should resist the temptation to change the form to suit their personal requirements. Above all, to close with the theme with which this book opened, one should have humility as one stands before its magnitude. As we have seen, speaking of God, Jesus urges us to "Be humble before Him, and yet great *in* Him" (T-15.IV.3:1), meaning that we are great because of our Identity as God's Son, and yet we are humble because He is our Creator and Source, and we need His help (through the Holy Spirit) to awaken to our reality as His Son. Likewise, we should feel the humility of recognizing the learning we need accomplish *before* we can remember our Identity as Christ. Trying to change, distort, or scale *A Course in Miracles* down to our size is an expression of the ego's arrogance, not our advanced spirituality. One would do well to remember a statement made by Bruno Walter, perhaps the greatest Mozart conductor of this millennium's closing century.

> It needs some maturity to understand the depth of emotion which speaks in Mozart's seeming tranquillity and measure. …I was…fifty when for the first time I was audacious enough to perform the G Minor [Symphony #40]. I…had such a feeling of responsibility and of the difficulty to

perform it.... And I wondered at all the young conductors who, without any qualms, just went ahead and conducted all these works which asked for such depth of feeling and such maturity of technique.*

Clearly, people do not have to be fifty before they can feel they have understood *A Course in Miracles*, or are prepared to teach it. However, we should be able to accept with humility the need to learn from this wonderful gift from Heaven, rather then to allow the ego's arrogance to tell us that, since the Love of God is all that we now experience, we have already learned and mastered everything the Course can teach. True humility, in the spirit of Bruno Walter's attitude towards Mozart, would have us welcome gladly the truth that in this world we have much to learn. Thus, we gratefully accept the spiritual tool and inner Guide that would teach us how to remove "the blocks to the awareness of love's presence" (T-in.1:7), and return home at last to the Love that lies—liberally paraphrasing the inspiring words of Dante's beatific vision of his *Commedia*—beyond the sun and all the other stars.†

---

* From a recorded conversation with Arnold Michaelis, included in the Columbia recording of Walter conducting various Mozart works (ML 5756).
† The original Italian reads: "L'amor che muove il sole e l'altre stelle." *Commedia: Paradiso*, XXXIII,145.

APPENDIX

A SIMPLE, CLEAR, AND DIRECT COURSE*

Kenneth and Gloria Wapnick

A common source of misunderstanding for students of
A Course in Miracles lies in not recognizing the original context for the scribing which was directly personal to Helen
Schucman and William Thetford. Jesus' "notes" (his word) to
Helen were a mixture of personal messages and the objective
teaching. Even though the more informal nature of the latter
dropped off as the scribing progressed, we continue to find
subtle references to Helen and her reluctance to learn the
Course all the way through, as seen for example in "The
Simplicity of Salvation," the first section in Chapter 31 of the
text. One reason for the writing of *Absence from Felicity: The
Story of Helen Schucman and Her Scribing of A COURSE IN
MIRACLES* was to clear up any potential confusion as to the
meaning of many passages, and of the Course itself. As is discussed at length in that book, Helen was in great conflict regarding *A Course in Miracles* as it was coming through her.
While she had no questions whatsoever about the "voice's"
identity as Jesus, nor of the absolute truth of his words to her,
the Course did arouse tremendous anxiety as its message was
totally antithetical to her personal thought system. She was
therefore in the uncomfortable position of writing down (over
a seven-year period!) a document that undermined her ego's
very existence.

As a result of her great ambivalence—loving and being devoted to Jesus on the one hand, and terrified on the other of the
implications to her ego of such devotion—Helen on occasion
would attempt to disprove the legitimacy of the Course's
author, not to mention his message. Jesus gently chided her
over these attempts, which, again, are documented in *Absence*

* "The Lighthouse," Newsletter of the Foundation for *A Course in
Miracles®*, Volume 4, No. 4, September 1993.

from Felicity. And when these attempts would fail, Helen would then argue that this Course was too difficult and demanded too much of her. While some of Jesus' responses to Helen were taken out of the published edition of the Course, as directed by Jesus himself, enough have remained to allow the reader to see the importance to Jesus of the simple, clear, and direct nature of the Course he was giving to Helen and to the world. It is the purpose of this article to underscore this very important aspect of *A Course in Miracles*—which emerges from Helen's direct and personal experience of scribing the Course from Jesus, which allowed her in turn to experience *his* relationship with the Course—as a help for students who are becoming confused about the "different interpretations" of the Course that are being offered by its students and commentators.

Simple, Clear, and Direct

As *A Course in Miracles* becomes more and more popular, one can sample among students an increasing number of written and spoken commentaries that purport to express what the Course teaches. However, it is difficult to reconcile many of these positions with the very clear and unequivocal position Jesus himself took regarding his Course, which he most certainly did not see as being complex, difficult to understand, or open to interpretation, as he reminded Helen many times. The following statements from *A Course in Miracles* are illustrative—though not exhaustive—of his attitude:

> This is a very *simple* course (T-11.VIII.1:1; italics ours).

> The reason this course is *simple* is that truth is simple (T 15.IV.6:1; italics ours).

> Like the text for which this workbook was written, the ideas used for the exercises are very *simple*, very *clear* and totally *unambiguous*. We are not concerned with intellectual feats

nor logical toys. We are dealing only in the very obvious, which has been overlooked in the clouds of complexity in which you think you think (W-pI.39.1:2-4; italics ours).

...how *direct* and *simple* the text is (W-pI.39.2:5; italics ours).

You have surely begun to realize that this is a very practical course, and *one that means exactly what it says* (T 8.IX.8:1; italics ours).

This course offers a very *direct* and a very *simple* learning situation, and provides the Guide Who tells you what to do (T-9.V.9:1; italics ours).

It is important to note here that by "simple" Jesus does not mean simplistic or simple-minded. *A Course in Miracles* is simple because it says only one thing, without deviation, and without compromise:

How *simple* is salvation! All it says is what was never true is not true now, and never will be. The impossible has not occurred, and can have no effects. And that is all (T 31.I.1:1-4; italics ours).

This next passage, dealing with the answer of forgiveness to all problems, can certainly also represent Jesus' view of *A Course in Miracles*—his answer to Helen and Bill's request for "another way":

...for here we have an answer, *clear* and *plain*, beyond deceit in its *simplicity*. All the complexities the world has spun of fragile cobwebs disappear before the power and the majesty of *this extremely simple statement of the truth* (W pI.122.6:6-7; italics ours).

In response to Helen's complaints about the difficulty of the Course he was teaching her, Jesus responded with the following passages, so that she would understand that his words— the reflection of the Holy Spirit's purpose and God's truth— could not be misunderstood and, moreover, require no interpretation:

> In fact, in order to be *simple* it [the Holy Spirit's purpose] *must* be unequivocal. The simple is merely what is easily understood, and for this it is apparent that it must be *clear* (T-17.VI.1:2-3; first and third italics ours).

> Reflections are seen in light. In darkness they are obscure, and their meaning seems to lie only in shifting interpretations, rather than in themselves. *The reflection of God needs no interpretation. It is clear* (T-14.IX.6:1-4; italics ours).

Therefore, "shifting interpretations" of what Jesus is teaching in *A Course in Miracles* can only come about when people are in the "darkness" of their wrong minds, and are unconsciously perverting the "reflection of God," which "needs no interpretation."

Finally, in light of Helen's (and all students') proclivity for projection of guilt onto God and him, Jesus made this very clear statement to her:

> I have made every effort to use words that are almost impossible to distort, but it is always possible to twist symbols around if you wish (T-3.I.3:11).

Different Interpretations

It should be evident from these few quotations how Jesus viewed his book. Nevertheless, it has not prevented students from believing that *A Course in Miracles* can be subject to *different* and equally valid "interpretations," nor from twisting its symbols around to suit their ego's wishes. Can you imagine Helen saying to Jesus: "I understand what you are saying to me and teaching in this Course, but I think there is another interpretation you can give to this section and to these ideas that you have just dictated." In all the years Helen and I (Kenneth) spent in going over the Course, both in preparation for the published edition, as well as in discussing different portions from the three books, it never once occurred to either of us that there might be *another* possible explanation for what Jesus was teaching so clearly and directly.

In this regard, I (Kenneth) remember in the very early years of the Course's publication having a discussion with Helen about an individual who was attempting to teach the Course without really understanding it, and maintaining that it was saying something it was not, taking sentences out of context to prove his point. Helen was furious and incredulous at the same time: furious at the person for his arrogance in teaching something he clearly had no comprehension of, but pretended that he did; and incredulous at the idea that there would actually be people claiming that *A Course in Miracles* said something it obviously did not mean, and arrogantly believing they were right.

While she was not always happy with the Course's teachings, Helen never forgot Jesus' statements about its simplicity, clarity, and directness. And as has been documented in *Absence from Felicity*, she had little tolerance for those who sought to distort the Course's teachings for the glorification of their own egos. Helen's integrity was such that even though she had difficulty in applying the principles of *A Course in Miracles* to her own life, which she always readily admitted to, she never once attempted to change what it said to meet her ego's needs. Specialness, after all, is only a problem when it is denied, leading inevitably to projection onto others. We are not asked by Jesus in his Course to be *without* the limitations imposed by our specialness, but only to *escape* the terrible burden of guilt we place upon ourselves (M-26.4:1-2), a burden which is maintained by our stubborn refusal to acknowledge the ego thought system we have made real and accepted within our minds. Honesty with oneself regarding the investment in specialness is essential to the process of forgiveness, for it undoes denial and projection, the ego's "double shield" that protects its guilt and therefore its own existence. That is why Jesus pleads with us in the text:

>   Watch carefully and see what it is you are really asking
> for. Be very honest with yourself in this, for we must hide
> nothing from each other.... Think honestly what you have
> thought that God would not have thought, and what you
> have not thought that God would have you think. Search
> sincerely for what you have done and left undone accord-
> ingly, and then change your mind to think with God's
> (T 4.III.8:1-2; T-4.IV.2:4-5).

Once again, *A Course in Miracles* is simple, clear, and direct
in its teachings. It is the wrong mind that weaves the obscuring webs of complexity.

It is always helpful as a point of reference, to ensure that
one does not get off-track when working with the Course, to
keep in mind the original instant of separation when we chose
against God and experienced the seeming effects of that
choice. That ontological moment not only contains the original error, but is the source of all the succeeding ones as well,
including the one we are discussing here. Yet, therein too is
found the only answer to all problems: the Holy Spirit's forgiveness. As the text explains:

>   Each day, and every minute in each day, and every in-
> stant that each minute holds, you but relive the single
> instant when the time of terror took the place of love.

And that instant is the

> tiny tick of time in which the first mistake was made, and
> all of them within that one mistake...[It also holds] the
> Correction for that one, and all of them that came within the
> first (T-26.V.13:1; 3:5).

And so we relive that moment when we believed in the reality of the separation, and took seriously the "tiny, mad idea."
Thus we became convinced that we could be different and
therefore separate from our Creator and Source, with Whom
we can only exist in perfect oneness and love. We believed in
our insanity that there could be *different* interpretations of reality, and that the simple, clear, and direct truth of God's

Heaven could be discussed and debated. And that, in fact, our interpretation was every bit as valid, *if not more so*, than God's.

Imagine the arrogance of the Son who believed not only that he could be right while God's truth was wrong, but also was convinced that his happiness resided in his *being* right. The clarity of this single error of separation quickly was obscured by the complexity of the ego's thought system. This complexity then was reflected in the projection of the separation thought which became the physical universe, wherein was contained the glorification of the Son's newly won separated individuality and triumph over God—his specialness as a self-created being, a seeming travesty of God's perfect and unified creation. The ego's attempt to use the world's complexity to conceal the origin of the one error is dramatically described in the following passage from the text:

> You who believe that God is fear made but one substitution. It has taken many forms, because it was the substitution of illusion for truth; of fragmentation for wholeness. It has become so splintered and subdivided and divided again, over and over, that it is now almost impossible to perceive it once was one, and still is what it was. That one error, which brought truth to illusion, infinity to time, and life to death, was all you ever made. Your whole world rests upon it. Everything you see reflects it, and every special relationship that you have ever made is part of it.
>
> You may be surprised to hear how very different is reality from what you see. You do not realize the magnitude of that one error. It was so vast and so completely incredible that from it a world of total unreality *had* to emerge. What else could come of it? Its fragmented aspects are fearful enough, as you begin to look at them. But nothing you have seen begins to show you the enormity of the original error, which seemed to cast you out of Heaven, to shatter knowledge into meaningless bits of disunited perceptions, and to force you to make further substitutions.
>
> That was the first projection of error outward. The world

217

arose to hide it, and became the screen on which it was projected and drawn between you and the truth (T-18.I.4:1–6:2).

The hallmark of this newly emergent dream of miscreation
is that truth is relative and subject to different interpretations.
This was the famous position taken by the Greek Sophists, who
became enshrined in history through Plato's Dialogues, where
their arrogance is exposed and countered by Socrates' repeated
demonstrations of their ignorance, and his teaching that truth is
absolute and not subject to whatever the Sophists would have
it be. This argument continues today, and students of *A Course
in Miracles* familiar with the section "The Laws of Chaos" will
recall this important statement of the ego's first law, which is
based in part upon the original Sophist argument:

> The *first* chaotic law is that the truth is different for every-
> one. Like all these principles, this one maintains that each is
> separate and has a different set of thoughts that set him off
> from others. This principle evolves from the belief there is
> a hierarchy of illusions; some are more valuable and there-
> fore true. Each one establishes this for himself, and makes it
> true by his attack on what another values. And this is justi-
> fied because the values differ, and those who hold them
> seem to be unlike, and therefore enemies (T-23.II.2).

Differences in interpretation of *A Course in Miracles* thus become the rallying cry of those hellbent on proving the reality
of their perceived separation from God and from certain members of the Sonship.

The Fear of Truth

The workbook says that "Nothing the world believes is
true" (W-pI.139.7:1), because the world was made "to be a
place where God could enter not, and where His Son could be
apart from Him" (W-pII.3.2:4). It follows then that when truth
presents itself to us within the dream, as in *A Course in
Miracles* for example, the ego mind must inevitably distort

and change it, since the ego *is* the thought that it can change the truth of God's creation into something else. And thus it is equally inevitable that we will not know who we are as Christ, God's *one* Son, because the dream we call the world of separation and differences was made by us to be a place where our true Home and Identity would be forgotten. Therefore, as long as we believe we are here, we will be forever uncertain of who we and our brothers truly are. And so Jesus says about the world: "It is a place whose purpose is to be a home where those who claim they do not know themselves can come to question what it is they are" (W-pI.139.7:2). The conclusion of the ego's plan is that all who come to this world enter as amnesiacs, having drawn a veil of forgetfulness across their minds to cover their true Identity, having substituted for it a parody of their true Self.

The explanation for our adamant refusal to accept the truth as true, therefore, lies in the investment we have in our individual identities. The ego tells us that without this—our specialness—we would then disappear into the "oblivion" of God. For accepting our reality as part of the unified Christ, is to accept the Atonement principle that the impossible never occurred. Therefore the ego—the belief in the reality of the separated and differentiated self—does not exist. To the extent that one believes in this false self—and everyone who comes into this world does believe in it—to that extent will the Course's teachings of undoing specialness be experienced as threatening and fearful. Jesus uses the circumstances of his own murder as an example of the ego's fear of the truth:

> Many thought I was attacking them, even though it was apparent I was not. An insane learner learns strange lessons. What you must recognize is that when you do not share a thought system, you are weakening it. Those who believe in it therefore perceive this as an attack on them. This is because everyone identifies himself with his thought system, and every thought system centers on what you believe you are (T-6.V-B.1:5-9).

It would logically follow then that the investment in preserving one's specialness would inevitably lead a student of *A Course in Miracles* to become frightened of what it truly teaches. A world of duality, differentiation, specialness, and individual identity cannot be long sustained in the presence of the teachings that reflect the perfect Oneness of God and Christ, and which lead the student to that state of oneness. Therefore, as students read the Course through the eyes of specialness, their wrong minds caution them to be careful of the truth which threatens their existence. The process can be described as follows: 1) having chosen the ego as our teacher, a message goes from the wrong mind to the brain not to see what is written; 2) we then are instructed to deny the Course's simplicity, clarity, and directness; and 3) we are then directed to substitute complexity, confusion, and divergence from the Course's message. Building upon Shakespeare's famous statement from "The Merchant of Venice" about the devil citing scripture for his purpose, Jesus states in the Course:

> Nothing the ego perceives is interpreted correctly. Not only does the ego cite Scripture for its purpose, but it even interprets Scripture as a witness for itself (T-5.VI.4:3-4).

> ...the ego, under what it sees as threat, is quick to cite the truth to save its lies. Yet must it fail to understand the truth it uses thus. But you can learn to see these foolish applications, and deny the meaning they appear to have (W-pI.196.2:2-4).

We thus can see that the ego, being no one's fool, realizes that it is better to "join" the truth, rather than oppose it. It counsels the unknowing students that they would be better served to bring the truth to illusion for interpretation, rather than, as the Course repeatedly advocates, to bring their illusions to the truth. The form this takes is that students, under the guise of loving and honoring Jesus' teachings, actually subvert the meaning of his words to read what *they* would like them to say, rather than what the words in truth do say. And all this without the students' conscious awareness of their ego's insidiousness.

Jesus discusses this ego dynamic in several places in the Course as an explanation for why students would choose to obfuscate, distort, or change the simplicity of his teachings. And clearly, it is not only Helen's resistance Jesus was addressing in these passages, but everyone who chooses to be so tempted. We begin with a passage that was specifically meant to help Helen undo her ego's attempts at obscuring the simple truths of the Course's teachings:

> This course is perfectly clear. If you do not see it clearly, it is because you are interpreting against it, and therefore do not believe it.... I am leading you to a new kind of experience that you will become less and less willing to deny. Learning of Christ is easy, for to perceive with Him involves no strain at all. His perceptions are your natural awareness, and it is only the distortions you introduce that tire you. Let the Christ in you interpret for you, and do not try to limit what you see by narrow little beliefs that are unworthy of God's Son (T-11.VI.3:1-2,6-9).

And yet it is the "little beliefs" of specialness that so often lead students of *A Course in Miracles* to interpret its message from their wrong minds, meanwhile believing otherwise. They are not aware that they have an unconscious investment in correcting Jesus, proving that he is wrong while they are right, still maintaining that they are not as God created them, and in fact know better than He who they truly are. To all of these fearful ones who would seek to substitute their littleness for the magnitude of Christ, Jesus counsels in this confluence of two passages from the Course:

> Ask not of one's petty strength—the tiny wings of the sparrow—how, with mighty power, the eagle soars (T 20.IV.4:7; M-4.I.2:1-2).

That the ego distorts *A Course in Miracles* is brought up again several chapters later, with Jesus emphasizing once more that without the ego's involvement his Course would be readily understandable:

> Being so simple and direct, this course has nothing in it that is not consistent. The seeming inconsistencies, or parts you find more difficult than others, are merely indications of areas where means and end are still discrepant.... This course requires almost nothing of you. It is impossible to imagine one that asks so little, or could offer more (T-20.VII.1:3-4,7-8).

Denying one's attachment to specialness, and therefore one's need to compromise the Course's clear, simple, and direct truth, follows inexorably from having chosen to study it through the lens of the wrong mind. This is an inevitable occurrence once one is in the dream we call the world, and is certainly not sinful nor unexpected. However, it *is* a mistake not to recognize these dynamics of specialness and bring them to Jesus, so that we, together with him, may look on them without judgment or guilt, thus dispelling their seeming darkness. Without Jesus' help, we would be oblivious to the ego's lies; and therefore they would continue indefinitely under the protection of denial, only to lead to further distortions and misinterpretations of the Course through the dynamic of projection: all this being painfully reminiscent of what was originally done with Jesus' message two thousand years ago.

In the section immediately following "The Laws of Chaos," Jesus discusses more specifically the ego's wrong-minded attempts to compromise truth by rationalizing away attack thoughts with smile-filled wrappings whose purpose is to conceal the gift of murder that lies underneath: another example of the ego's ongoing efforts to bring illusion into truth so that we would think they are the same. This of course reflects the original mistake of equating our illusory ego selves with God. Thus he writes:

> This course is easy just because it makes no compromise. Yet it seems difficult to those who still believe that

compromise is possible. They do not see that, if it is, sal-vation is attack (T-23.III.4:1-3).

No compromise is possible with the simple truth, and the following three passages are Jesus' even more pointed reminders to his students that they are truly terrified of his Course, and so are unwilling to "pay the price" of giving up their specialness. In their insanity they would choose the "freedom" of their individual uniqueness and self-importance over the "imprisonment" of the truth that would only make them free:

> We have repeated how little is asked of you to learn this course.... And being true, it is so simple that it cannot fail to be completely understood. Rejected yes, but not ambig-uous. And if you choose against it now it will not be because it is obscure, but rather that this little cost seemed, in your judgment, to be too much to pay for peace (T 21.II.1:1,3-5).

> This course has explicitly stated that its goal for you is happiness and peace. Yet you are afraid of it. You have been told again and again that it will set you free, yet you sometimes react as if it is trying to imprison you. You often dismiss it more readily than you dismiss the ego's thought system. To some extent, then, you must believe that by not learning the course you are protecting yourself. And you do not realize that it is only your guiltlessness that *can* protect you (T-13.II.7).

> Eyes become used to darkness, and the light of brilliant day seems painful to the eyes grown long accustomed to the dim effects perceived at twilight. And they turn away from sunlight and the clarity it brings to what they look upon. Dimness seems better; easier to see, and better recog-nized. Somehow the vague and more obscure seems easier to look upon; less painful to the eyes than what is wholly clear and unambiguous. Yet this is not what eyes are for, and who can say that he prefers the darkness and maintain he wants to see? (T-25.VI.2)

223

And so given this tremendous ego need to change *A Course
in Miracles* to protect itself, it stands to reason that it would be
impossible for any student to learn the Course as long as the
ego-identification is maintained at all. We can therefore understand that the flight *into* different interpretations is really a
flight *from* the clear and simple teachings of the Course. As
Jesus says:

> Complexity is of the ego, and is nothing more than the
> ego's attempt to obscure the obvious (T-15.IV.6:2).

> You who have not *yet* brought all of the darkness you
> have taught yourself into the light in you, can hardly judge
> the truth and value of this course (T-14.XI.4:1; italics ours).

> It is impossible to learn anything consistently in a state of
> panic. If the purpose of this course is to help you remember
> what you are, and if you believe that what you are is fearful,
> then it must follow that you will not learn this course. Yet
> the reason for the course is that you do not know what you
> are (T-9.I.2:3-5).

And in this telling passage—taken from the section "The
Treachery of Specialness"—on the seeming power of specialness to drown out the Voice for truth, Jesus underscores the
importance of undoing our identification with the ego's lies:

> You are not special. If you think you are, and would de-
> fend your specialness against the truth of what you really
> are, how can you know the truth? What answer that the
> Holy Spirit gives can reach you, when it is your specialness
> to which you listen, and which *asks and answers*? Its tiny
> answer, soundless in the melody that pours from God to
> you eternally in loving praise of what you are, is all you lis-
> ten to. And that vast song of honor and of love for what you
> are seems silent and unheard before its "mightiness." You
> strain your ears to hear its soundless voice, and yet the Call
> of God Himself is soundless to you (T-24.II.4; italics ours).

Humility and Arrogance

While certainly the thought system of *A Course in Miracles* is difficult to embrace at first, because of its total undermining of the ego thought system, students need to cultivate an attitude of humility in recognizing that the solution to the problem of not understanding does not rest in "different interpretations" of the teachings, but rather in the recognition of the fear of losing one's specialness in the presence of truth. Humility would accept the fact that one's ego would inevitably attack the Course by striving to change it; arrogance would deny such attack with a series of rationalizations and interpretations that simply confuse the issue still further.

As an aid in developing this attitude of humility, students would do well in calling to mind the words Helen heard herself speak one morning as she came out of her sleep: "Never underestimate the power of denial." Jesus "borrowed" that idea later for the Course, where in several places he cautions his students against underestimating the ego's power: the intensity of its drive for vengeance, the extent of its insanity, and our need to be vigilant against it (T-5.V.2:11; T-7.III.3:5; T-11.V.16:1; T-11.VI.5:1; T-14.I.2:6; T-16.VII.3:1).

Because of this great temptation to underestimate the power of identifying with the ego, Jesus speaks to his students as if they were children, who need to be taught by an older and wiser brother about what is true and what is false. Children believe they understand when they do not, and so Jesus cautions us:

> Of all the messages you have received and failed to understand, this course alone is open to your understanding and can be understood. This is *your* language. You do not understand it *yet* only because your whole communication is like a baby's (T-22.I.6:1-3; second italics ours).

Rather than stubbornly insisting that they know what is right, and that they have the wisdom of judging the difference between truth and illusion, students of *A Course in Miracles* would do well to approach its teachings with humility, wonder, and a sincere desire to *learn* from it, rather than trying to *teach* it (and others) what it says. Recalling that Jesus views his students as children who cannot discern truth from illusion, as their eyes are clouded with the specialness that is protected by denial and projection, one would gladly and humbly accept the loving hand that Jesus extends as a gentle guide on the journey home. The readiness to turn away from specialness and learn the curriculum still lies in the future, and awaits one's growth into spiritual maturity and out of the fears of childhood that root one in the past:

> This course makes no attempt to teach what cannot easily be learned. Its scope does not exceed your own, except to say that what is yours will come to you when you are ready (T-24.VII.8:1-2).

We thus urge all students to realize that this Course is a very difficult spiritual curriculum precisely *because* it is so simple, clear, and in direct opposition to the ego's thought system. And so we say in closing: Respect your fear of *A Course in Miracles* as a direct threat to your specialness, and do not deny the illusions you have made and cherish as a substitute for the resplendent truth of God. If indeed *A Course in Miracles* is your spiritual path, then let *it* lead you, by stepping back and letting the simplicity, clarity, and directness of Jesus' own words be your guide. Only then can he truly help you forget the hatred of specialness you have made real, and recall at last the simplicity of the love that has patiently awaited your remembrance.

CAPITALIZATION IN *A COURSE IN MIRACLES**
Kenneth Wapnick, Ph.D.

The capitalization in *A Course in Miracles* has been a source of quizzical wonderment for many students. At times it can seem to have been done on a whim, and its seeming inconsistencies more of a hindrance than a help as students struggled to decipher the meaning of sentences. Yet, to paraphrase the famous phrase from *Hamlet*, there yet has been a method to its apparent madness. Since awareness of the capitalization of the Course will inevitably become part of any student's use of this Concordance, a complete explanation of the capitalization principles used in *A Course in Miracles* is presented here now, appearing for the first time in print.

We begin with a discussion of the capitalization philosophy of Helen Schucman, scribe of the Course, as described in the book on Helen and her scribing of *A Course in Miracles*: *Absence from Felicity: The Story of Helen Schucman and Her Scribing of "A Course in Miracles."* It should be noted at the outset that with the very few exceptions discussed below, the capitalization was not dictated by Jesus. It was thus left to Helen to determine how words should be capitalized.

> One can see an "evolution" in Helen's style as one traces the Course from its original dictation in the notebooks, through Bill's [William Thetford, Helen's close friend and colleague] first typing and Helen's subsequent retypings. The process culminated in Helen's feeling that every word even remotely (a slight, but only slight, exaggeration on my [Kenneth Wapnick] part) associated with God should be capitalized, including pronouns and relative pronouns. I should mention that while here again Jesus left Helen with the freedom to do as she wished, he did make some

* From the *Concordance of A COURSE IN MIRACLES* (Foundation for Inner Peace, Viking-Penguin, 1996), pp. xiii-ix.

exceptions. Under his specific instructions, all pronouns referring to him were to be lowercase (in the earlier manuscript Helen always capitalized them), to reflect his unity with us. Jesus instructed Helen always to capitalize the term "Son of God," to emphasize the inclusion of all of us as part of God's one Son, in contradistinction to traditional Christianity's exclusion of all but Jesus from God's special Sonship. Pronouns referring to the Son, however, were to be lowercase, to emphasize our separated state. The exception, of course, would be when "Son of God" refers to our true Identity as Christ, where the pronouns would be capitalized. Also, Jesus asked Helen to capitalize all pronouns referring to the Trinity-God, Christ, and the Holy Spirit-otherwise the reader might not always know for whom (or Whom) the referent was meant.

In the manuscript from which Helen and I were editing, Helen's capitalization was quite inconsistent. While I did originally try to talk her out of what I believed to be the excessive stylistic emphasis on God's divinity, I soon abandoned this fruitless enterprise and ended by saying to Helen that I would capitalize the Course words any way she chose to have them be, but that the capitalization should be consistent. This clearly appealed to her sense of logic, and so we set out in writing the rules of capitalization we would follow, and kept to these as best we could (pp. 364-66).

RULES OF CAPITALIZATION

Trinity

Nouns for the three Members of the Trinity-God, Christ, and the Holy Spirit-are always capitalized, along with their pronouns.

God

Nouns relating to God-Mind, Heart, Will, Everlasting Arms, Holiness, Presence, etc.-are capitalized, but the pronouns for these nouns are not capitalized, unless these nouns are used as synonyms for God. Some words are capitalized when used as synonyms for God, but not capitalized when used more generally, even though they clearly relate to God. Examples of this principle would be *Truth*, *Life*, *Light*, and *Innocence*.

Christ

Synonyms for Christ are capitalized—for example: *Effect*, *Identity*, and *Self*. However, with the exception of *Love*, words associated with Christ are not capitalized, as, for example, *face*, *eyes*, *hands*, and *vision*.

Holy Spirit

Synonyms for the Holy Spirit are capitalized—for example: *Teacher*, *Guide*, *Answer*, *Voice for God*—as are their pronouns. *Love* is capitalized when it is associated with the Holy Spirit.

Jesus

The first person (i.e., "I") used throughout *A Course in Miracles* is Jesus. Words associated with him are not capitalized; for example: all pronouns, *brother*, *man*.

Exceptions

When a capital letter is needed for clarity and emphasis, exceptions to these principles are made. For example:

> *What*: Although demonstrative pronouns are not capitalized, this is allowed when it specifically refers to Christ, as in T-31.V.17:9.

> *Itself*: Pronouns for *Will* are not capitalized. However, one itself referring to Will is capitalized for clarity, so that readers would be able to distinguish this from other *itselfs* in the same sentence (W-pII.253.2:2).

Pronouns

Compound pronouns such as *both*, *either*, *they*, or *those* are capitalized when one or both subjects are part of the Trinity. An exception to this rule is when one of the two subjects refers to the ego, as in T-24.II.5:2.

229

text

text (continued)

text (continued)

workbook for students

workbook for students (continued)

manual for teachers

INDEX OF REFERENCES TO *THE GIFTS OF GOD*

FOUNDATION FOR *A COURSE IN MIRACLES*®

TEACHING ORGANIZATION OF THE FOUNDATION FOR INNER PEACE

ACADEMY ✦ RETREAT CENTER

Kenneth Wapnick received his Ph.D. in Clinical Psychology in 1968 from Adelphi University. He was a close friend and associate of Helen Schucman and William Thetford, the two people whose joining together was the immediate stimulus for the scribing of A COURSE IN MIRACLES.® Kenneth has been involved with A COURSE IN MIRACLES® since 1973, writing, teaching, and integrating its principles with his practice of psychotherapy. He is on the Executive Board of the Foundation for Inner Peace, original publishers of A COURSE IN MIRACLES.®

In 1983, with his wife Gloria, he began the Foundation for A COURSE IN MIRACLES,® and in 1984 this evolved into a Teaching and Healing Center in Crompond, New York, which was quickly outgrown. In 1988, they opened the Academy and Retreat Center in upstate New York. In 1995, they began the Institute for Teaching Inner Peace through A COURSE IN MIRACLES,® an educational corporation chartered by the New York State Board of Regents. The Institute is under the aegis of the Foundation, administering its workshops and Academy courses. The Foundation also publishes a quarterly newsletter, "The Lighthouse," which is available free of charge. The following is Kenneth and Gloria's vision of the Foundation and description of the Center.

In our early years of studying *A Course in Miracles,* as well as teaching and applying its principles in our respective professions of psychotherapy, and teaching and school administration, it seemed evident that this was not the simplest of thought systems to understand. This was so not only in the intellectual grasp of its teachings, but perhaps more importantly in the application of these teachings to our personal lives. Thus, it appeared to us from the beginning that the Course lent itself to teaching, parallel to the ongoing teachings of the Holy Spirit in the daily opportunities within our relationships which are discussed in the early pages of the manual for teachers.

One day several years ago while Helen Schucman and I (Kenneth) were discussing these ideas, she shared a vision that she had had of a teaching center as a white temple with a gold cross atop it. Although it was clear that this image was symbolic, we understood it to be representative of what the teaching center was to be: a place where the person of Jesus and his message in *A Course in Miracles* would be manifest. We have sometimes seen an image of a lighthouse shining its light into the sea, calling to it those passers-by who sought it. For us, this light is the Course's teaching of forgiveness, which we would hope to share with those who are drawn to the Foundation's form of teaching and its vision of the Course.

This vision entails the belief that Jesus gave *A Course in Miracles* at this particular time in this particular form for several reasons. These include:

1) the necessity of healing the mind of its belief that attack is salvation; this is accomplished through forgiveness, the undoing of our belief in the reality of separation and guilt.

2) emphasizing the importance of Jesus and/or the Holy Spirit as our loving and gentle Teacher, and developing a personal relationship with this Teacher.

3) correcting the errors of Christianity, particularly where it has emphasized suffering, sacrifice, separation, and sacrament as being inherent in God's plan for salvation.

Our thinking has always been inspired by Plato (and his mentor Socrates), both the man and his teachings. Plato's Academy was· a place where serious and thoughtful people came to study his philosophy in an atmosphere conducive to their learning, and then returned to their professions to implement what they were taught by the great philosopher. Thus, by integrating abstract philosophical ideals with experience, Plato's school seemed to be the perfect model for our teaching center.

We therefore see the Foundation's principal purpose as being to help students of *A Course in Miracles* deepen their understanding of its thought system, conceptually and experientially, so that they may be more effective instruments of Jesus' teaching in their own particular lives. Since teaching forgiveness without experiencing it is empty, one of the Foundation's specific goals is to help facilitate the process whereby people may be better able to know that their own sins are forgiven and that they are truly loved by God. Thus is the Holy Spirit able to extend His Love through them to others.

A teacher is defined in the Course as anyone who chooses to be one, and so we welcome to our Foundation all those who wish to come. We offer lectures and workshops for large groups as well as courses for smaller groups that would facilitate more intensive study and growth.

The Foundation, about 120 miles from New York City, is situated on ninety-five acres surrounding beautiful Tennanah Lake in the Catskill Mountains. Its country location and comfortable accommodations provide a peaceful and meditative setting in which students may carry out their plans for prayer, study, and reflection.

RELATED MATERIAL ON *A COURSE IN MIRACLES*®

By Kenneth Wapnick, Ph.D.

Books and Pamphlets

CHRISTIAN PSYCHOLOGY IN *A COURSE IN MIRACLES*.® Second edition, enlarged. Discussion of the basic principles of the Course in the context of some of the traditional teachings of Christianity. Includes a new Preface and an Afterword.
ISBN 0-933291-14-0 • #B-1• Paperback • 90 pages $5.
Audio tape of the first edition of the book, read by Kenneth Wapnick
#B-2 $5.

Available also in Spanish:
ISBN 0-933291-17-5 • #B-1s • Paperback • 114 pages $5.

A TALK GIVEN ON *A COURSE IN MIRACLES*.® An Introduction. Fifth edition. Edited transcript of a workshop summarizing the principles of the Course; includes the story of how the Course was written.

Available also in Spanish:
ISBN 0-933291-10-8 • #B-3S • Paperback • 152 pages $5.

Available also in Portuguese:
ISBN 0-933291-27-2 • #B-13s • Paperback • 117 pages $5.

Available also in German:*
EINFÜHRUNG IN *EIN KURS IN WUNDERN*® • ISBN 3-923662-33-5

Available also in Dutch:
INLEIDING TOT *A COURSE IN MIRACLES*® • ISBN 90-202-8135-6

GLOSSARY-INDEX FOR *A COURSE IN MIRACLES*.® Fourth edition, revised and enlarged. A study guide: summary of the Course's theory with a listing of all major terms; glossary of 139 terms and index of most important references; index of more than 800 scriptural references as found in *A Course in Miracles*,® cross-referenced to the Bible. The book is keyed to both the first and second editions of the Course.
ISBN 0-933291-03-5 • #B-4 • Hardcover • 734 pages $20.

---

* *All German translations may be ordered from*:
Greuthof Verlag und Vertrieb GmbH • Herrenweg 2 • D 79261 Gutach i. Br. • Germany • Tel. 07681-6025 • FAX 07681-6027.

Available also in Spanish:
ISBN 0-933291-20-5 • #B-4s • Paperback • 245 pages $10.

Available also in German:
GLOSSAR ZU *EIN KURS IN WUNDERN*® • ISBN 3-923662-35-1

FORGIVENESS AND JESUS: The Meeting Place of *A Course in Miracles*® and Christianity. Fourth edition. Discussion of the teachings of Christianity in the light of the principles of the Course, highlighting the similarities and differences; the application of these principles to issues such as injustice, anger, sickness, sexuality, and money.
ISBN 0-933291-13-2 • #B-5 • Paperback • 355 pages $16.

Available also in German:
DIE VERGEBUNG UND JESUS • ISBN 3-923662-42-4

THE FIFTY MIRACLE PRINCIPLES OF *A COURSE IN MIRACLES*.® Third edition. Combined and edited transcript of two workshops; line-by-line analysis of the fifty miracle principles, with additional material.
ISBN 0-933291-15-9 • #B-6 • Paperback • 115 pages $8.

Available also in Spanish:
ISBN 0-933291-19-1 • #B-6s • Paperback • 139 pages $8.

Available also in German:
WUNDER ALS WEG • ISBN 3-923662-38-6

AWAKEN FROM THE DREAM. Gloria and Kenneth Wapnick. Presentation of the Course's major principles from a new perspective. Includes background material on how the Course was written.
ISBN 0-933291-04-3 • #B-7 • Paperback • 133 pages $10.

THE OBSTACLES TO PEACE. Edited transcript of tape album; line-by-line analysis of "The Obstacles to Peace"—sections central to the Course's theory—and related passages.
ISBN 0-933291-05-1 • #B-8 • Paperback • 295 pages $12.

LOVE DOES NOT CONDEMN: The World, the Flesh, and the Devil According to Platonism, Christianity, Gnosticism, and *A Course in Miracles*.® An in-depth exploration of the non-dualistic metaphysics of *A Course in Miracles*,® and its integration with living in this illusory world.
ISBN 0-933291-07-8 • #B-9 • Hardcover • 614 pages $25.

A VAST ILLUSION: Time According to *A Course in Miracles.*® Second edition. A weaving together of various passages from the Course to present a coherent statement of time, including its metaphysical nature, the role of the miracle and forgiveness in collapsing time, and finally the end of time. (Edited and expanded transcription of the tape album "Time According to *A Course in Miracles.*®")
ISBN 0-933291-09-4 • #B-10 • Paperback • 343 pages $12.

ABSENCE FROM FELICITY: The Story of Helen Schucman and Her Scribing of *A Course in Miracles.*® Discussion of Helen's lifetime conflict between her spiritual nature and her ego; includes some of her recollections, dreams, letters, and personal messages from Jesus—all never before in print; an account of her own experiences of Jesus, her relationship with William Thetford, and the scribing of the Course.
ISBN 0-933291-08-6 • #B-11 • Paperback • 521 pages $16.

OVEREATING: A Dialogue. An Application of the Principles of *A Course in Miracles.*® The Course's approach to all addictions with specific focus on food addictions and preoccupation with weight. (Edited and slightly expanded version of the tape "Overeating.")
ISBN 0-933291-11-6 • #B-12 • Paperback • 35 pages $3.

A COURSE IN MIRACLES® AND CHRISTIANITY: A DIALOGUE. Kenneth Wapnick and W. Norris Clarke, S.J. Discussion identifying the radical differences as well as the similarities between the thought systems of the Course and biblical Christianity. Topics discussed include: The Origin of the World; Jesus: Nature and Role, The Meaning of the Crucifixion and the Resurrection; The Eucharist; and Living in the World.
ISBN 0-933291-18-3 • #B-13 • Paperback • 113 pages $5.

Available also in Spanish:
ISBN 0-933291-22-1 • #B-13s • Paperback • 117 pages $7.

THE MOST COMMONLY ASKED QUESTIONS ABOUT *A COURSE IN MIRACLES.*® Gloria and Kenneth Wapnick. Question and answer format addressing the most frequently asked questions concerning the meaning and application, as well as the overall curriculum of *A Course in Miracles.*®
ISBN 0-933291-21-3 • #B-14 • Paperback • 142 pages $8.

Available also in Spanish:
ISBN 0-933291-28-0 • #B-14s • Paperback • 155 pages $8.

Available also in German:
DER HIMMEL HAT KEIN GEGENTEIL • ISBN 3-923662-37-8

Video Tape Albums

SEEK NOT TO CHANGE THE COURSE. Reflections on *A Course in Miracles.*® Talk given by Gloria and Kenneth Wapnick, including questions and answers, on some of the more common misunderstandings about the Course.
#V-1 • 135 mins. • VHS $30 • PAL (non-U.S.) $40 • Audio tape version $10.

FOUNDATION FOR *A COURSE IN MIRACLES*® Conference and Retreat Center. Gloria and Kenneth Wapnick speak about the Course's beginnings, the origin and purpose of the Foundation, and their vision of its development in the future. A visual and verbal portrait of the Center.
#V-2 • 24 mins. • VHS $10 • PAL (non-U.S.) $20.

THE REAL WORLD (Three-hour unedited workshop). Gloria and Kenneth Wapnick. Explanation of the process of attaining the real world beginning with the metaphysics of *A Course in Miracles*® and the undoing of the ego by the Holy Spirit. The culmination of this process is the real world—the state of mind in which both the problem and the answer disappear, leaving only the memory of God's Love, exemplified in our world by Jesus.
ISBN 0-933291-99-X • #V-3 • 3 hrs. • VHS (US) $30 • PAL (non-US) $40.

THE REAL WORLD (Two-hour edited workshop). Gloria and Kenneth Wapnick. Edited version of the video listed above. Interspersed throughout the workshop are excerpts of an interview with Gloria and Kenneth. Audience questions have not been included in this version.
ISBN 0-933291-98-1 • #V-4 • 2 hrs. • VHS (US) $20 • PAL (non-US) $30.

AN INTERVIEW WITH KENNETH AND GLORIA WAPNICK. A one-hour interview conducted by Corinne Edwards at the Miracle Network in Chicago in December 1995. Topics discussed include: Helen Schucman and her experience of writing down *A Course in Miracles*® as dictated by Jesus; Kenneth's experience with the Course and his relationship with Helen Schucman and William Thetford; the nature of the Course, its core teachings, and their contrast with Christianity; the application of the principles of the Course to specific life situations, and common misunderstandings of the principles and mistakes made in applying them.
#V-5 • 1 hr. • VHS (US) $15.

Audio Tape Albums
Classes and Workshops

CHRISTIAN PSYCHOLOGY IN *A COURSE IN MIRACLES*® Audio tape of first edition of book of the same title, read by Kenneth Wapnick.
ISBN 0-933291-50-7 • #B-2 • 1 tape $5.

THE SIMPLICITY OF SALVATION. Intensive overview of the Course. The two levels of discourse in the Course; in-depth summary of the major principles; comparison of the Course and Christianity; the story of how the Course was written.
ISBN 0-933291-51-5 • #T-1 • 8 tapes $48.

ATONEMENT WITHOUT SACRIFICE: Christianity, the Bible, and the Course. Workshop exploring the relationship between *A Course in Miracles*® and the Judaeo-Christian tradition, with special emphasis placed on the role of sacrifice and suffering.
ISBN 0-933291-53-1 • #T-3 • 2 tapes $10.

THE EGO AND FORGIVENESS. Introductory overview of the Course. The ego's thought system of sin, guilt, fear, and special relationships, and its undoing through the Holy Spirit's thought system that includes forgiveness and holy relationships. (Album consists of first two tapes of "The End of Injustice.")
ISBN 0-933291-55-8 • #T-5 • 2 tapes $10.

SPECIAL RELATIONSHIPS—PART 1. Line-by-line commentary on sections discussing specialness; explains the unloving nature of most relationships, and how to transform them.
ISBN 0-933291-59-0 • #T-9 • 8 tapes $48.

SPECIAL RELATIONSHIPS—PART 2. Continuation of Part 1, developed through commentary on later chapters in the text including "The Healed Relationship," "The Treachery of Specialness," and "The Forgiveness of Specialness."
ISBN 0-933291-60-4 • #T-10 • 6 tapes $36.

JESUS AND *A COURSE IN MIRACLES.*® Discussion of passages in the Course in which Jesus refers to himself: as the source of the Course; his historical teaching example as the manifestation of the Holy Spirit, and perfect model of forgiveness; and his role as our teacher, without whom the undoing of the ego's thought system would be impossible.
ISBN 0-933291-62-0 • #T-12 • 5 tapes $30.

CAUSE AND EFFECT. The importance of this principle in understanding how forgiveness undoes the ego's thought system of guilt and punishment; line-by-line analysis of text sections on our dreams of suffering and victimhood.
ISBN 0-933291-63-9 • #T-13 • 8 tapes $48.

PSYCHOTHERAPY: PURPOSE, PROCESS AND PRACTICE. Line-by-line commentary on this supplement to the Course, scribed by Helen Schucman from Jesus.
ISBN 0-933291-64-7 • #T-14 • 7 tapes $42.

THE GIFTS OF GOD. A discussion of the inspired poetry of Helen Schucman, scribe of the Course; includes personal reminiscences about Helen.
ISBN 0-933291-65-5 • #T-15 • 3 tapes $18.

SEEK NOT TO CHANGE THE COURSE: Reflections on *A Course in Miracles.*® Gloria and Kenneth Wapnick. Audio version of video tape of the same name.
ISBN 0-933291-66-3 • #T-16 • 2 tapes $10.

LOVE DOES NOT OPPOSE. Gloria and Kenneth Wapnick. The importance of non-opposition as the basis of forgiveness in special relationships.
ISBN 0-933291-67-1 • #T-17 • 8 tapes $48.

THE SONG OF PRAYER. Line-by-line commentary on this supplement to the Course, scribed by Helen Schucman from Jesus; the role of prayer as a reflection of the process of our acceptance of the true meaning of Jesus' presence in our lives; Jesus' relationship with Helen as the model for understanding the nature of prayer.
ISBN 0-933291-68-X • #T-18 • 10 tapes $60.

THE ORIGIN OF *A COURSE IN MIRACLES.*® The story of the scribing of *A Course in Miracles;*® reflections on Helen Schucman and William Thetford.
ISBN 0-933291-69-8 • #T-19 • 1 tape $6.

I WILL BE STILL AN INSTANT AND GO HOME. A collection of two talks and a meditation by Kenneth Wapnick, and one talk by Gloria Wapnick and Kenneth—given at various Sunday services.
ISBN 0-933291-70-1 • #T-20 • 1 tape $6.

JESUS AND THE MESSAGE OF EASTER. The Course's view of Jesus, and the meaning of his crucifixion and resurrection.
ISBN 0-933291-71-X • #T-21 • 8 tapes $48.

THE AUTHORITY PROBLEM. The authority problem with God and its reflection in our everyday life.
ISBN 0-933291-72-8 • #T-22 • 5 tapes $30.

OUR GRATITUDE TO GOD. Our gratitude to God, Jesus, and to each other; the obstacles and resistances to this gratitude.
ISBN 0-933291-73-6 • #T-23 • 5 tapes $30.

SICKNESS AND HEALING. Discussion of the cause and purpose of sickness in the ego thought system; analysis of healing as occurring in the mind—the healing of the belief in guilt, by turning to the Holy Spirit and forgiving.
ISBN 0-933291-74-4 • #T-24 • 8 tapes $48.

WHAT IT MEANS TO BE A TEACHER OF GOD. Discussion of the ten characteristics of a teacher of God; also includes discussion of magic and healing.
ISBN 0-933291-75-2 • #T-25 • 6 tapes $36.

OVEREATING: A DIALOGUE BASED UPON *A COURSE IN MIRACLES.*® The ego dynamics involved in food addictions and weight problems; forgiveness through the Holy Spirit as the solution.
ISBN 0-933291-76-0 • #T-26 • 1 tape $6.

TO JUDGE OR NOT TO JUDGE. The Course's teachings on judgment; the process of recognizing our need to judge, and letting Jesus or the Holy Spirit judge for us.
ISBN 0-933291-77-9 • #T-27 • 4 tapes $24.

HEALING THE UNHEALED HEALER. The characteristics of the unhealed healer; healing through joining with Jesus in understanding all forms of sickness and problems as calls for love.
ISBN 0-933291-78-7 • #T-28 • 8 tapes $48.

THE REAL WORLD: OUR HOME AWAY FROM HOME. A discussion of our true home in Heaven, the ego's home in the world, and the Holy Spirit's correction of the ego's world: the real world.
ISBN 0-933291-79-5 • #T-29 • 8 tapes $48.

TRUE EMPATHY: THE GREATER JOINING. The world's version of empathy contrasted with the Holy Spirit's true empathy.
ISBN 0-933291-80-9 • #T-30 • 8 tapes $48.

JESUS: THE MANIFESTATION OF THE HOLY SPIRIT. A discussion of Jesus and the Holy Spirit in the context of the difference between appearance and reality, and the importance of Jesus as our guide in leading us out of the dream; includes a discussion of the relationship of Jesus to Helen Schucman and to *A Course in Miracles*.®
ISBN 0-933291-81-7 • #T-31 • 5 tapes $30.

THE LAWS OF CHAOS: OUR WAR WITH GOD. An in-depth exploration and discussion of the five laws of chaos that form the foundation of the ego's thought system, and powerfully express the ego's defenses against the Love of God.
ISBN 0-933291-82-5 • #T-32 • 12 tapes $72.

"THERE MUST BE ANOTHER WAY." The words that led to the birth of *A Course in Miracles*® provide the theme of this workshop which discusses forgiveness as the "other way"—rather than specialness— of relating to ourselves, each other, and to God.
ISBN 0-933291-83-3 • #T-33 • 1 tape $6.

THE METAPHYSICS OF SEPARATION AND FORGIVENESS. Summary of the teachings of *A Course in Miracles*,® specifically showing how the principle that the thought of separation and the physical world are illusions becomes the foundation for the understanding and practice of forgiveness in our daily lives.
ISBN 0-933291-84-1 • #T-34 • 1 tape $6.

THE WORKBOOK OF *A COURSE IN MIRACLES*:® ITS PLACE IN THE CURRICULUM—THEORY AND PRACTICE. Discussion of the metaphysical principles underlying the lessons, the mind-training aspects of the workbook, Jesus' gentle teaching method, and students' common misuses of the workbook. Two charts and an annotated outline of the workbook included.
ISBN 0-933291-85-X • #T-35 • 8 tapes $48.

MAKING THE HOLY SPIRIT SPECIAL: THE ARROGANCE OF THE EGO. Presentation of the major Course teachings on the role of the Holy Spirit—and Jesus as His manifestation—and the importance of Their Presence in our lives. Discussion of the contrasting attitudes of arrogance and humility in asking help of the Holy Spirit, as well as

what it means to hear His Voice. The idea that the Holy Spirit acts in the world is shown to rest on misunderstandings of the principles and language of the Course, as well as on our unconscious desire for specialness.
ISBN 0-933291-86-8 • #T-36 • 7 tapes $42.

THE MEANING OF JUDGMENT. Discussion based on "The Forgiving Dream" from the text, centering on four forms of judgment: 1) the dream of judgment against ourselves; 2) looking with Jesus at this ongoing judgment of guilt without further judgment; 3) judging all things in accord with the Holy Spirit's judgment; 4) joining with Jesus in the judgment of God's Love that is the only reality.
ISBN 0-933291-87-6 • #T-37 • 1 tape $6.

THE WEB OF SPECIALNESS. The metaphysical basis of specialness as an attack on God and as a defense against our true Identity as His Son, followed by a detailed explanation of the intricacies and subtleties of specialness in the context of a commentary on sections from Chapter 24 in the text. A discussion of the process of identifying the pervasive and insidious patterns of specialness in all areas of daily life, the fear, resistance, and deception encountered in this process, and the process of forgiving our specialness through the willingness to join with Jesus in looking at it honestly and without judgment.
ISBN 0-933291-88-4 • #T-38 • 12 tapes $72.

DUALITY AS METAPHOR IN *A COURSE IN MIRACLES*.® A comprehensive study of what is to be taken literally and what is to be taken metaphorically in *A Course in Miracles*,® and the distortions that result from not recognizing this difference between symbol and fact—explained in the context of the metaphysics of duality and separation, and what Jesus teaches about the world, joining, forgiving, prayer, the Holy Spirit, himself, and the only reality: the non-dualistic oneness of God and Christ.
ISBN 0-933291-89-2 • #T-39 • 8 tapes $48.

RULES FOR DECISION. A line-by-line analysis of the seven rules for decision from the section "Rules for Decision" in Chapter 30 of the text. A comprehensive study of the Course's concept of decision making, and discussion of what it means to choose Jesus, rather than the ego, as our teacher.
ISBN 0-933291-90-6 • #T-40 • 8 tapes $48.

I WANT THE PEACE OF GOD. A commentary on passages from Lesson 185, "I Want the Peace of God," and from "What Is the Peace of God?" in the manual for teachers. The commentary focuses on the idea that to say and mean the words "I want the peace of God" reflects the willingness to look openly with Jesus at our secret wish *not* to be peaceful. Only by choosing against our desire to attack can our decision to be peaceful have meaning, allowing the peace of God to be our only reality.
ISBN 0-933291-91-4 • #T-41 • one tape $6.

FORGIVING JESUS: "Stranger on the Road." Discussion of our need to forgive Jesus because he is right and we are wrong about ourselves. The context is Helen Schucman's poem "Stranger on the Road," which expresses her experiences of the crucifixion and the resurrection, and reflects her conflicts—shared by practically all students of the Course—in developing a relationship with Jesus.
ISBN 0-933291-92-2 • #T-42 • 2 tapes $10.

THE BIBLE FROM THE PERSPECTIVE OF *A COURSE IN MIRACLES.*® Kenneth and Gloria Wapnick. A presentation of the Bible and the Course as mutually exclusive spiritual paths, demonstrating that attempts to graft the Bible on to the Course result in the distortion and corruption of the meaning of both systems. The Course, with its non-dualistic God, and Jesus who teaches Atonement without sacrifice, is presented as the correction of the biblical thought system.
ISBN 0-933291-93-0 • #T-43 • 6 tapes $36.

THE THEOLOGY OF *A COURSE IN MIRACLES.*® Kenneth and Gloria Wapnick. A presentation of the unique non-dualistic theology of *A Course in Miracles*® contrasted with the dualistic theology of Judaism and traditional Christianity. The workshop focuses on the Course's radically different teachings on God, Jesus, sin, salvation, and Atonement, and the importance of these for the practice of forgiveness.
ISBN 0-933291-94-9 • #T-44 • 2 tapes $10.

THE INHERITANCE OF GOD'S SON. Kenneth and Gloria Wapnick. A line-by-line commentary on this important section from the text of *A Course in Miracles.*® Discussion of the ways in which, through guilt and blame, we obscure our inheritance as God's perfect sinless creation, and the undoing of these defenses by joining with Jesus through forgiveness of ourselves and others.
ISBN 0-933291-95-7 • #T-45 • 2 tapes $10.

THE SIGN OF CHRISTMAS IS A STAR. Kenneth and Gloria Wapnick. The theology of Christmas discussed in the context of two radically different views of Jesus: traditional Christianity which portrays him as the only Son of God, special and different from everyone else, sent by God to atone for the sins of humanity; *A Course in Miracles,*® in which Jesus presents himself as the reflection in our minds of the light of Heaven, reminding us of our true reality as the sinless children of God, the Identity of Christ we all share as one.
ISBN 0-933291-96-5 • #T-46 • 2 tapes $10.

THE HOLY CHRIST IS BORN IN ME TODAY. Kenneth and Gloria Wapnick. The world's veneration of Jesus' birth explained as the reinforcement of the ego's specialness, which always seeks to substitute idols for the true God. This approach is contrasted with that of *A Course in Miracles,*® in which Jesus teaches that the acceptance of his presence is but the rebirth in awareness of our oneness as Christ, the true meaning of Christmas.
ISBN 0-933291-97-3 • #T-47 • 2 tapes $10.

FROM TIME TO TIMELESSNESS. Originally a lecture given as an introductory overview to an Academy course held at the Center in October 1995. A summary of the role that time plays in the ego's strategy of protecting its individuality through its thought system of sin, guilt, and fear, which translates in the temporal world of form as past, present, and future. The role of Jesus in undoing our belief in time, retracing our steps up the ego's ladder and returning us to our true home in eternity, is also discussed.
ISBN 0-933291-49-3 • #T-48 • 1 tape $6.

CLIMBING THE LADDER HOME. The process of leaving and then returning to our home in Heaven explained in the context of the self-concepts we cherish—their purpose and their undoing. Each step down the ladder is identified as a self-concept requiring denial of the preceding step, with the climb back up the ladder explained as the process of disengaging from all the ego's concepts of self by turning to Jesus and correcting the mistake at each rung of the ladder.
ISBN 0-933291-48-5 • #T-49 • five tapes $30.

HOW WILL THE WORLD END? Workshop based on the section of the same name in the manual for teachers. The focus is first on the nature of the world and its purpose in the ego's plan to replace God and His Kingdom, with its crowning achievement being the involvement of God, the Holy Spirit, and Jesus in the solution of problems in the world. It is then shown that the "ending" of this world will occur when the need to believe in the illusion of our separation from God and Heaven is withdrawn through acceptance of the Holy Spirit's forgiveness.

ISBN 0-933291-47-7 • #T-50 • 2 tapes $10.

THE IMPORTANCE OF JESUS. The importance of Jesus in the ego's plan of atonement contrasted with his importance in the Holy Spirit's plan. It is explained in depth how the Jesus of *A Course in Miracles* replaces the image of the biblical Jesus portrayed throughout history, who was so thoroughly rooted in the world's dream of the body.

ISBN 0-933291-46-9 • #T-51 • 2 tapes $10.

LEARNING FROM THE HOLY SPIRIT: A Commentary on Workbook Lesson 193: "All things are lessons God would have me learn." The significance of this lesson in its integration of the theory of *A Course in Miracles* and its practical application is discussed. This class explains in depth what it means to see our lives as classrooms, with Jesus or the Holy Spirit as our teacher, along with common mistakes made by students of denying feelings and experiences, and believing that God and the Holy Spirit send us lessons to improve our individual lives in the dream.

ISBN 0-933291-46-0 • #T-52 • 2 tapes $10.

THE MEANING OF FORGIVENESS. Forgiveness as the central teaching of *A Course in Miracles*. In this workshop, its true meaning is explained in contrast to the distortions coming from the world's version, which has made forgiveness into a scourge rather than the path home to God. Through readings and discussion of examples, all forms of victimization are shown to be rooted in the projection of responsibility for our belief that we are separated from God's Love. Forgiveness, therefore, begins with looking at our experiences of victimization with Jesus, who then helps us see both their cause and their healing, which lie only in our mind's decision, either to be joined with his love or to remain separate from it.

ISBN 0-933291-44-2 • #T-53 • 2 tapes $10.

Ordering Information

For orders *in the continental U.S. only*, please add $3.00 for the first item, and $1.50 for each additional item, for shipping and handling.

For orders to *all other countries* (SURFACE MAIL), and to *Alaska, Hawaii,* and *Puerto Rico* (FIRST CLASS MAIL), please add $4.00 for the first item and $1.00 for each additional item.

New York State residents please add local sales tax. (New York law requires sales tax on shipping and handling charges.)

VISA and MasterCard accepted.

Order from:

Foundation for *A Course in Miracles*®
1275 Tennanah Lake Road
Roscoe, NY 12776-5905
(607) 498-4116 • FAX (607) 498-5325

* * * * *

A COURSE IN MIRACLES and other scribed material
may be ordered from:

Foundation for Inner Peace
P.O. Box 598
Mill Valley, CA 94942
(415) 388-2060

A COURSE IN MIRACLES, Second edition:

Three volumes: Hardcover $40

One volume (complete): Hardcover $30 • Softcover $25

*PSYCHOTHERAPY: PURPOSE, PROCESS AND PRACTICE: $3

*THE SONG OF PRAYER: PRAYER, FORGIVENESS, HEALING: $3

THE GIFTS OF GOD: $21

CONCORDANCE OF A COURSE IN MIRACLES: $49.95

*These two pamphlets are also available combined in one softcover volume entitled *Supplements to A Course In Miracles.* Order from:
Viking/Penguin: 1-800-526-0275 • FAX 1-800-227-9604
Penguin USA: 120 Woodbine Street • Bergenfield, NJ 07621

Additional copies of this two-volume set may be ordered from:

Foundation for *A Course in Miracles*
1275 Tennanah Lake Road
Roscoe, NY 12776-5905

Send a check or money order (in US funds only) for $22.00 plus
shipping: please see preceding page for shipping charges.

☐ I am interested in receiving a newsletter

☐ I am interested in receiving a catalog of books and tapes

☐ I am interested in receiving a schedule of workshops and classes

☐ Place me on your mailing list to receive your annual catalog and quarterly newsletter

PLEASE PRINT NEATLY

Name _____

Address _____

City, State, Zip _____

Foundation for A *Course in Miracles*®
1275 Tennanah Lake Road
Roscoe, NY 12776-5905

Place
postage
here